JP Movement

Emergency and India's Second Freedom

JP Movement

Emergency and India's Second Freedom

M G Devasahayam

Vitasta

Published by Renu Kaul Verma for
Vitasta Publishing Pvt. Ltd.
2/15, Ansari Road, Daryaganj,
New Delhi - 110 002
info@vitastapublishing.com

ISBN 978-93-80828-61-9

First Edition 2012
Third Reprint 2025

MRP 495

Layout by Vitasta Publishing Pvt. Ltd.
Cover Design by Aditya Kumar Rai
Printed by Manipal Technologies Limited, Manipal

This Book is dedicated to the forgotten patriot and legend Jayaprakash Narayan on whom his Australian biographer couple Allan & Wendy Scarfe has written this beautiful epitaph:

> "Not everyone's personal life can match the nobility of his ideas. But Jayaprakash's did.... His ideas were creative, compassionate, original and powerful.... But the man in his courage, integrity and humanity was greater still"

This was the man for whom Freedom had become a passion of life and he would not see it compromised for bread, for security, for prosperity, for the glory of the state or for anything else.

This Book salutes those who pursue this passion and would not compromise their Freedom, come what may!

Content

Preface

The term 'Emergency' that symbolised India's descent from democracy to dictatorship three-and-a-half decades ago has made a grand re-entry into middle class drawing rooms, specially amongst youth. What is significant is that the reference to Emergency is being made by a generation for whom it was an era in the distant past. They did not experience its excesses, nor would have cared about it till a short while ego. Now they do.

Soon after declaration of Emergency in June 1975, Prime Minister Indira Gandhi placed a document "Why Emergency?" before Parliament. This 'white paper' depicted Jayaprakash Narayan (JP) as the villain and put the entire blame for declaration of Emergency on the mass movement that he led.

It is time, therefore, to remember Winston Churchill's famous words: "Those that fail to learn from history, are doomed to repeat it." The purpose of this book is to provide the learning about JP Movement and the dark days of Emergency, which are inexorably intertwined with the sunshine of India's second freedom.

The trigger for bringing back memories of Emergency is Anna Hazare's middle-class surge with a generous sprinkle of youth demanding the enactment of stringent Jan Lokpal legislation to combat the massive scams and corruption that have engulfed the country and have led to public fury. Anna went on a 12-day fast at Ramlila grounds, with a few thousand crowds in attendance, and made Parliament pass a 'Sense of the House' resolution to draft a 'practical, implementable and constitutional' Lokpal Bill and enact the same into law within a short period of time. This was preceded by an aborted fast by yoga guru, Baba Ramdev at the same venue.

In contrast, during the seventies, JP led a most massive anti-government movement India has ever seen on the issues of corruption, price-rise and unemployment–concerns similar to the present ones that brought people to the streets. This movement culminated in the very same Ramlila grounds on the evening of 25 June 1975 under the auspices of Janata Morcha wherein more than a million people participated. Addressing the rally, JP said that a 'grave situation' had arisen in the country due to rampant corruption and called for mass action. After giving out the call '*sinhasan khali karo janata aa rahi hai*' (vacate the throne, people are coming), JP warned the country against the 'threat of fascism posed by Prime Minister Indira Gandhi's actions'.

Mrs Gandhi responded exactly as JP predicted–imposed Emergency in the country that extinguished democracy and replaced it with her brand of dictatorship. During midnight hours almost all leading lights of India's political spectrum–JP, Morarji Desai, Atal Behari Vajpayee, LK Advani, Chandra Shekhar, Piloo Mody etc.– were arrested under Defence of India Rules and whisked away to secretive places!

Minor variants of repressive acts of this period (25 June 1975 and 21 March 1977) were reenacted on 16 August 2011 at Delhi's Ramlila grounds when in a desperate demonstration of panicked overreaction, the UPA Government let loose the Delhi Police to arrest Anna Hazare and leaders of his anti-corruption movement to pre-empt their protest fast. Just a day after India celebrated its 65th Independence Day, Indian democracy once again stood defiled. The Opposition and social activists were quick to point out that the crackdown was reminiscent of Emergency. But the spontaneous and angry reaction of the people courting arrests all over the country gave a clear warning to the government that the people are determined to ensure that those dark days do not revisit India.

Baba Ramdev and Anna Hazare have done a commendable job in rousing people's dormant conscience against corruption and misrule and prodding government into possible action. But portraying these as 'second freedom struggle' is bizarre and preposterous. This goes against the very grain of freedom and 'people's movement'. Touting such a line indicates either total lack of knowledge of country's post-independence history–JP Movement, Emergency, extinction of Freedom and its restoration through massive people's power–in the seventies or a deliberate attempt to suppress historical facts that ushered in India's real second freedom.

So the true history of Emergency and India's second freedom need to be told in authentic terms. That precisely is the purpose of this book and it is for the readers to make their own informed judgement.

Every political movement has a reference point. The French Revolution had Marie Antoinettes quip 'Let them eat cake'; the American war of independence was imbued by the idea of republicanism and Fidel Castro's famous 'Condemn me! It does not matter, history will absolve me' during the 1953 trial had Cubans up in arms. All of them ended successfully. According to leading social scientists, there are only two reference points for contemporary India–national movement for independence and Emergency. One associated with liberation, the other with totalitarianism. National movement is the memory of what should be done and Emergency of what should not be done. To them "what is happening now is a cheap imitation of those intense years of the seventies."

Those 'intense years of the seventies' turned out to be a battle between the forces of Autocracy and Democracy. Prime Minister Indira Gandhi was the icon of Autocracy and 'Sarvodaya' leader Jayaprakash Narayan was the icon of Democracy. For a brief while–June 1975 to March 1977–autocracy triumphed, with the country under active state of Emergency. But in the eyeball-to-eyeball confrontation that ensued between the two icons during the Emergency-time election in March 1977 the latter (JP) won thereby restoring democracy in the country. This was real 'second freedom' and I have been a witness, indeed a participant in these 'intense years'.

Let us briefly go back to those days that made post-independence history. On the Midnight Hour of 25-26 June 1975, when India slept, Nehru's own daughter, Prime Minister Indira Gandhi, shattered and nearly destroyed the nascent democratic framework so painfully put together. This she did through a piece of paper proclaiming Emergency carried by her private secretary to the President, which was promptly signed:

> "In exercise of the powers conferred by clause (1) of Article 352 of the Constitution, I, Fakhruddin Ali Ahmed, President of India, by this Proclamation declare that a grave emergency exists whereby the security of India is threatened by internal disturbances."

Emergency that followed extinguished freedom and democracy, suspended fundamental rights of citizens, fettered freedom of the press and resorted to illegal detention and abuse of citizens. Enactment of draconian laws followed suit. Most institutions of governance when asked to bend prostrated themselves and crawled. This showed that the institutions of India's nascent democracy had not yet become robust enough to withstand an assault.

The wheel seems to have come full circle and there is a parallel to the situation in India today. Emergency was a direct sequel to the massive upsurge against corruption and misrule started by the students of Bihar and Gujarat in 1974, and later spearheaded by JP. Launching his massive 'war against corruption,' JP had said: "As I diagnose the root cause of the country's critical state of health, I identify it unhesitatingly as corruption and precipitous fall in the moral standards of our politics and public life." In response, Indira Gandhi proclaimed that 'corruption was universal' and crushed the Movement by imposing Emergency and destroyed democratic governance to protect the corrupt. Now also the civil society revulsion is against corruption in its most rotten form while Government is protecting the corrupt and crushing those protesting against this venality.

Emergency ripped apart the delicately crafted and carefully nurtured democratic fabric of a poor nation wherein lived one/sixth of the human race. As the Civil Rights stalwart Rajni Kothari puts it: "It was a state off-limits, a government that hijacked the whole edifice of the state, a ruling party and leader who in effect treated the state as their personal estate. It was the imposition of a highly concentrated apparatus of power on a fundamentally federal society and the turning over of this centralized apparatus for personal survival and family aggrandizement....And it happened in this country after 28 years of democratic functioning." Then in less than 22 months, freedom and democracy returned to this parched land when the people ruthlessly voted out the Emergency regime and its minions!

To understand this phenomenon we need to closely look at two icons of this darkest phase of India's history that led to the country's Second Freedom–Prime Minister Indira Gandhi, representing autocracy and Sarvodhaya stalwart Jayaprakash Narayan representing democracy.

At this point suffice it to say that while the former was the epitome of power and pelf, the later abjured all desire for power, but wielded immense moral authority. They became intractable adversaries on the night of 25/26th June 1975. Emergency brought about an eyeball-to-eyeball confrontation between 'autocrat' Indira and 'democrat' JP. By the time the confrontation ended in March 1977, JP had won and India had regained its Freedom.

Indira is among the most written-about celebrity in the world. But not so JP, who has been given the affectionate title of 'Lok Nayak'. Judged from hindsight, in the service of the nation 'Lok Nayak' is at par with the 'Mahatma'. The intensity of passion and fire roused by JP's daring escape from Hazaribagh Jail in 1942 gave fresh life to the Quit India movement launched by Mahatma Gandhi, leading to Independence in 1947. Thirty years later, in 1977, when the Mahatma was no more, JP almost single handedly put a distressed nation together, crafted a political blueprint, defied a well entrenched native empire far more powerful than the alien British, and restored India back to democracy.

During the freedom struggle in all JP had spent over five years in jail, which has been well chronicled by JP himself or his co-prisoners. But JP had no co-prisoners in Chandigarh since it was virtual solitary-confinement in the ward of a super-specialty hospital declared as jail. JP did try and keep a diary of events in between bouts of demoralization, depression and ill health, but could manage only 60 days of entry during the 140 days he was in detention. And most of these entries are brief and patchy.

Till midnight of 25 June 1975, JP was a Messiah and the only hope of India's teeming millions for deliverance from stinking corruption and misrule. That was when India was a democracy. From that fateful midnight on under Indira's autocratic regime he was a villain and Enemy No:1 of the State. The 20 weeks JP was in detention saw the Indian nation and its people reeling under the weight of emergency excesses and deprivation of freedom and fundamental rights. These weeks also saw a frail old man in his seventies brooding in the solitary confines of the PGI ward, summoning up the last reserves of the indomitable spirit that had egged him to scale the high walls of Hazaribagh jail and flare up the freedom struggle.

While the Emergency drama was for the whole world to see, the opportunity of witnessing the intense struggle of the 'revolutionary in chains' was only mine. Not only did I see, I felt it and for a while I was part of it. This was so because, though I was part of the elite IAS and the District Commissioner of Chandigarh (therefore the custodian of JP in Jail), I was primarily a citizen who valued freedom more than anything else.

George Santayana, the Spanish-American philosopher, essayist and poet wrote these words of wisdom: "Progress, far from consisting in change, depends on retentiveness. When change is absolute there remains no being to improve and no direction is set for possible improvement: and when experience is not retained, as among savages, infancy is perpetual. Those who cannot remember the past are condemned to repeat it."

This is precisely happening in India, more so in the ruling Congress party. Nothing has been learnt from the experience of Emergency and nothing has been retained. In the manner of the dark days of Emergency, an extra-constitutional centre of power controls much of what transpires in the Union Government. It is also no secret that Indira's dynastic successor and Congress president, Sonia Gandhi, who became that supra-constitutional authority after the 2004 general election with a back-bending and pliable man as Prime Minister, regularly exercises her veto power and keeps a tight rein on the Government. And when a prime minister is alive and kicking, party minions are serenading for a 'dynastic greenhorn' to take over pronto.

This comes naturally for the Congress party that does not see this as violative of any principle, constitutional or otherwise, because the presence of such extra-constitutional entities is part and parcel of the party's concept of democracy and governance. Since the Nehru-Gandhis play a pivotal role in the affairs of the Congress, the party runs on the premise that members of the dynasty need no formal office or mandate to run the affairs of state!

In the event today, India's governance and government have become rotten and is marked by several despicable realities:

- No other Democracy in the world has an unelected Prime Minister but India.
- No other Democracy in the world has a 'dynastic greenhorn' and his toadies breathing down the Prime Minister's neck claiming 'divine right to rule'.
- No other Democracy in the world has its Prime Minister, President, political parties and Parliament as tolerant and acquiescing to horrendous corruption and misrule as in India.
- No other government in the civilised modern world receives orders from an extra constitutional authority as obsequiously as does the Indian Government.
- No other government in civilised world is ever seen staggering indecisively and so clownishly as our very own Government.
- No other Democracy in the world has as many as nearly a third of its Members of Parliament facing serious criminal charges, which is a record.
- No other Democracy (government of the people, by the people and for the people) has so brazenly 'transformed' into Kleptocracy (government of the thieves, by the thieves and for the thieves)

No other government can boast of so many scams and scandals as the UPA Government. Indeed India has morphed from world's largest Democracy to largest 'Kleptocracy' through the autocracy route. As is natural kleptocrats look at citizens as enemies and adversaries. Home Minster opposes 'elected members' dealing with civil society and Congress worthies consider them as tyrants posing huge threat to democracy!

Land struggle is raging all over the country. With such 'kleptocrats' ruling the country, communities across are struggling and people's fight against the 'kleptocratic power' is raging. These farmers, adivasis, dalits urban poor and working class of Bharat have sacrificed their life on the altar of 'destructive development', while trying to defend the piece of mother earth to which they belong and from which they seek their livelihood. These struggles are not only to protect their livelihood but central to this is defending the basic tenets of our democracy. The overall struggle is for deepening of democracy in the country–to establish the rule of law, to ensure right to life and livelihood with dignity, to ensure democratic control over natural resources–*zameen, jal, jangal, and Khaniz* (land, water, forest and minerals).

To suppress the people, fascist forces of Emergency is re-emerging and asserting them selves in a crude manner by heaping insult, injury and death on the citizens. On the eve of the 36th Anniversary of Emergency, veteran journalist Kuldip Nayar wrote in anguish: "The new generation must understand that today's non-governance or mis-governance is the fallout of what Indira Gandhi had done 36 years ago by destroying an established democratic order....How do you make the new generation relate to Emergency imposed some 36 years ago this week? I have been asked this question many a time.... I do not have an answer."

Opening chapter of the Book juxtaposes the two personalities–JP and Indira-who are the dramatis personae of this Book. The next two chapters dwell upon the way Emergency papers were suppressed, how they were dug out and what they reveal. This story is told in the language of the media. After that the Book is a lucid narration of author's first-person account of Emergency days when 'autocrat' Indira ruled from the 'Delhi Durbar' and 'democrat' JP suffered in 'solitary confinement' at Chandigarh. Final chapters deal with the collapse of Emergency, defeat of autocracy and regaining India's Freedom, all made possible by the Rebel-Recluse, Jayaprakash Narayan….

This Book would provide the answer to Kuldip Nayar's anguishing lament and will tell the truth and relate the Emergency and India's Second Freedom to the new generation. The Book does it by placing both the icons–that of autocracy and democracy - in perspective leaving it to the people in general and the youth in particular to understand, appreciate and judge….

And also to keep the flame burning…. As a leader of the JP Movement once said: "These movements never die. Just when you think you've put it out, it catches fire somewhere else." Now read on….

— M G Devasahayam
October 2011

Foreword

On the night of 25th June 1975 and the wee hours of the 26th, Indira Gandhi imposed Emergency and Bharat's democracy entered a dark era. The dictatorial Prime Minister suspended all fundamental rights on the flimsy ground of an imagined revolution against the state. Loknayak, as JP was fondly called, was arrested on 26 June and sent to Haryana. From there, he was taken to the All India Institute of Medical Sciences (AIIMS) on 29th June due to his failing health. The need for specialized medical care finally forced the state to take him to the Post Graduate Institute of Medical Education and Research (PGIMER) in Chandigarh on 1st July. His ordeal was lessened there because of a compassionate young MG Devasahayam who was the District Magistrate of Chandigarh and would talk hours with JP and discuss various social and political issues facing the country.

Devasahayam was JP's custodian in Jail. He met JP almost on a daily basis. He was responsible for JP's security arrangements, monitoring of his health, screening of visitors, and keeping the Central Government informed about JP's situation.

While most of the things he did came by way of a call of duty as a bureaucrat, he seized the opportunity to talk to one of the greatest souls of Bharat at a time that became a turning point in the history of the country. Instead of treating JP as a guest of the government, he looked up to him as a man who had inspired millions of people to take up the cudgels for their rights. For him, JP was a living connection with and embodiment of the ideas and ideals that Gandhiji instilled in those who fought for our freedom.

The result was the natural absorbing conversations that make several chapters of this book. JP comes through as a man surprised at the intensity of the reaction that he had produced. From a low point, he gradually recovered his old self, and in spite of his ill health, showed the determination to right the wrong that was done to Bharat.

Through Devasahayam, we hear fascinating glimpses of JP's association with Indira Gandhi and Jawaharlal Nehru, and his turbulent relationship with the former. JP reminiscences about Kamaraj, discusses the political leaders he knew, and dissects the events that led to the imposition of Emergency. In jail, he hones his strategy to unite opposition parties for elections. He weeps for the people of Bihar, devastated by floods.

The Emergency was imposed to crush anti-corruption movement led by JP. The movement also epitomized the combined anger of people against price-rise and misrule of the then Congress government and a clamour for empowerment and answers to their pitiable existence.

Prime Minister Indira Gandhi, the flamboyant daughter of a democrat father, undermined democratic institutions and norms, debased politics, allowed corruption to assume unprecedented proportions and victimized those who stood for principles and integrity. This has been the single most important cause of the relentless putrefaction of Bharat's public life from the time of the Emergency and the country's descent into 'Kleptocracy'.

JP was a Titan. His life exemplified the ethos of idealism and he generously worked for welfare of the people as a legendary freedom fighter, a Socialist party worker, a leader of the Sarvodaya movement, a peacemaker in Nagaland, and the conscience of Bharat in the 1970s, before, during and after the Emergency. He emerged as the tallest figure in the history of modern Bharat post-Independence.

JP's personality was ever youthful and that is why he had the determination of never say die attitude. That is the reason I feel he was found out experimenting and learning from experiences, He was not captive of any dogma or fetters of ideologies and was keen to correct himself and move forward in the thought process. He never harboured any illusion that he was all knowledgeable and that he was the last word on every subject. He was always keen to learn from young activists.

In the first decade of the post-independence era he could realize that the constructive plank of the movement should not be neglected and he had the courage enough to get engaged in constructive activities in northern Bihar be it part of Saharsa or Musahari in Saharan district. He integrated the ethos of Marxism and socialism into more comprehensive ethics based ideology of Sarvodaya. His courage can be estimated by his response at a particular stage that 'if the Jan Sangh is fascist, then Jayaprakash Narayan is also a fascist'. Only such magnanimity could bring together a variety of political forces, Right or Left notwithstanding, and fine tune it into a viable, successful and political weapon to defeat the authoritarian forces. He had told the ultra Left that 'you may not agree with me on non-violence as a principle but understanding the challenges of the time the Leftist should strategically shun violence and adhere to peaceful means for national reconstruction'.

When he was the member of the Congress Party, he attempted to ensure that it kept to the ideals of socialism. We remember him as the daring revolutionary who escaped from jail and went underground during the 1942 Quit India Movement, and then underwent hideous torture in Lahore jail on being captured. We remember him as the socialist stalwart who suddenly walked out of electoral politics into the Sarvodaya movement, fashioning a philosophy centered on Gram Swaraj and the politics of 'people's power'. His aim was to work for the common man.

Then, suddenly in the mid-1970s when gloom pervaded the country, this 73-year-old man became the beacon of hope for a disenchanted nation. A new generation listened to his indictment of the corruption and misrule of the then Indira Gandhi Government. And thus started the maelstrom that came to be known as the JP Movement. It shook the polity to its core and forced its regeneration through a mass upsurge. The JP Movement was at its most impressive and the strongest in Bihar.

The movement had the support of the entire spectrum of non-Congress political parties, barring the Communists.

To break the backbone of this massive Movement, National Emergency was clamped on the country on 25 June 1975. In an overnight swoop, most leaders of the movement were put behind the bars. During the Emergency era (1975-77), the government committed all kinds of excesses including forced sterilization of people since officials were given targets. All norms of democracy were throttled and there was complete censorship of the Press. Most institutions of parliamentary democracy were on the verge of collapse since those considered powerful were keen to genuflect before the might of Indira Gandhi.

These led to an upsurge against the Congress when elections were announced in 1977. People showed their support for JP and defeated the Congress by a massive mandate when elections took place in March 1977. A fragile looking JP won over dictatorial Indira Gandhi. Devasahayam has vividly captured the eyeball-to-eyeball confrontation that obtained between Indira Gandhi and JP and the former's defeat.

Tenacity and stamina of the JP Movement was proven during the three years when it faced different challenges. JP's stellar leadership matched up to the challenges. He never got into the issue of political and non-political and retrieved himself successfully from the high pitch of politics. From April 1974 to August 1974, it sounded anti-political. But come November, JP was the leader to pick up the gauntlet and enter the arena of politics accepting the challenge of Shrimati Indira Gandhi. From 1977 onwards, his ill health made him much more uneasy and agitated and he could not assume the desired role that time.

This first person account of the movement by Devasahayam makes for an interesting reading. He has been able to break into the government fortress and bring out 'Secret Emergency documents' hidden from the public for over three-and-a-half decades. This will add lot of value to research on JP and open a new perspective.

The timing of this book is significant. Emergency clouds are looking large over the country once again. After nearly 40 years, the situation that led to the JP movement is getting repeated in this decade.

This means that basic issues remain still unaddressed. In the pattern of governance, square peg in the round hole situation has neither been sensitively assessed, nor been sincerely addressed in the post Independence era. Only some patchworks by way of constitutional amendments have been attempted.

Dissent is being crushed and police, the CBI and various other agencies of the state are being used by the government to settle scores with adversaries. The way police resorted to midnight crackdown on Baba Ramdev and his supporters on 4 June 2011 at Delhi's Ramlila Maidan showed that the present government was not bothered about democracy or public opinion.

The government also tried to bully the Anna Hazare led movement against corruption and used all chicanery to defame those leading the movement. It is an irony that after coming to power, the democratically elected government try to kick the very same ladder because of which they could reach to the top.

But this movement needs to be extra cautious since it will have to pass through the various twists and turns. If the response of this movement to the callous, reluctant and dishonest approach of the government is to consistently avoid tangible results of the agitation, then the million dollar question hangs in the air as to whether the movement would end up merely as a fruitless pressure group or achieve some tangible results. Also, significant is whether or not the agitation will into the forays of power politics? Comparing a single issue movement with JP movement is unfair. The new movement is yet to prove the stamina and determination of the cause and cohesiveness of the leadership. For the benefits of those who want to understand JP, I need to remind that when JP was questioned by Indira Gandhi about his faith in democracy, he did not agitate but decided to spread the movement. He then used all his skills for networking politicians across the country and for bringing them in the fold. While this gave a fresh momentum to the movement, he had his own plans to forge a new force of youngsters so that overdependence on political parties could be countered.

Corruption has reached new heights. Ministers and parliamentarians are in jail for their misdeeds but the people who might have benefitted from the loot continue to be in power shamelessly. Morality of those in government and administration has never been so slow. Added to these is the issue of ever increasing price rise.

The problems of national integration and lack of cohesion in society have been always brushed under the carpet. While quick fix solutions are being attempted, systemic change based on the pedestals of indigenous thinking and decentralization is yet to be effectively initiated. And systemic change conducive to Bharatiya ethos and compatible with the needs of the times is yet to emerge and get popularized in youth. Today's youth is forward looking in this regard. There is enough vitality courage and perseverance witnessed in the present youth which is the silver lining in the sky.

As a mark of respect to the indomitable JP, the time has come once again to fight for restoration of democratic values and a corruption free society. The country is poised for complete transformation–*vyavastha parivartan*–through reforms at all levels. And a mass movement is needed to achieve this desired goal. I am happy to write a forward to Devasahayam's book which I hope will act like fuel to the fire. Also, I wish to give full credits to the publisher for bringing this book.

— K N Govindacharya

Emergency Icons: 'Autocrat' Indira Vs 'Democrat' JP

INDIRA PRIYADARSHINI NEHRU was born on 19 November 1917, and was the only child of Jawaharlal and Kamla Nehru. The active participation of both her parents in India's independence struggle drew Indira to politics at an early age. It was as if politics and politicians always surrounded her.

By the time she was about twelve years old, she headed what came to be known as the Vanar Sena (Monkey Brigade). This brigade consisted of children who warned the independence movement leaders of their arrest. Being its leader, she delivered speeches while other children actually warned the people who were going to be arrested. The Congress figured that the British would not suspect children of participating in such activities.

She was soon sent to England for her studies where she joined the Somerville College, Oxford. She also spent time in Switzerland, primarily because her mother needed to be there due to her ill-health. Kamla Nehru passed away in 1936.

In 1938, Indira returned to India and joined the Indian National Congress. Soon afterwards, in 1942, she married journalist Feroze Jehangir Gandhi and had two sons–Rajiv and Sanjay. Soon after the couple was married, they were sent to prison on charges of subversion by the British. Her one and only imprisonment lasted from 11 September 1942, until 13 May 1943, at the Naini Central Jail in Allahabad.

India won its independence from British in 1947. In that same year, Jawaharlal Nehru became India's first Prime Minister. Since her mother's death, Indira acted as her father's hostess and confidante and travelled with Nehru. Simultaneously, she was steadily making her presence felt in the political arena. In 1953-57, she was chairman of the Central Social Welfare Board. In 1955, she became a member of the Congress Working Committee and Central Election Committee, the Central Parliamentary Board in 1956, and was the president of the All-India Youth Congress from 1956 to 1960.

After the death of Jawaharlal Nehru in1964, the then Prime Minister, Lal Bahadur Shastri, appointed Indira Gandhi as the Minister for Information and Broadcasting. This position was the fourth highest-ranking position in the Cabinet as radio and television were important sources of information for the largely illiterate population of India. As a minister, she encouraged the making of inexpensive radio sets and started a family planning programme.

Shastri suddenly died of a heart attack in 1966. The contenders for his post could not agree among themselves and, therefore, felt that Indira Gandhi would be the best bet for the position. Hence, she became the Prime Minister in 1966, till India held the next elections in 1967. She won the election and became the first woman Prime Minister of India. In 1971, Gandhi was re-elected. Her slogan of *Garibi Hatao* (abolish poverty) had become extremely popular.

She rode a wave of success in 1971 with India's victory in the Indo-Pak war and the launching of India's first satellite into space. And, with the testing of a nuclear device in 1974, she earned the reputation of a tough and shrewd politician among the middle class.

At the same time, by 1973, large-scale demonstrations began to take place across Delhi and northern India. A large section of the population felt that she was not living up to her promises of *Garibi Hatao*. High inflation, rampant corruption and poor standards of living led to social unrest. Student agitation and the resultant JP movement were the fallout of this unrest.

In an attempt to control population growth, the Indira government implemented a voluntary sterilization programme. Her adversaries, however, criticized the programme and Indira began to face strong opposition to her administration in general.

By 1975, Indira Gandhi had to face charges of corruption. In June 1975, the High Court of Allahabad found her guilty of using illegal practices during the last election campaign. She was ordered to vacate her seat. There were demands for her resignation. She responded by declaring a state of emergency on 25 June 1975.

During this Emergency, the Supreme Court of India overturned the Allahabad High Court's judgment. Through the powers ensured to her through the Emergency, she ordered the arrests of the main Opposition leaders. In her opinion, she had declared an emergency for the good of India. The constitutional rights of citizens were extinguished and the Press was under strict censorship overnight. Meanwhile, her younger son, Sanjay Gandhi, ordered the removal of slum dwellings and, in an attempt to curb India's growing population, initiated a highly-resented programme of forced sterilization.

In early 1977, Indira thought she had eliminated her Opposition and called for fresh elections. Her Congress Party lost badly at the polls. She was voted out of power and a newly formed coalition of political parties came to power. Many declared that she was a spent force. But Indira came back to power again in 1980. The same year, however, her son Sanjay was killed in an airplane crash.

In the post-Emergency period, the Prime Minister Gandhi was preoccupied by efforts to resolve the political problems in the state of Punjab. In her attempt to crush the secessionist movement of Sikh militants, led by Jarnail Singh Bhindranwale, she ordered an assault upon the holiest Sikh shrine in Amritsar, the Golden Temple. It was from here that Bhindranwale and his armed supporters waged their campaign. Operation Bluestar, waged in June 1984, led to the death of Bhindranwale, and the Golden Temple was stripped clean of Sikh terrorists. However, the shrine was damaged and Indira earned the undying hatred of Sikhs. In November of the same year, Indira was assassinated at her residence by two of her own Sikh bodyguards, who claimed to be avenging the insult heaped upon the Sikh nation.

Her death led to sectarian violence across India during which over a thousand people died, most of them Sikhs. Instead of following democratic principles of electing a senior leader as prime minister, the Congress Party chose dynastic succession by installing Indira's son Rajiv Gandhi, an Indian Airlines co-pilot, who had absolutely no grounding or experience in politics, governance or administration.

Indira Gandhi was remarkable for her ambition for personal power, her endurance and political tenacity. On the international front, she built up the image of a tough Third World leader and a forceful spokeswoman for the rights of poorer nations. On the domestic front, however, her autocratic methods often clashed with her democratic principles. She had an authoritarian streak and rarely tolerated dissent. In many respects, Indian democracy was irreparably harmed during her rule. Apart from her infamous imposition of the internal emergency, the use of the Army to resolve internal disputes greatly increased in her time.

On its 125th anniversary in 2010, her own Congress Party finally spoke the truth about Indira. This is what the book titled *A Centenary History of the Indian National Congress* says about their 'great' leader:

> "She (*Gandhi*) attempted to reach down to the bottom level and restructure the party from the top into an 'oligarchy' controlled with the help of her close aides. This led to the breakdown of the 'machine' character of Congress, which had been the strength of the party in some states....By the mid-1980s, considerable damage had occurred to the organisation and electoral base of the party from which it has not yet fully recovered. Her attempt to control the party led to absence of internal democracy leading to collapse of branches of the party in key states such as UP."

The book brought out by a group of editors, headed by senior party leader Pranab Mukherjee, delves deep into some of the unpleasant chapters in Congress history, including the Emergency, and covers the period from 1964 to 1984 of which a fairly large portion is devoted to Indira Gandhi. Let us look at some of the passages:

> "Paradoxically, just when the conditions in the country and the party were ripe for achieving Gandhi's vision of change, she got pushed into personality-oriented politics that resulted in centralisation and personalisation of power in her hands."

> "Indira adopted 'personality based politics' rather than consensus based politics. She dismantled the party, removed the intermediate leadership and the process of the consultative decision-making and re-built it without a democratic structure with office-bearers personally responsible to her."

> "Indira had inherited a fairly well-organised party machine with several capable leaders in the states across the country. But her bypassing of the party machinery inaugurated the decline of single party dominance, and a process of long term decay of the party organisation, particularly in north India. Impact of these developments contributed to the virtual collapse of the party in the 1990s... these developments cumulatively impacted on the social and regional base of the party and its electoral fortunes."

With her elder son Rajiv Gandhi succeeding her as Prime Minister, the dynastic dominance in the Congress Party comprising servile sycophants continued. His wife and the current 'numero uno' has taken to her mother-in-law in all manners and mannerism. The way she dresses, the choice of her handloom sarees, the masculine watch on her wrist, the briskness of her walk, the manner in which she sits on the dais at the AICC sessions, the intonation of her "*Jai Hind*"–these are all reminiscent of Indira Gandhi. As if to reflect this, slogans have been coined to underscore the similarities between the two–*Sonia Gandhi kaisi hai, Indira Gandhi jaisi hai* (like Indira, like Sonia!).

SARVODAYA LEADER JAYAPRAKASH NARAYAN (JP) was the front-line foot soldier of Mahatma Gandhi during the freedom struggle. He never sought power and did not enjoy it even for a day. Well before Indira was anywhere near politics, JP had been offered the posts of Union Cabinet Minister, Prime Minister and President of India in quick succession and he turned down each one of them. Though considered the natural successor to Nehru as prime minister, JP chose to withdraw from power politics, to engage in the more enduring struggle against poverty, social evils and violence. JP was an iconoclast with compassion and a product of the Magadha legacy which "not only produced relentless fighters and exterminators of kings" but "hearkened at the same time to the devout teachings of Vardhamana Mahavira and Gautama Buddha."

The man who could have become the second prime minister of India, and possibly finished off the Nehru-Indira dynasty rule for ever, unwittingly became its perpetrator by declining to take office. Instead, he became, after Mahatma Gandhi, the second redeemer of the nation, freeing the country from the shackles of a home-brewed dictatorship, which was imposed by an unprincipled Indira Gandhi. Sometimes leaders scale such lofty heights of national eminence that they become too big for mundane office. In post-Emergency India, JP never occupied any official seat of power and was regarded as the nation's patron saint.

Jayaprakash Narayan was born on 11 October 1902, in Sitabdiara, a village on the border of Uttar Pradesh and Bihar. Whenever the Ganga changed course, JP's ancestral house has been shown alternately in Bihar and UP. He became a natural leader among the village boys. Jayaprakash was married to Prabhavati, daughter of lawyer and nationalist Brij Kishore Prasad, in October 1920. Prabhavati was very independent-minded and, on Gandhiji's invitation, went to stay at his ashram while Jayaprakash continued his studies. Because of Prabhavati's vow of celibacy while JP was away in the USA, and his honouring the same on return, the couple did not have any children and therefore had no family.

As he grew up and cut his teeth in public life, JP wanted to overhaul the entire Indian society. For him, the political system had to be responsive to the aspirations of the poorest of the poor; the glaring inequalities that our economic system breeds had to end; the educational system should be geared to the needs of the nation; the canker of corruption in India's political and administrative system had to be eradicated; the various social ills that afflict our country had to end. This, in simplistic and pragmatic terms, is what JP meant by "Total Revolution." The kind of sweeping reforms JP had in mind appear like a utopian abstraction, but nobody can contest their fundamental desirability. Evidently, the initiative for such a revolution has to come from society as a whole, not just the government.

JP was a dreamer and an idealist to a fault. It was Maulana Abul Kalam Azad's fiery oratory and his call to, "lift up to the skies like leaves before a storm" that drew JP to the freedom movement. Jayaprakash took the Maulana's words to heart and left Patna College with just 20 days remaining for his examinations. He joined the Bihar Vidyapeeth, a college run by the Congress. After exhausting the courses at the Vidyapeeth, Jayaprakash decided to go to America to pursue his studies. To pay for his education, Jayaprakash picked grapes, set them out to dry, packed fruits at a canning factory, washed dishes, worked as a mechanic at a garage and at a slaughterhouse, sold lotions and accepted teaching jobs. All these jobs gave Jayaprakash insights into the problems of the working class.

JP's sojourn in America for seven years at the prestigious universities of Berkeley, Iowa and Wisconsin only increased his passion for freedom. He was a student of professor Edward Ross, the father of sociology and while at Wisconsin, was introduced to Karl Marx's *Das Capital.* His Ohio professor observed in the young man "germs of leadership" and "aggressiveness of thought." When he returned to India in November 1929, he was "a mature young man with an enquiring mind, original in his thinking, and with the fierce, idealistic desire to devote himself to serve society."

For JP, freedom transcended beyond politics and included freedom from hunger, poverty and ignorance. This conviction was the hallmark of JP's struggle throughout his life before and after Independence. Power and office did not appeal to him and he remained a revolutionary in thought and action. Though Jayaprakash was a believer in the Communist school of thought, he joined the Congress Party at the invitation of Jawaharlal Nehru and fought for independence shoulder to shoulder with the likes of Ram Manohar Lohia, Ashok Mehta, Achyut Patwardhan and Acharya Narendra Dev.

On the attainment of independence, when people scrambled for loaves of office, JP stood apart, concentrating his efforts on leading the Congress Party towards the socialist path. He politely turned down Pandit Nehru's repeated invitations to join his cabinet. Instead, he turned his attention to the trade unions he led. With the help of the unions, he was able to get many facilities for the workers such as minimum wage, pension, medical relief and housing subsidy. Seeing the totalitarian ways and bloody purges unleashed in Soviet Russia, JP turned away from Communism.

He decided to dedicate himself totally to Mahatma Gandhi's ideal of *sampoorna swarajya* and pursue his efforts towards 'people's participatory governance' and corruption-free, value based public life. In 1954, he blended himself with Vinoba Bhave's Sarvodaya movement. He gave up his landed property and withdrew from all political activity to devote the rest of his life to the movement. He set up an ashram in poor and backward Hazaribagh, trying to give Gandhian concepts a new dimension by using modern technology to uplift the villages. Even Prime Minister Nehru's suggestion in the late fifties that JP could be his successor did not lure him back to politics.

In his eventful political career, JP always served as a carrier of expectations, a catalyst of mighty happenings, although he never claimed, and rightly so, to be the creator or the moulder of such events. After his early wanderings in search of an ideology, which could combine his urge for nationalism with his yearning for a better social order where poverty could be banished, he shot into the limelight in Indian politics when he founded the Congress Socialist Party in 1934. The inspiration for it, of course, came from Jawaharlal Nehru's groping for a way to instill in the Congress a commitment to social change in the struggle for Independence. Jayaprakash took the initiative for setting up a definite group within the Congress itself.

Those were the years when some of the finest intellectuals-turned-activists in the national movement like Narendra Dev, Yusuf Meherally, Achyut Patwardhan and Rammanohar Lohia joined hands with him, or more correctly, spurred him on in the new endeavour. Side by side, the outlawed Communists, after a protracted phase of persecution and sectarianism, also felt the need to build bridges with comrades-in-arms against foreign rule. It was this combination of the urge for socialism with the restlessness of militant nationalism that soon made the Congress Socialist Party a force to reckon with, so much so that it commanded in strength more than one-third of the AICC, with its influence spilling over to many more.

JP was arrested for speaking against Indian participation in the Second World War in February 1940 and sent to the Deoli detention camp in Rajasthan. He was again arrested in 1942 for participating in the Quit India Movement. In November 1942, Diwali night, JP, along with five others, escaped the high-security Hazaribagh jail by scaling a 17-foot-high wall while the guards remained distracted by the festivities. A reward of Rs 10,000 was offered for JP's capture, dead or alive. He escaped to Nepal and organized a guerilla army called the Azad Dasta. JP and Ram Manohar Lohia were captured briefly but rescued by the Azad Dasta members, who set fire to a hut to distract the guards. Both freedom fighters escaped to Bihar. Finally, the British closed in on JP in Amritsar when he was on his way to Rawalpindi to meet Khan Abdul Gaffar Khan. He was taken to Lahore Fort, notorious as a "torture chamber" on 18 September 1943. Sixteen months of mental and physical torture followed. JP was put in solitary confinement for the first month. Then came interrogations, physical torture and humiliation. He was released from jail on 12 April 1946.

AP Sinha, a jail-mate and close friend whom JP tried to persuade to join the Hazaribagh escapade, had this exhortation to make to the latter prior to the escape: "JP, I am sorry I cannot make the break with you. I want to come for the love of you and keep you company and support you. But my health is poor and I'm not sure I could be effective. I'm too deeply Gandhian. All I'll do is to hide myself. I'm only used to attending political meetings and passing resolutions. I would not be able to give you the help you need. Let me help to cover your getaway. *You have got the passion that can make people's spirits soar up. You can inspire them to self-sacrifices, to accept sufferings. You are a great national leader.*"

Independence finally came on 15 August 1947. Within a year Gandhiji was assassinated. The Socialists lost to the Congress in the 1952 elections. Nehru invited JP to join the Cabinet. When Nehru could give no assurances on the implementation of JP's 14-point plan to reform the Constitution, the administration and the judicial system, nationalize the banks, redistribute land to the landless, revive swadeshi, and set up cooperatives, he refused the offer.

On 19 April 1954, at a meeting in Gaya, JP made the dramatic announcement of dedicating his life (*jeewan daan*) to Vinoba Bhave's Sarvodaya movement. He renounced all self-interest, gave up his land in Sitabdiara, and withdrew from all personal activity to devote the rest of his life to the movement. Prabhavati was delighted at this declaration. It was then that JP set up his ashram in Hazaribagh.

JP believed that every village should be like a small republic–politically independent and capable of taking its own decisions. It was a marriage of Gandhian-Indian concepts and modern western democracy. His thoughtful, well-researched and brilliant book, *The Reconstruction of Indian Polity* won him the Ramon Magsaysay Award.

In June 1971, Sarvodaya workers in Muzaffarpur, Bihar, received a letter threatening to kill them. The area was continuously threatened by Naxals, who were militant young men. JP walked into the heart of Naxal territory armed only with love and sympathy. He knew that the cause of violence was the frustration of the youth because of poverty and unemployment. He lived in Musahari block for many months and experimented with measures to alleviate the problems of the Naxals.

Jayaprakash was also a key person in acquiring the surrender of dacoits in the Chambal Valley.

On 15 April 1973, Prabhavati died of cancer leaving Jayaprakash alone and devastated.

But, true to his idealism and passion, JP returned to active politics in 1974 at the ripe age of 72 when student unrest against corruption, unemployment and high inflation spread like wild fire, threatening to turn violent and go beyond control. In the face of terror and repression unleashed on the students by the governments of Bihar and Gujarat, JP, who had spurned the office of prime minister, took charge and thus was born the 'JP Movement' that shook corrupt and authoritarian governments to their very foundation.

As part of the movement, on 8 April 1974, JP led a silent procession at Patna. The procession was lathi-charged and this created a mass upsurge against corruption and autocratic rule. On 5 June 1974, riding the crest of a popular upheaval against all that was rotten in governance and public life, JP declared at a massive rally in Patna:

> "This is a revolution, friends! We are not here merely to see the Vidhan Sabha dissolved. That is only one milestone on our journey. But we have a long way to go... After 27 years of freedom, people of this country are wracked by hunger, rising prices, corruption... oppressed by every kind of injustice... it is a total revolution we want, nothing less!"

There is an interesting anecdote about how JP was brought into the Bihar movement. According to Ramnath Goenka, owner of the *Indian Express* Group, this was done via Tirupati. When JP had reservations about leading the Bihar movement on health grounds, saying he would not live for long. Ramnathji, along with Nanaji Deshmukh and Ramdhari Singh Dinkar (the famous Hindi poet), took him to Tirupati where Dinkarji prayed to the Lord to give the remaining years of his life to JP. All of them returned to Madras (now Chennai), and Dinkarji died in the lap of JP in Ramnath Goenka's house. Thus, was born the JP Movement, which changed the grammar of the national politics in the mid-1970s.

When, on 12 June 1975, the Allahabad High Court held Prime Minister Indira Gandhi guilty on charges of corrupt practices in the election, JP advised her to resign until her name was cleared by the Supreme Court. Instead, she clamped the Emergency on the nation.. JP was the first to be arrested under the Defence of India Rules.

Finally, in January 1977, fresh elections were declared. Under JP's guidance and leadership, several parties united to form the Janata Party and, in the March 1977 elections, defeated dictatorship and returned democracy to the country.

JP was physically weak and helpless by that time. He felt his work was done, but he had to sorrowfully witness the collapse of the Janata Party Government. He died on 8 October 1979. People hailed him as Lok Nayak or Leader of the People though he considered himself only a *lok sevak* or a servant of the people.

The Emergency Papers

Kuldip Nayar wrote in his article, 'Transparency in system' (June 2011): "What happened during the Emergency, which lasted from June 1975 to March 1977, is a shameful story of a takeover by a prime minister to save power and her skin. Prime Minister Indira suspended the Constitution, gagged the Press and imposed personal rule to overcome the handicap of disqualification from Parliament… Only a few dare to point out the excesses of those days because the impression is that when you do so, you are tagged anti-Congress, and will be out of favour with the rulers… The entire story is yet to come out. In fact, the demand for making papers of those days public, raised again and again, goes unheeded." Nayar is partly right and partly wrong. Initially the demand did go unheeded, but then Government had to heed. Let us look at media reports and editorials on this:

Emergency! No govt record of our darkest days*

Chennai: So where are the records of India's darkest days, the political period that seemed to spell curtains for democracy, the Emergency of 1975-1977? If replies to an RTI query are to be believed, no one knows where to find the communications between then President Fakhruddin

* *Times of India*, 8 August 2010.

Ali Ahmed and the government before and after the Emergency. And no one has any idea where to look for the relevant documents, notings and records of various decisions. These are not with us, says the ministry of home affairs, passing the buck to the National Archives of India (NAI). The NAI, which is the repository of non-current records of the government of India, says nothing was transferred to it. So where did the records go?

The presumption is that they (the officers) have either destroyed them or they don't want to give it away. In this context, one can only assume that all the allegations (pertaining to the Emergency period) against Indira Gandhi and Sanjay Gandhi were true, said M G Devasahayam, an ex-IAS officer who served as Chandigarh district magistrate during the Emergency.

On February 25, Devasahayam, who now lives in Chennai, set off a chain of extraordinary events with extraordinary implications when he sent an RTI application to Sanjukta Ray, deputy secretary and chief principal information officer in the prime ministers office (PMO). He asked for information on the presidential proclamation of June 6, 1975, declaring a state of Emergency in the country that lasted up to March/ April 1977. The PMO replied on March 4, transferring the queries for appropriate action under Section 6(3) of the RTI Act, to the ministry of home affairs, the nodal ministry for enforcing the Emergency.

On April 7, P K Mishra, a director in the home ministry, said the information sought was more than 25 years old and not available with the ministry. As per Rule 5 of the Public Records Rules, 1997, the relevant records and documents may be available in the National Archives of India, he said, adding that a copy of Devasahayam's application had been forwarded to the NAI.

The NAI's response was prompt but the mystery only deepened. On May 11, Rajesh Verma, assistant director, NAI, wrote to Devasahayam, saying, during a preliminary search, the requisite information sought could not be located... since it has not been transferred to the NAI.

On May 27, Devasahayam dashed off a complaint under Section 18 of the RTI Act to chief information commissioner Wajahat Habibullah but says his good friend and batch mate... remains silent. Devasahayam says he wants the information, which is not under the Official Secrets Act, because the country is yet to get over the hangover of the dark days. All that is going on now and the corruption in the system has flowed from then.

The 15 questions listed in the application pertain to the competent authority's duly attested clean copy of all relevant records or documents, including the noting portion, on causes leading to the declaration of Emergency and its nature; on the proceedings, recommendation and resolution adopted by the Union Cabinet to declare the state of Emergency and the names of those who attended the Cabinet meeting; on how the recommendation was conveyed to the President and by whom; orders, directions, guidelines, wireless, telex and telegraphic messages issued by the government from time-to-time for imposing and monitoring the state of Emergency; for imposing and monitoring press censorship; for arresting and detaining citizens under the Maintenance of Internal Security Act (MISA) and other relevant laws during the period and the number of persons detained under the MISA and the names of prominent political personalities among them and all documents relating to the end of Emergency and the notification concerned.

Devasahayam, who has written a book, *'India's 2nd Freedom, an Untold Saga'*, also listed queries on Jayaprakash Narayan, social reformer and revolutionary, his arrest and detention, letters exchanged between him and the government, including Indira Gandhi and the alleged Operation Medicine, the death drill in the event of JP dying in detention and the copy of the interim and final reports submitted by Dr Nagappa Alva Commission (1977-78), which enquired into the medical treatment given to JP (whose kidneys failed while he was in detention) at the Post Graduate Institute of Medical Education and Research (PGI), Chandigarh and action taken thereafter.

"Some of the information I seek I already have, as I served as district magistrate in Chandigarh before, during and after the Emergency. But I need nationwide records and information", said the 1968 batch IAS officer. The country is yet to get over the hangover of the dark days.

Even now, we have not come out of it. All that is going on now, the corruption in the system, has flowed from the Emergency days. This will be the focus of my next book", he said.

Experiments with untruth*

The Congress and its government at the centre have overturned the old adage that truth will be out. The facts relating to two major events of post-independence history will never be known. One of these is the Emergency of 1975-77, which was the country's first experience with authoritarianism. And the other is the Henderson-Brooks report on the 1962 border conflict with China. What is curious about the official silence about the Emergency is that there are apparently no records at all about the whys and wherefores of its proclamation. The Henderson-Brooks report is at least known to exist although the government says that it cannot be released because of its "extremely sensitive" nature. But there is not a scrap of paper in the ministries and archives about the Emergency.

This unexpected disclosure came to light after an RTI application was submitted by a former IAS officer, MG Devasahayam, to the PMO seeking details. Then began the typical bureaucratic game of passing the buck. The PMO referred the matter to the home ministry and the latter to the national archives. But the end result was zilch. Nothing emerged from their exertions — or the lack of them. Yet, the non-discovery will not surprise those who have had the misfortune of living through those days of India's experiments with untruth.

The first probable reason why nothing exists on paper is that the original orders were verbal. It was several hours after the Emergency was proclaimed in President Fakhruddin Ali Ahmed's name that the Union cabinet presided over by Indira Gandhi gave its post-facto approval. Only Swaran Singh, who was the defence minister, "wondered aloud", as noted by Granville Austin in his book, *Working a Democratic Constitution: A*

---

* Editorial in *New Indian Express*, Chennai on 10 August 2010.

History of the Indian Experience, whether it was necessary to take such a drastic step. But "the others remained silent and Indira did not reply". That tense and craven silence in the cabinet room on the morning of June 26, 1975, shows why the RTI application has drawn a blank. The transition is a secretive process enveloped in uncertainty and suspicion and perhaps also a guilt complex. Any notes will be nothing but exercises in falsification and, therefore, useless as historical documents.

How they surfaced and the Impact*

Chennai: Nearly three weeks after a report was published in TOI (August 8, 2010) about the mysterious disappearance of documents and records relating to the Emergency period, the National Archives of India (NAI), a repository of non-current records of the government of India, said it had located a few files received from the ministry of home affairs some time ago.

Owing to the sensitive nature of the documents, they had been classified and subsequently declassified by the MHA before appraisal and transfer to NAI and had been kept separately, in light of instructions from the ministry. Hence, they do not figure in the general list of files transferred to the home department and all the officers of the records division were not aware of their availability, Verma said in a letter to MG Devasahayam, whose RTI application seeking Emergency-related documents had drawn a blank....

...On August 20, the NAI wrote to Devasahayam, referring to the report that appeared in TOI rather than his RTI application saying they were able to lay their hands on some files. Since the physical condition of the files is not good, we are taking steps to have them repaired by the preservation department before they are made accessible for consultation under the Public Record Act and Rules, Verma said in his letter.

Devasahayam said, "I am surprised that the physical condition of the records with NAI is not good. I too have several communications and records of that period. But they are in a good condition, consider-

---

* *Times of India*, Chennai on 02 September 2010

ing that they are just 30 years old. In his reply to NAI on August 30, Devasahayam sought to know if he could get the information he had asked for in his RTI application to the PMO and if he could have access to the files for inspection."

The Immediate Impact

Papers were obtained in September 2010 and they were simultaneously put on the public domain by the National Archives of India. Provoked, Era Sezhiyan dug out his archives, brought out the full Shah Commission Report and published the same. Here is a media report:

MP's Book on Elusive Report*

What has the Shah Commission Report on the Emergency got to do with a popular story from the 'Skanda Purana?'

At least the "resurrected" version of the panel's report in a new format by veteran former MP Era Sezhiyan's "Shah Commission Report, Lost and Regained," has an odd mystical similarity with the tussle between Lord Ganesh and his brother Murugan for the "divine mango of knowledge."

The legend as recounted in the Purana speaks of sage Narada bringing the mango fruit and giving it to Shiva in Kailash. But a contest is set for the Lord's two sons—Ganesh and Murugan—that whoever encircled the Universe thrice first would get the fruit.

Murugan speeds through the universe thrice on his peacock. But a more pragmatic Ganesh circumambulates Lord Shiva and Parvathy thrice, as their parents are believed to identical with the universe itself and thus wins the fruit. A parallel to this tale was drawn by the former MP during the launch of his new book on the Shah Commission Report on the Emergency by senior BJP leader L K Advani.

Sezhiyan explained why he undertook this task now of compiling and editing the Commission's three-volume report submitted to the government way back in 1978.

---

* *Deccan Herald,* Chennai, 19 December 2010

Former civil servant M G Devasayaham, who took care of Jayaprakash Narayan when he was district commissioner in Chandigarh during the Emergency days, had been moving heaven and earth for the past several months through RTI applications to get some original documents related to the Proclamation of Emergency, for a detailed work.

But the Centre's dilly-dallying was enough to vex Devasahayam. When Sezhiyan came to know about the former IAS officer's plight and of another RTI activist Agarwal's vain effort, he began to dig up his library for the Shah Commission Report.

After the Congress Government in 1980 reportedly withdrew all the copies of that report, only two copies were said to have existed—in a library each in London and Australia, respectively. As Sezhiyan's library had all the three volumes, he felt that for the benefit of a whole new generation, this was the best moment to re-publish the same with his introduction as a constitutional expert.

The Shah Commission report has incorporated the key documents that Devasahayam had been hunting for from the National Archives, like Murugan encircling the Universe thrice. But Sezhiyan, like Lord Ganesh, just went round his own library and got the "fruit" he wanted.

Emergency Files: What they Reveal

On this subject, I shall let the media speak first.

Emergency papers found, Minus Indira Signature*

New Delhi: Six months after pleading ignorance about their whereabouts, the National Archives have come up with records of the infamous Emergency. Tell-tale gaps in the information though could well have been responsible for the delayed disclosure about a phase that the present rulers have much to be embarrassed about.

The original paperwork related to the proclamation of Emergency on June 25, 1975 and its draconian enforcement for 21 months has come into public domain, thanks to the tenacity of RTI applicant M G Devasahayam, who had Jayaprakash Narayan in his custody for six months as the then deputy commissioner of Chandigarh.

Though his application was shunted from the Prime Minister's Office to the home ministry and then to the National Archives, what forced the authorities to give up their blocking tactics was Devasahayam's recourse to a complaint under RTI as that could have had penal consequences for those denying information.

---

* *Times of India,* New Delhi, 10 December 2010

The reams of documents given to Devasahayam betray extraordinary attempts to distance Indira Gandhi from much of the illegal decisions responsible for the Emergency and its excesses. Though the signatures of other dramatis personae, President Fakhruddin Ali Ahmed downwards, are available on the Emergency records, there is none of Indira Gandhi herself in any of them.

The omission of Indira Gandhi's signature is most glaring in the file relating to the manner in which she had bypassed the Cabinet while asking Ahmed to sign the Emergency proclamation late in the night on June 25, 1975. While the original proclamation bearing Ahmed's signature is available, there is only a typed copy of the PM's top secret letter that had recommended imposition of Emergency under Article 352 of the Constitution.

According to the file, the copy of Indira Gandhi's historic letter was obtained by the home ministry from the President's Secretariat. The original letter signed by Indira Gandhi was probably taken out of the file at some point and kept away in her personal papers, which are in the control of her family.

Whatever the reason for the missing original, the file nails the claim made by Indira Gandhi in her letter that she had information suggesting that there is an imminent danger to the security of India being threatened by internal disturbance. The file does not contain a shred of material backing such threat perception on the fateful day.

In fact, the file reveals that the first assessment of the alleged threat of internal disturbance was made more than a fortnight after the imposition of Emergency. It was in the form of a report on the situation before and after June 25, 1975 from the Intelligence Bureau, submitted on July 11. This shows that India's hard-fought democracy was suspended on the perception of one individual, without any institutional checks....

What the files reveal?

- Proclamation of Emergency was not preceded by a comprehensive assessment of the 'grave emergency that threatened the security of India' as mentioned in the promulgation. There was no assessment or report on the files. There was no report on any "internal disturbance", major threat to law and order, or widespread mass violence from any State Government or Central/State agency.

- Prime Minister Indira Gandhi's letter to the President on June 25, 1975 night, saying that information had reached her that 'there is an imminent danger to the security of India being threatened by internal disturbance'. This meant that Emergency was declared and a functioning democracy was turned into a personal autocracy on the basis of lies and falsehood by the Head of Government to Head of State.
- Signatures of the President of India and Home Minister appear at various places in the file subsequent to the declaration of Emergency, Prime Minister Indira Gandhi's signature appears nowhere. Even the original letter sent by her to the President asking him to promulgate Emergency was taken back and is not available on the file. Only a typed copy is available.
- This meant that Indira was well aware of the seriousness and deviousness of the steps she was taking or was being forced to take. And so she distanced herself from the beginning, remote controlled and fired from other people's shoulders. This is the root cause for the severe damage to India's institutions of governance from which the country now suffers.

On 18 January 1977, Indira Gandhi made a public announcement that the general election to Parliament would be held in March 1977. Thereafter, on the direction of the Prime Minister, a group comprising the Additional Secretary and Joint Secretary, the MHA and the Joint Director, IB, constituted to advise on relaxation of the Emergency, examined the desirability of its revocation. On 12 February the group recommended revocation of the external emergency imposed on 3 December 1971, and the internal emergency promulgated on 25 June 1975.

Yet within three days, on 15 February under direction from Union Home Secretary (S L Khurana), a 'detailed' note suggesting continuation of the Emergency and Press censorship was prepared by the MHA and given to the Home Minister. In the event, the Emergency was lifted by a Cabinet Resolution only on 20 March 1977 (approved and signed by B D Jatti, Vice President, officiating as President on 21 March 1977) after the elections were over and the Janata Party was voted to power with a thumping majority.

This is confirmation of a parallel power centre under Sanjay Gandhi working for continuation of the Emergency by sabotaging the elections and restoration of normalcy. This is the same power centre that sabotaged the reconciliation efforts between JP and the Prime Minister, though Indira was in favour of it. But for this sabotage, Emergency would have been revoked within six months of its proclamation, thereby saving the nation from a great democratic tragedy.

It is the same S L Khurana who invoked the 'Union War Book' to maintain internal security and who initiated a note on 27 June 1975, suggesting issuance of a notification under Article 359 depriving citizens of the right to move the courts under Articles 14, 21 and 22 of the Constitution. This note was forwarded to the President by Home Minister Brahmananda Reddy on the same day and got approved. Both signed the file, the Cabinet approval was obtained and the notification, signed by Khurana, was issued that very day!

These matters were brought under the scrutiny of the Shah Commission and these documents confirm the findings of the Commission. But the Commission's Report was suppressed soon after the Congress came back to power in 1980. The impression given out was that this report was not available anywhere. But, as we have seen, the report has resurfaced and been published as a book.

Records do not show any process or procedure adopted before Fakruddin Ali Ahmed, the then President, signed the Emergency proclamation. This order was typed and signed on a plain sheet of paper without even a seal of the President's Office!

A proclamation of such enormous magnitude should have been preceded by a comprehensive assessment of the 'grave emergency that threatened the security of India'. Based on such assessment, the Union Cabinet should have considered the matter dispassionately and, if necessary, recommended imposition of internal emergency to the

President. No such assessment or recommendation is available on the files. There is no report of any "internal disturbance", major threat to law and order, or widespread mass violence from any State Government or Central/State agency.

The only piece of paper, prior to declaration of the Emergency, available on the file is a typed copy of a 'Top Secret' letter written by Prime Minister Indira Gandhi to the President on 25 June 1975 (time not indicated, and as per Shah Commission records, it was around 10.30 pm). This letter starts as below:

"As already explained to you a little while ago, information has reached us that there is an imminent danger to the security of India being threatened by internal disturbance. The matter is extremely urgent..." There is no record of any such 'information'!

The letter, that claimed to enclose copy of the draft proclamation, urges the President to proclaim internal emergency under Article 352 (1) of the Constitution. The letter concludes thus:

"I recommend that such a proclamation should be issued tonight, however late it may be, and all arrangements will be made to make it public as early as possible thereafter." This was virtually an order and the President was not even given time to think!

K Balachandran, then Secretary to the President, deposed before the Shah Commission that the Prime Minister's letter 'did not have the draft proclamation enclosed'. Subsequently, the President had told Balachandran that RK Dhawan, then Special Assistant to the PM, had brought the proclamation to him, he had signed it and 'Mr Dhawan had taken it back with him along with the Prime Minister's letter.' According to Akhtar Alam, President's Special Assistant, this happened around 11.20 p.m.

There is nothing else on the file. From Brahmananda Reddy's statement before the Shah Commission, it is revealed that the Prime Minister talked to the President over the telephone before sending the letter. There is no noting, no other process, nothing whatsoever prior to this letter. The letter from the Prime Minister to the President available in the records is not a signed copy of the letter. It is only a 'Copy obtained by JS (IS) from President's Secretariat'.

The Union Cabinet met at 6 am on 26 June and meekly gave ex-post-facto approval to the 'promulgation of the Emergency'. On the same evening, at 8.30 pm, the Cabinet met again and gave approval for 'imposing press censorship'. On 28 June, the Cabinet approved amendment to the Defence of India Act and Rules. On 29 June, the Cabinet met again to approve the Maintenance of Internal Security (Amendment) Ordnance, 1975.

The senior bureaucracy just caved in without even a mild protest. The first action taken by the MHA on 26 June was by Joint Secretary P P Nayyar addressing a secret 'crash wireless message' to all Chief Secretaries informing them of the Emergency promulgation. The message said that "some leaders have been arrested" and directed the officials to "enforce internal security schemes with immediate effect and take steps to maintain law and order at all costs including preventive arrests, pre-censorship of news, prevent circulation of newspapers/leaflets, prevention of any dispatch of news overseas, and maintaining liaison with the Army" by making full use of powers under the Defence of India Act and Rules. On the same day, Khurana addressed secret letter to all Secretaries to the Government of India to invoke the 'Union War Book' to maintain internal security. The first noting on the file was on 26 June by S Balakrishnan, Joint Secretary (L) of MHA. This note, acknowledging proclamation of the Emergency as a *fait accompli,* dealt with extension of the proclamation to Jammu and Kashmir. This was accordingly done.

In all, the following preventive arrests were made during the Emergency period:

Emergency MISA detenus:	16,345
Detenus from banned organizations:	4,671
Detenus from political parties:	1,659
Anti-social elements:	9,724
Economic offenders:	291
Total:	**32,690**

These official figures appear to be way off the mark. Shah Commission gives a figure of 110,806.

After most of the arrests were made, the Intelligence Bureau prepared a 'Top Secret' Report on July 11, 1975, justifying promulgation of the Emergency and upholding Indira Gandhi's contention that instead of 'demolishing democracy' by declaring the Emergency, she was only putting 'democracy back on the rails'. Most of the content of this report was reproduced in a booklet titled '*Why Emergency*', and laid on the table of Parliament when the Resolution to Approve the proclamation of Emergency was moved on 21 July 1975. The main justification given consisted of the speeches made by JP at various places during his nationwide tour in 1974-75 as part of the JP movement to mobilize people against corruption and his 'incitement to the armed forces and the police.' The report also refers to the railway strike that took place more than one year before, in May 1974. The resolution was bulldozed through the Parliament.

An intriguing part of the documents obtained through the RTI Act is that, whereas signatures of the President of India and Home Minister appear at various places in the file, subsequent to the declaration of Emergency, Prime Minister Indira Gandhi's signature appears nowhere. Even the letter sent by her to the President asking him to promulgate the Emergency was taken back. This speaks volumes about the way the nation was governed during its darkest of days!

Documents obtained make the following things clear:

- No Constitutional or civil authority – Union Cabinet, Home Minister, Cabinet Secretary, Principal Secretary to Prime Minister, Home Secretary etc. – or any State Government was involved in the decision to promulgate Emergency. It was the decision of a few individuals forming a coterie.
- The President functioned as a rubber-stamp, cowed down by a mere telephone call from the Prime Minister. He signed the proclamation on a piece of paper brought by the Special Assistant to the Prime Minister without the mandatory resolution from the Cabinet. There was no application of mind on his part.
- Arrests of senior leaders were made even before the President signed the proclamation.

- There was no whimper of protest by the Union Cabinet, senior bureaucracy and parliamentarians belonging to the ruling Congress Party.

India Becomes an Autocracy

There are several perceptions and opinions of prominent people, including JP, about the causes and factors leading to the Emergency. But the pronouncement of Justice J C Shah, the one-man Commission appointed to enquire into the Emergency excesses, could be considered objective and reliable. This is what he said: "Indira, in her anxiety to continue in power, brought about a situation which directly contributed to her continuance in power and also generated forces which sacrificed the interests of many to serve the ambitions of the few. Thousands were detained and a series of totally illegal and unwarranted actions followed involving untold human misery and suffering."

Repudiating the spurious theory of 'grave threat to national security', Justice Shah was emphatic that "there was no evidence of breakdown of law and order in any part of the country, nor of any apprehension on that behalf. The economic condition was also well under control and had in no way deteriorated. There was not even a report of an apprehension of any serious breakdown of the law and order situation or deterioration of economic condition from any public functionary. The public records of that time, both secret and public, and newspapers spoke with unanimity that there was no unusual event or even a tendency in that direction to justify the imposition of Emergency".

Proving Justice Shah absolutely right, at the dawn of 26 June 1975, the Union Territory of Chandigarh was as normal as any other dawn. As usual, I had gone for my morning tennis game and was back home around 8 am. My wife Aspil informed me that M L Bhanot, Senior Superintendent of Police, had called and said it was urgent. As was my wont, I switched on the radio to listen to the morning news. But instead of news, I heard a tight and tense voice of the Prime Minister addressing the nation and saying something about the 'grave threat to the country and the need for drastic steps'. I felt that something was amiss and called up Bhanot to find out what was happening. What he told me shook me a bit.

As in the rest of the nation, the night of June 25-26 was one of high drama in Chandigarh, though on a smaller scale. It reflected the deep depravity into which the governance of the country had been pushed in the name of 'national security'. On verbal directions from the Delhi Durbar, Giani Zail Singh, Chief Minister of Punjab, had called up N P Mathur, Chief Commissioner of Chandigarh, past midnight to say that an emergency had been declared and the Press had to be severely disciplined. He was specific that *The Tribune* should be sealed and not be allowed to come out that morning. Zail Singh even wanted the arrest of Madhavan Nair, infirm but fiercely independent editor of the newspaper, a household name in the northwestern States of Punjab, Haryana, Himachal Pradesh, Jammu and Kashmir and the Union Territory of Chandigarh.

Deeply rattled, Mathur called Union Home Secretary SL Khurana, who had nothing to say. The same was the response from Srinivasa Varadan, Additional Home Secretary. Mathur's attempts to contact the Union Home Minister and Minister of State Om Mehta did not bear fruit. As Chief Commissioner, Mathur was the head of the Chandigarh Union Territory and had to get his orders or instruction from Government of India and not the Chief Minister of Punjab. Mathur would have been in the right if he had ignored the instructions and carried on as usual. At best, he could have called me and passed on the buck since, as the district magistrate, I was responsible for law and order and issuance of orders, if any, regarding the sealing of *The Tribune* or arresting its editor.

In his panic, Mathur obviously forgot these minor procedures and instead called Bhanot and passed on the instructions of Zail Singh. Bhanot was certainly not willing to carry out the wishes of the Punjab Chief Minister blindly. Nevertheless, he went through the motion of going to *The Tribune* premises and advised those on duty not to print any news unpalatable to the powers-that-be. He also posted a small posse of policemen to keep a watch on the Press.

Obviously, this did not have much impact on the paper and the morning edition came out as usual. This infuriated Chief Minister of Haryana, Bansi Lal, who also resided in Chandigarh. In his inimitable style, he threatened that, if the Chandigarh administration was not willing to raid *The Tribune* seal its premises and arrest its editor, he will get it done through the Haryana police. For this purpose, he would not even hesitate to "take over" the premises and buildings, if need be! Indeed, the heady brew of the Emergency had commenced its task of intoxicating persons in power!

As the district magistrate, I had been kept in the dark about the happenings during the hours of darkness. I made a mental note that this was not going to happen again, lest governance got messed up in the name of an emergency. Information was trickling in about the nocturnal signature of the President declaring the Emergency without the Union Cabinet's endorsement and the preventive detention of top leaders like JP, Morarji Desai, Atal Behari Vajpayee and others even before the declaration was signed. Though news censorship had been clamped, *The Tribune* displayed in their spot news the arrest of JP and Morarji Desai. As we in the Chandigarh administration – chief commissioner NP Mathur, home secretary GV Gupta, legal remembrancer AP Chaudhury, senior superintendent of police ML Bhanot and myself, the district magistrate – got together for the first Crisis Group meeting, we were clueless as to what was happening and what we needed to do.

With rumours spreading like wild fire, there was the danger of the law-and-order situation in the Union Territory going out of control.

Prompted by the Delhi Durbar, the Chief Ministers of Punjab and Haryana were breathing down our neck and could virtually take over the administration and also seal *The Tribune* if they decided to gang up. To ward off these eventualities, I decided to take charge despite absence of any official communication from the Central Government regarding the imposition of the Emergency or any other instruction.

I swiftly obtained a copy of the Emergency notification from the deputy director, Intelligence Bureau, Chandigarh. Moving fast, I imposed prohibitory orders under Section 144 of the Criminal Procedure Code throughout the Union Territory. On my recommendation, S K Tuteja, director, public relations, Chandigarh administration, was appointed as censor officer, invoking provisions of the Defence of India Rules. A joint planning committee was constituted under the internal security scheme for continuous monitoring of events. These and the other steps initiated by us helped in warding off the onslaughts from Zail Singh and Bansi Lal, both vying for the privilege of being close to the Delhi Durbar.

Initial defiance of the Emergency came in different shapes: the look of stupor on the faces of the people, their choice epithets against the Emergency masters and the 'sound of silence' from the Press. *The Tribune* was published with bland, censored news. Hindi and Urdu newspapers from Jalandhar came out with blank pages with the words *'Censor ki bhet'* (gift of the censor) printed on all pages. *The Hindustan Times* from New Delhi left the entire editorial columns blank, recalling the pre-Independence days of struggle against alien rule. *Veer Pratap*, a Hindi daily from Jalandhar, was more poignant. In the 26 June issue, the editorial page was blank, with a Urdu couplet rubber stamped all over. Translated, it meant: *"I can neither voice anguish nor petition; it is my fate to choke and die"*.

As news of the 'Emergency in action' started coming in, one was left with the feeling that the country's hard-earned freedom from foreign hegemony was being extinguished and a parliamentary democracy was being turned into personal autocracy. As the Constitution of India, particularly the fundamental rights, stood suspended, citizens had no personal liberty. The Maintenance of Internal Security Act (MISA), enacted in the wake of Indo-Pak War of 1971, was amended to vest district magistrates with awesome powers to arrest and detain any one without showing cause. All that needed to be done was to compile a reasonable dossier of activities injurious to law and order or the "security of the state".

We, the bunch of civil servants running the Chandigarh administration, had nothing to prove and no laurels to seek from the political masters. So we decided to be very objective and cautious in exercising the Emergency powers, particularly of preventive detention under MISA. The decision was not to arrest anyone under the MISA unless there was indisputable and convincing evidence of threat to law and order or security of the state. In the initial days, the Chandigarh police confined itself to routine rounding up of anti-social elements under Section 107/151 of CrPC.

Though we went through the internal security drill with special instructions to college principals and the Punjab University authorities to remain vigilant, the silence was eerie. The 'Emergency' was nowhere in evidence and everything was calm and quiet. One could only discern an undercurrent of fear and anxiety in the minds of the people as they went about their routine chores.

Different people have described the Emergency in different ways. Some have said that the Emergency was a 'shock-treatment' for India's democracy and therefore good. Many differed. But a compilation of activities of the President, Parliament and the Executive during the Emergency would reveal as to how democracy in India was being ravaged. Having by and large reduced the legislature and the executive to impotency, courts were made the primary targets during the Emergency session of Parliament held in July and August 1975. With his proclamation, the President had already suspended enforcement of Fundamental Rights under Article 14 (Equality before Law), Article 21 (Protection of Life and Personal Liberty) and several clauses of Article 22 (Protection against detentions).

As if these were not bad enough, a series of constitutional and statutory amendments were effected:

- Courts were barred from pronouncing on the validity of a proclamation of Emergency or President's Rule or an ordinance;
- The MISA was amended to prevent courts from giving relief to detainees even by virtue of common law or natural law;
- The election law was amended to bar courts from adjudicating matters regarding the date of appointment, resignation, dismissal etc. of a government employee;
- The judgment of Allahabad High Court unseating Indira was declared null and void by a constitutional amendment;
- Courts were stripped of their authority to deal with disputes relating to the election of the President, the Vice-President, the Speaker and the Prime Minister;
- The Representation of the People Act and the MISA were included in the Ninth Schedule and thereby made immune to judicial review;
- The MISA was amended so as to provide that those detained during the Emergency need not be furnished with the grounds of detention. They could be indefinitely kept in prison without an idea as to why they had been jailed.

The Emergency agenda of ravaging democracy to concentrate power on one individual is aptly described by Nayantara Sahgal in her book, *Indira Gandhi's Emergence and Style*: The essence of Emergency was the pinnacle-power - a position above the multitude, unaccountable and unchallengeable - it sought to guarantee the Prime Minister. This was accomplished by three amendments to the Constitution and an Act of Parliament. The 38th Amendment put the declaration of Emergency beyond the scrutiny of the courts. The 39th Amendment made election disputes relating to the Prime Minister, President, Vice President and the Speaker non-justiciable. This wiped out the Allahabad High Court judgment with retrospective effect and ensured a Supreme Court judgment in her favour. On 7 November 1975, a five-judge bench of the Supreme Court, with no legal option but to exonerate her, upheld her 1971 election to Parliament. The proposed 40th Amendment conferred complete immunity on the Prime Minister, President, Vice-President and Speaker, in respect of past or future criminal offences. An Act banned the publication of 'objectionable matter' making criticism of the Prime Minister, President, Vice-President, Speaker and Council of Ministers a penal offence. The inclusion of these other dignitaries resembled light musical accompaniment to the somber theme of prime ministerial power, finally established through a drastically amended Constitution in 1976."

The Emergency was bad in itself. But the worst thing was that it ripped apart the delicately crafted and carefully nurtured democratic fabric of a poor nation wherein lived one-sixth of the human race. Basic violations of the democratic spirit and the crude attempts to legitimize a new type of regime and new criteria of allocation of rights and obligations were more central to what the Emergency was about than the arrest and torture of a few thousand individuals. It was about the abrogation of any sense of boundary or restraint in the exercise of power, and the striking growth of arbitrariness and arrogance with which citizens were turned into subjects that was at issue.

On the ground, during the 20 months of active Emergency, people moved in hushed silence, stunned and traumatized by the draconian goings on. Across the nation, groveling administrators, academicians, advocates and accountants vied with each other to sing paeans to the Emergency rulers, some signing pledges of loyalty and servitude in blood! Whisky-swilling and pipe-smoking social climbers and sycophants chanted in unison, "Discipline is preferable to Democracy" just because trains were running on time and they got parking space in New Delhi's Connaught Place! The bulk of the civil service crawled when asked to bend. Higher echelons of the judiciary bowed to the rulers and were willing to decree that under the Emergency regime, citizens did not even have the right to life. Politicians of all hue and colour, barring honourable exceptions, lay supine and prostrate. There was gloom all around and it looked as if everything was over and the world's largest democracy was slowly but surely drifting into dictatorship.

Far more pertinent than the act of imposition of an Emergency regime was the manner in which the nation almost capitulated, to a man, with so few exceptions in such a vast land. There were no doubt protests and acts of both courage and imagination. All these were individual heroics, which is all that these individuals were capable of. They hardly had any great impact on the course of things. But there was one man popularly known as JP and the action of this individual did have a great impact not only on India's polity but on the country's history as well.

JP: Indira's Prisoner

Perhaps the most eventful chapter in post-independent history of India commenced on 1 July 1975, when JP, the enemy number one of the autocratic Indian state under the Emergency, was brought to Chandigarh for confinement, healthcare and safe custody.

That morning, Tuteja dropped into my room and said that something was brewing in Delhi and the 'most important leader in custody' would be my 'honoured' guest at the PGI. I did not take it seriously, but nevertheless called Dr P N Chuttani, Director PGI, for confirmation. He was down with flu and had no clue. He wished the news was not true since it would spoil his 'golf holiday' in Gulmarg, scheduled for the next week! I left it at that.

Suddenly there was a flurry of activities and telephone calls back and forth leading to our Crisis Group meeting at 6 pm. What Tuteja mentioned as "floating news" now became official. JP was being shifted to Chandigarh and he would be brought in a special aircraft that evening itself. Mathur was excited and a bit surcharged. Mathur had worked with JP during the Bihar famine and they belonged to the same Kayastha caste. Instructions from Union Home Ministry were that JP was to be received at the Chandigarh airport and put up at the PGI.

We, Gupta, Bhanot and I, swung into action and landed at the

PGI guesthouse where JP would be lodged, pending regular arrangement. Dr YN Mehra, ENT specialist and superintendent of the Nehru Hospital attached to the PGI, was already there along with his team. We had a quick conclave and instructions were given to spruce up the main bedroom on the ground floor, repair the air-conditioner and vacate the adjacent room and the building opposite, all in a jiffy. Within minutes, work started in full swing.

We quickly firmed up the security and policing arrangements. It was decided to notify the guesthouse as a temporary jail under Section 417 CrPC and post jail officials at the inner perimeter. The police was to man the outer perimeter and provide the necessary security. As a matter of abundant caution, it was decided to disconnect the telephone line.

The ETA of the flight bringing JP was 9.30 pm at the Air Force technical bay. Therefore, we had enough time to listen to Indira's address to the nation, unveiling her famous 'Twenty-point Economic Programme' meant to transform India's economy and banish poverty from its soil. It was a typical case of packing 'old wine in a new bottle' and a wish-list of clichés. This rehashed programme was to serve as the 'economic balm' for the political body blow delivered in the form of Emergency. This document became the Bible of sycophants and a convenient cover to justify the ravaging of India's democracy under the slogan 'Bread is more important than freedom.'

Be that as it may, Bhanot and myself reached the Air Force station at 9.15 pm. Station commander Air Commodore Bhasin and his colleague Wing Commander Nanda were already there. We briefed them about the mission and who was coming since they had no information. They told us about the delay in the flight and the revised ETA of 10.30 p.m. The wait was long and we spent the time strolling on the runaway.

At 10.35 pm, the aircraft landed and we were on the tarmac near the ladder. First the superintendent of police from Delhi accompanying JP came down to hand over the relevant papers to his counterpart in Chandigarh. Then I saw the frail old man coming down the steps, clad in immaculate white. I shook hands with JP, introducing others and myself in the reception team. I felt that the old man was perplexed and my introductions had not registered with him.

My staff car pulled in near the ladder and I asked JP to sit inside as I attended to the paper work like the 'Transfer Warrant' at the lounge. When I returned after five minutes, JP was still standing outside, leaning on the door of the car. He was concerned about the safety of his luggage consisting of two brief cases. The SP from Delhi showed both the bags to JP and put them in the luggage boot. We proceeded to the PGI guesthouse accompanied by Dr ML Bhatia who had come from All India Institute of Medical Sciences (AIIMS) and reached around 11 p.m.

The guesthouse was ready in all respects. Dr Mehra and his team, along with the jail doctor, conducted a quick medical check up on JP and found everything okay. They also had a discussion with Dr Bhatia. Since JP said that he had had his meal, we took leave of him after assigning the guesthouse caretaker and one of my orderlies (Manohar Lal) to attend to JP. JP asked me whether I was going back to Delhi. I clarified that I was the DC of Chandigarh and Bhanot was the SSP. Now, JP understood and profusely apologized for the mix up.

During our meetings in the evening, Gupta had conveyed the directive from the Delhi Durbar that, on "depositing" JP in the guesthouse, I should report to Bansi Lal, a key member of the Emergency coterie. As I returned home, my wife told me that Bansi Lal had called and left a message that I should talk to him urgently. When I called him up, his attitude was haughty and his instructions were terse, *"Yeh salah apne aapko hero samajtha hai. Us ko wahin pade rehne do. Kisi se milne ya telephone karne nahin dena. Aap hi khatam ho jayaga* (This damn fellow thinks he is a hero. Let him lie there. Don't allow him to meet anybody or telephone any one. He will be finished this way). The same night, Gupta conveyed to me another message from Bansi Lal that JP should not be allowed to take a walk in the open between sunrise and sunset. Though this callous attitude and crude language of Bansi Lal as well as his direct interference put me off, I did not give it much importance and ignored them. But later events were to reveal as to how ominous these remarks and these instructions were!

I was at the guesthouse early next morning. JP was sitting in his room in a spotless white kurta. He received me with a warm handshake though he did not recognize me and I had to introduce myself all over again. On my query about his health, JP replied that he felt alright except for some fatigue since he did not sleep well in this new place. He volunteered information that his health problems were cardiac trouble and diabetes, but both were under control. He expressed his distress about the inability to take a good morning walk and on being lonely in a guesthouse. He suggested shifting to a ward, where he could have company and where attendance also would be prompt. I promised to do the needful. At this stage, Bhanot walked in and joined the conversation. We spent some more time and then left.

The Crisis Group met in the forenoon and was joined by Chuttani and Mehra. The main agenda was shifting JP to the ward, if possible on the same day. Chuttani was as keen on this as JP himself, but for a different reason. He did not want the guesthouse where senior visitors stayed to be unavailable to them for a long time. The question was which ward. I suggested the VIP ward on the fifth floor and Bhanot concurred. Chuttani summarily vetoed this and instead suggested the completed but uncommissioned special ward, which was vacant then. After a quick joint inspection, we felt that, though not ideal from the security point of view, the place would be okay with some minor improvements. The room for JP's stay was to be fitted with air-conditioner and wire meshing. The glass was to be painted to ensure privacy, secrecy and security. Work started immediately and it was decided to shift JP by 9 pm.

In the evening, both Bhanot and I went to the PGI, inspected the ward and escorted JP from the guesthouse to the ward. It was past 9 p.m. and JP had started dozing. As we started moving, JP mumbled something to the effect that this was his fifth shifting in as many days. I said it was at his request and only to take care of his health better. His response was pointed and poignant and gave a glimpse of his state of mind: "I am 73. I do not know how long I am going to live. I wonder what use my life is going to be in captivity. Everything seems to be finished." As we walked up the ramp to the ward, the hospital staff and police personnel watched the old man in awe and admiration. We lodged him comfortably in the ward and returned home.

Next morning, again I was with JP promptly, as he was returning from a walk in the corridors, accompanied by assistant jail superintendent R D Sharma. He was looking brighter and said he was feeling better and had slept well. Over a cup of tea, we had a general conversation and I asked him what kind of reading material he would like to have. He asked for some light reading like fiction, travelogues, poetry and detective novels. I asked him about the preference of authors. He replied: "You know better and please send me books which you know are okay." He was relaxed and happy about the room and other arrangements. He was curious to know as to how a South Indian had landed as the District Commissioner of Chandigarh. I spent a few minutes explaining about the IAS, its cadre allotment system bringing me to Haryana and the process of deputation to the Chandigarh administration.

Though JP was well-ensconced in the special ward, Bhanot and I were not comfortable with this arrangement from the overall security point of view. First, the PGI was a huge public institution frequented by hundreds of patients and visitors day and night. Secondly, the ward was on the elevated ground floor, easily accessible from the main entrance. Most of all, it was right opposite the large campus of the Punjab University teeming with thousands of young students, some of whom could be hot-headed. Fortunately, it was holiday time, but trouble could start when the university reopened in the next couple of weeks. We pointed this out at the Crisis Group meeting that day and it was decided to prepare alternative accommodation for JP at the sub-jail at Burail, on the suburb of Chandigarh.

Accordingly, we visited the sub-jail the same day and decided on some major additions and alterations to make JP's confinement comfortable and to provide for one or two doctors to stay alongside. All this was to be done by 6 July.

In the afternoon of 3 July, I received the first request seeking an interview with JP from advocate J P Goel, forwarded to me from the Delhi administration. I rejected the request on the ground that he was not an advocate nominated by JP.

Next day, Mohinder Singh saw JP in the morning and Sharma accompanied him on his morning walk. To both of them, JP complained of the lack of open air. The corridor, where he was allowed to walk, was stuffy and warm. He found out from them that there was a jail in Chandigarh and requested to be transferred there so that he could have his walks in the open air. This was discussed at the Crisis Group meeting and it was decided to expedite the work in the jail. Immediately after the meeting, the Crisis Group visited the jail, inspected the work and expressed satisfaction. The works that included a new toilet and air conditioning had a budget of a few lakh of rupees and Mathur sanctioned it. He had kept in the picture the Union Home Secretary, who had approved the idea of shifting JP to the jail premises.

Late that night, we received the Government of India orders banning the RSS, the Anand Marg, the Jamia Islamia and other militant and communal organizations with instructions to seal their offices, freeze bank accounts, attach properties and arrest active elements of these organization. The legal remembrance drafted the orders. Magistrates and police officers were assembled and given suitable directions to implement the orders. Towards implementation of the ban decree, I issued the first set of orders under the MISA for detaining six persons belonging to these banned organizations.

Because I had not met JP in the morning, he sent word through Mohinder Singh that he wanted to see me. I made a mental note to see him next day. There had been several telephone calls from JP Goel to my residence. About 10 pm, I took the call. Goel requested permission for former Justice V M Tarkunde, of the Maharashtra High Court, now practising in the Supreme Court, and Rajeshwar Prasad, brother of JP from Bombay, to interview him the next day. I said this could not be decided over telephone as there were procedures to be followed. Goel said they would come to Chandigarh, and I said OK.

6 July was a Sunday. Due to my slight indisposition, I was late in getting ready to go to the PGI to see JP. About 10am, Rajeshwar Prasad, Tarkunde and Goel came to see me, seeking an interview with JP. I asked them to give their request in writing, which they did separately. Since

this was the first set of such applications and the matter was sensitive, I wanted to examine it thoroughly before taking any decision. So I asked them to come back at 1 pm. They returned at 1 pm sharp and I was ready with the orders. Being the brother of JP, Prasad was allowed the interview for one hour – from 3 to 4 pm - in the presence and within the hearing of executive magistrate Mohinder Singh, and deputy superintendent of police S P Dewan. Prasad was advised to converse in English or Hindi and not in Bhojpuri or Oriya as was the practice when the two brothers met. Tarkunde and Goel were told that interviews for them could be allowed only if JP gave a letter appointing them as his counsel and requiring a meeting to discuss possible petition to a court of law. Accordingly, both of them wrote to JP, offering their services to take up the matter of his detention at the Delhi High Court and gave them to Mohinder Singh.

In his book, *JP: Mission Partly Accomplished*, Minoo Masani describes the backdrop of these three gentlemen landing up together in Chandigarh: "There were alarming stories during the next two or three days (following proclamation of Emergency) about JP and Morarjibhai being on a hunger strike and even a rumour that they were being forcibly fed. I was awakened more than once in the middle of the night by anxious callers who wanted to know if it was true that JP had passed away. Not knowing the answer made this a doubly harrowing experience. I see from my diary that I did two things. One was to suggest to JP's brother Rajeshwar Prasad that he should travel up to Delhi, find out where JP was and ask for an interview with him. Then I wrote a letter to Mr VM Tarkunde, introducing JP's brother."

During the interview with his brother, JP opened up and narrated the happenings ever since he was abruptly taken into custody on the night of June 25/26 from the Gandhi Peace Foundation where he was staying. He was not even given time to pack up his frugal belongings. He was taken to the tourist lodge at Sohna in the Gurgaon district of Haryana. As he was taken to the lodge, he saw Morarji Desai also alighting from another vehicle. Both of them were put up in the same lodge but never allowed to meet each other. A police party headed by a DSP was guarding him and the Chief Medical Officer of the district came for medical check-up every day. On the CMO's advice he was shifted to All India Institute of Medical Sciences within a couple of days. From there, he had landed up where he was now.

Prasad described his arrival at Delhi and the difficulties he went through in locating JP because the district magistrate of Delhi was evasive. JP asked Prasad how things were in the country and what was happening in Bihar. Prasad said that people were in the dark since there was strict censorship of the Press. JP was upset and stated that Indira was trying to destroy the nation. On this, Mohinder Singh intervened and advised that conversation of this type was not permissible. Overcome by emotion, JP retorted: "You do not know. This woman is vicious. I don't think I will be getting out of jail alive under the rule of this lady." After this outburst, JP composed himself and the rest of the conversation was strictly personal, confined to friends and relatives. There were poignant and touching references to Gulab Yadav, personal attendant of JP.

Prasad and Mohinder Singh came back around 5 pm, carrying a letter from JP requesting an interview with Tarkunde and Goel. It was granted for 30 minutes in the presence, but out of hearing, of the officials, as per rules.

JP had been restless in the morning after reading some news items praising the Emergency and the deceit being practised by Indira. He had despaired: "What is this lady doing to the country? She was like my child. I knew her father and grandfather. Panditji would have given his life to preserve democratic institutions." Another reason for the restlessness was my not meeting him despite a specific request. This he had mentioned to Chuttani, virtually cautioning that 'he should not be compelled to resort to things he would not ordinarily do' (indicating a possible hunger-strike). On being told about this, Mathur got jittery and called me at 2 pm, asking me to go and see JP immediately. I could not do so since I had a minor surgery scheduled for the afternoon in the General Hospital to remove my left toenail, which was getting septic due to an injury. In any case, the meeting with his brother and advocates would take care of the old man's moods!

As soon as these advocates returned, I went to see JP at about 7 pm. He looked relieved of the uncertainties and tension haunting him for the past few days. The meeting with his brother and advocates had a salutary effect and JP looked happy and relaxed. He asked me about the facilities available for interviews. I said there could be two interviews in a week, and for this week the quota was over. JP responded by saying that his small circle of relatives and friends lived in far off places like Patna, Calcutta, Bombay and Delhi and they would not be able to avail themselves of this facility. He was going to write to the Government requesting transfer to a place near Patna or Delhi so that he would not feel like being kept in 'solitary confinement'. Though he very much wanted Gulab Yadav to stay with him, he would not ask for it since it would be tantamount to detaining Yadav under the MISA. JP said that he was very much attached to Gulab, who had come with Prasad, and requested permission to see him for a few minutes.

I asked JP whether he was getting newspapers and reading them. He said that he did not wish to read them because they were stale and one-sided. Instead, he asked for the annotated edition of Valmiki's *Ramayana*. He asked about writing letters and I said rules allow him to write four letters a week. "This is too much. I am a poor letter-writer," he responded.

As a special gesture Gulab Yadav was allowed to meet JP for a few minutes. Mohinder Singh took Gulab from the residence of senior advocate and Congress (O) leader C L Lakhanpal and both met for about five minutes. Gulab touched JP's feet and both embraced each other, breaking into tears. Hardly were any words exchanged. Mohinder Singh said that JP felt greatly relieved after meeting Gulab.

Deification of Autocrat and 'Death Drill' for Democrat

"Indira is India and India is Indira," squealed pipe-smoking, scotch-swilling Congress president D K Barooah in utter veneration of the autocrat who had hijacked the world's largest democracy overnight. This was the man described by JP as the "hard-core sycophant" being used by Indira.

The President of India prostrated and signed the proclamation of Emergency without even a whimper. After the proclamation, the Union Cabinet convened like a bunch of zombies and gave post-facto approval to the Emergency. The Congress succumbed in total servitude and servility. The higher echelons of bureaucracy vied with each other to 'implement' the draconian freedom-killing Emergency measures like the MISA arrests, Press censorship and autocratic amendments to preventive detention laws without raising a single query!

While autocrat Indira was revelling in deification, for the old war-horse JP it was preparations for his possible 'death in detention'. With the impending reopening of colleges and the Punjab University, on July 7, the Crisis Group had a general discussion with Dr R C Paul, Vice Chancellor to make an assessment on the student front. The Vice Chancellor was candid and did not expect much trouble. But he did not rule out the possibility of JP's presence at the PGI, right across the campus, being exploited by fiery elements.

After the Vice-Chancellor left, Mathur casually asked us, as if in an after thought, to formulate a 'contingency plan' in consultation with military authorities to be put into effect in the event of JP's death in Chandigarh. He called it the "death drill". I felt bad about it and was surprised as to how a sober person like N P Mathur could use such a crude word. Mathur belonged to the Bihar cadre of the IAS and was well acquainted with JP. There seemed to be some bitterness between them, though Mathur kept saying that both, he and JP, were Kayasthas and he had worked with the old man during the Bihar famine. Was Mathur scared or just play-acting? I wondered. Since Mathur did not sound serious, Bhanot and I also did not take it seriously either. But, as we left the meeting, Mathur again took up the issue of preparing a 'death drill' for JP and he sounded serious. Obviously, he had instructions from the 'Delhi Durbar'.

Given the seriousness, I and Bhanot got together in Gupta's room to formulate the 'death drill'. It was agreed upon that the most important thing to be done in the event of JP's death was to remove the body as fast as possible outside Chandigarh. Bhanot's contention was that if the body was not shifted immediately, there might develop a very explosive situation given the proximity of the university. A consensus evolved that the dead body should be shifted to the Air Force terminal lounge and the whole Air Force area sealed off. Bhanot was not in favour of calling the Army to cordon off the PGI in the event of the old man's death. He said police could manage it and calling in the Army would only add to the confusion. It was agreed that Mathur should get clearance from GoI to requisition only an Air Force plane to carry the body to Delhi or some other place. In consultation with GoI we should decide in advance as to where JP's body was to be taken in the event of his death. It was also agreed upon not to associate the Army in the planning at this stage.

Next day, the Crisis Group discussed the 'death drill'. Mathur's suggestion of bringing in the Army at an earlier stage was stoutly opposed by Bhanot and me. I, with my Army background, would certainly not like the forces to meddle in such a delicate situation. For Bhanot it was a matter of professional ego. Anyway, we won the round and there was to be no Army at this stage. I took up the matter of shifting JP to the sub-jail, now that the special accommodation was ready in all respects. The urgency was brought home because the date for the reopening of the university campus and colleges was drawing closer.

JP's 'death drill' was indeed being taken seriously and Mathur discussed the same with top Home Ministry officials, including K F. Rustomji, Special Secretary Ministry of Home Affairs, and SL Khurana, Union Home Secretary during his visit to Delhi. The 'death drill' was to be known by the code word 'Operation Medicine'. This code word and the contingency plan would be known only to ten people in the whole country - Prime Minister, Union Home Minister, Union Minister of State for Home Affairs, Cabinet Secretary, Union Home Secretary, Special Secretary to Ministry of Home Affairs, Mathur, Gupta, Bhanot and me.

Rustomji had undertaken the task of finalizing the plan in consultation with the Prime Minister and Home Minister as to who would be informed when the death occured and where the body was to be taken and how. On activating the code word, a special plane would be placed at the disposal of the Chandigarh administration. Only three copies of the contingency plan would be typed-two copies to be retained with GoI and one copy sent to the Chandigarh administration.

In Chandigarh, as soon as death occurred, the emphasis would be on how fast the body was shifted to the airport. Mathur was keen on the proper make up and tying of the *aarti*, since JP was an international figure and his dead body could not be handled in a careless manner. He repeated this procedure 2-3 times. Bhanot suggested that a small ambulance car could be taken right into the ward through the bridge. As soon as death occurred, all the persons in the PGI, patients, the medical and para-medical staff, would be quarantined inside. Only the essential and key persons would be at work. The body would be placed in a stretcher, put inside the ambulance van and shifted to the Air Force station as quickly as possible. When this exercise went on, the entire PGI would be sealed off completely. The body would be removed though the PGI back door and not through the Madhya Marg, where the university campus is. Bhanot was of the opinion that *aarti* etc. should be done only at the airport lounge, and we ought not to waste time on this at the PGI, lest the news leaked out and a flare up started.

It was decided not to call in the Army at this stage. Bhanot was confident that his police could handle the matter with the help of the battalion of Indo-Tibetan Border Police and the companies of the CRPF, already positioned at Chandigarh. Mathur said that GoI wanted Chief Ministers of Punjab and Haryana to be informed as soon as the death occured so that they could take precautionary measures in their States. Bhanot said we should not inform them immediately after the death, but do so as we moved the body away from the PGI.

'Operation Medicine' was amended after further discussions with the Centre. Mathur said that in the event of JP's death, he was to be cremated in Chandigarh itself. His relatives would be brought to Chandigarh by plane. This meant, we would have to bear the full brunt. Gupta was of the opinion that in order to placate the people, we would have to give JP a state funeral. Mathur said Madame Prime Minister wouldn't allow that. At least, the necessity of giving an open and decent funeral was agreed upon. Bhanot was in favour of a quick and quiet cremation. Mathur said that was not possible since GoI wanted the relatives to participate. Bhanot said he could keep JP's death a secret for 24 hours. We were of the opinion that it was not possible. In any case 'Operation Medicine' had to undergo substantial changes as it developed.

I did not feel very comfortable with our action plan. We were planning the contingency of the 'death and cremation' of a hale-and hearty man who had, just about couple of weeks ago, aroused the conscience of millions of people and had given them new hope. What an irony of fate! This overplaying of the 'death drill' left me with a few nagging doubts. Deep within, I was disturbed and I could not fathom why. Was JP brought to Chandigarh to prepare for his 'death'? Who was behind this 'drill' – the 'Delhi Durbar', the Ministry of Home Affairs or just Mathur? Why was Mathur so worked up about this? Was there a pre-orchestrated plan in bringing JP to Chandigarh at all? I made a mental note to find the answers.

After the Crisis Group meeting, Bhanot came to my room. He wondered why all this fuss about 'Operation Medicine'. JP's death would make hardly any difference to Indira Gandhi. I asked him what was his general assessment of the situation. He said that there was no likelihood of any trouble and Indira's rule was perfect and complete. According to him, there would be some important developments after the parliament session. There would be a major cabinet change in the Center and in some State Chief Ministers and ministers would be eased out. He predicted, Indira would twist the ears of chief ministers, ministers, and top bureaucrats and put them in their places. Indira would go from strength to strength and there would be no challenge to her authority. After some time, she might install Sanjay Gandhi in her place. Bhanot was fondly dreaming of an absolute police raj. After all, Bhanot was only a policeman!

It was strange that we were preparing the 'death drill' of the man whose detention order was expiring that day (12 July)! In the Crisis Group, I had reiterated that we had not yet received the confirmation orders of the Delhi administration on the detention of JP. I made it clear that the DM, Delhi's orders had validity only for 15 days and that was scheduled to expire midnight that night. If the Delhi administration did not pass a confirmatory order by then, JP would be deemed to be free and detaining him would be illegal confinement. I was blunt in pointing out that keeping JP in custody would tantamount to illegal detention and I would be constrained to release him.

Mathur asked Gupta as to what came out of his talk with J K Kohli, chief secretary of the Delhi Administration. Gupta sounded as if he was disgusted. When he had talked to Kohli in right earnest and seriousness on this subject, all that Kohli had told him was that the matter was being looked into by the Ministry of Home Affairs, Government of India and appropriate action was being taken! Kohli had pleaded with Gupta to bear with him for a few more days and hold on to JP!

This was the rottenness and heartlessness of the Emergency regime and 'Delhi Durbar' and the pathetic plight of senior bureaucracy in the Delhi administration and the Central Government.

JP's Musings and the Chandra Shekar Interlude

The first set of letters written by JP - one addressed to the Union Home Secretary and the other to his brother-in-law in Calcutta – were received through the SSP. This was a wrong practice and I made a mental note to advise JP in the matter. The letter to the Union Home Secretary was a request for shifting him (JP) to a place near Patna, his hometown.

My meeting with JP on Tuesday, 8 July, helped break the ice between us. After dressing my left toe in the morning, I went to the PGI to see him. He was in a relaxed mood and was busy writing a letter. He told me that he was feeling better, though a bit tired at times. He thanked me for allowing Gulab to see him and said he felt quite relieved on that count. He said that though the advocates had only 30 minutes with him on Sunday, they had discussed certain salient points regarding the challenging of his and others' detentions in the court. He said he may have to consult the advocates again and would be making a request shortly, which I promised to consider. I advised him not to give the letters he wrote to policemen but instead, to give them to the jail superintendent (Mohinder Singh) or assistant jail superintendent (R D Sharma), one of whom would be seeing him every day.

The conversation drifted on to newspapers (the day's newspapers were lying on a nearby chair). He said he had asked Sharma not to supply them. He said he got upset while reading the one-sided and highly distorted news versions due to strict government censorship. He was particularly upset to read that some Central Minister had accused him of being a foreign agent out to create chaos and anarchy.

JP went into a pensive mood and asked: "How is it possible that when almost all leaders have been arrested there is no reaction? Papers say that everything is normal and people are happy. How can it be?" On his own he went on: "There never had been any plan to create anarchy or lawlessness in the country. The mass movement was confined only to Bihar and, that too, against political and administrative corruption which is rampant." He felt particularly bad about a news item, which said that in Bihar, some 'Sangarsh Samiti' members had assaulted government officials who had gone to unearth the stock of some hoarder. "How is it possible?," he lamented. "De-hoarding was one of the main tasks of the Sangarsh Samiti. This is pure spinning."

Propelled by an inner urge, JP opened up. The only mass movement they had planned was to launch peaceful *satyagraha* to demand the resignation of Indira Gandhi in the wake of the Allahabad High Court decision against her and the Supreme Court's refusal to grant absolute stay of this order. The Opposition was compelled to organize meetings and launch satyagraha because of the stage-managed rallies, demonstrations, and meetings organized by Indira and her sycophants using public funds. It was the duty of the Opposition to show that there was an equal, if not more, number of people who wanted her resignation in view of the court's decision and the need to maintain democratic institutions and traditions. This certainly could not be taken as spreading anarchy in the country. "Hasn't the Opposition any duty and responsibility in a democracy", he asked in anguish.

JP was particularly sore about the arrest of Morarji Desai who had not uttered a single word in favour of violating law and order, and Chandra Shekhar, Indira Gandhi's own party colleague and a member of the Congress Working Committee. He said that most of the Congressmen, though they did not approve of the way Indira was functioning, did not have the moral courage to express their opinion openly. They were afraid of losing the Congress ticket in the next election. "What is the use of a Congress ticket?" he asked. "It is the people who would be voting for them and not Indira." Chandra Shekhar was the only exception and being idealistic, spoke out his mind. For this, he was being punished so cruelly.

The very day JP spoke so highly of him, Chandra Shekhar, who had been detained under MISA, was brought to Chandigarh. His only sin was his refusal to endorse Emergency and issue a statement condemning JP and hailing the ruling coterie. Initially he was detained in the Rohtak [Haryana] jail along with several others like Ashok Mehta, Piloo Mody and Raj Narain. But due to certain peculiar reasons, he was brought to Chandigarh that day and we made arrangements for his confinement in the sub-jail. Though his stay in Chandigarh was brief before being shifted to Patiala, it was quite eventful.

One incident that left a lingering bitterness in him, is worth narrating. On 10 July in the afternoon about 3 pm, six people – Chandra Shekhar's brother Kirpa Shankar Singh along with his brother-in-law, two friends and two kids - Shekhar's son [aged 6] and nephew [aged 7] came to me and asked for an interview with the Young Turk. Only the previous evening, we had received strict instructions from the Union Home Ministry through a wireless crash message totally prohibiting interviews with friends and banning interviews even with close relatives "except in an extreme situation on humanitarian grounds like serious illness of detainee." In the face of such a harsh rule, I deemed it prudent to consult the Crisis Group as to whether I should grant the requests for interview. The Crisis Group asked me to reject the requests, including that of the children, and advised me to be 'cussed in the matter'. However I took a risk to partially disregard the rules and the Crisis Group advise by allowing the kids to have a good meeting with Mr Chandra Shekhar that very evening. Nevertheless, on hearing from the kids of what had happened, Chandra Shekhar went into a rage and threw a tantrum.

Next day, he shot off two letters, one to Union Home Minister Brahmananda Reddy and the other to Haryana Chief Minister Bansi

Lal. The letter to Reddy was sarcastic and taunted his near impotency in the Emergency regime. Both the letters vehemently protested his perceived 'solitary confinement' and denial of interviews with his close relatives. I met Chandra Shekhar in jail the next day. As I walked in, he was reading the book, "Man's search for meaning". Contrary to the tenor of his letters, he was polite and respectful. His eyes wandered and were piercing, as if something burned within him. Despite my explanation and quoting Government of India rules and the prevailing atmosphere, he persisted with his protest against 'solitary confinement' and denial of interviews with his closest relatives. He repeatedly wondered as to why he was shifted from the Rohtak jail and why a battery of doctors attended on him there, especially when he was hale and hearty. This he saw as an effort to segregate him from other prisoners.

After my meeting with Chandra Shekhar, I had a look at the new accommodation prepared for JP. The room had come up very nicely and with air conditioner and good flooring, it looked like a room in any of the best guest houses. In the event of JP being shifted to the sub jail, a doctor had to be on duty permanently with necessary apparatus. It was decided to prepare a room with attached toilet in the barrack itself, adjacent to the special room. I gave instructions to Mohinder Singh accordingly.

At the Crisis Group meeting in the afternoon of 11 July, the main topic was the letters received from JP and Chandra Shekar. It was decided to dispatch JP's representation to the Union Home Secretary and Chandra Shekar's letter to Brahmananda Reddy immediately and accordingly both these letters were sent by special messenger to the Union Home Ministry. Regarding the other two letters, I pointed out that these were of purely private nature and it would not be possible to withhold them. After much discussion, it was decided that these letters should be forwarded to the Delhi administration with copy to the Home Ministry. Regarding Chandra Shekar's request to be lodged with the other detainees, it was decided to defer the same since Mathur said he would again pursue the matter regarding his transfer to Patiala jail.

When I met JP the next day, he told me that he was feeling light hearted after his conversation with me the day before. He was better now and in his opinion, the slight sense of weakness and nausea he had felt was due to the strong diabetes medicine he was taking. He said he should not make it a habit. He could not always hope to have the same kind of superior medical attention he was getting now. As such, he would like to go back to his original diabetic medicine. He asked me what happened to his representation to the Union Home Secretary regarding his transfer. I told him that we had sent the letter to Delhi through a special messenger and we are yet to get any reply. He said that he hardly had any hope of his request being accepted. "They are afraid to send me to a place near Patna", JP commented and added that he would be writing a detailed letter to the Prime Minister soon.

JP wanted to open up the conversation a little and asked me about the election petition concerning the PM. As per the press reports, the appeal was to come up for hearing on 14 July and I also told him that Raj Narain had filed a special appeal against the order of the Allahabad High Court rejecting some of his pleas. He asked me as to who the PM's counsel was. I told him Jagannath Kaushal, advocate general of Haryana would be the main counsel. JP was of the opinion that Tarkunde and J P Goel would be the advocates for Raj Narain and they would be consulting Nani Palkhivala also. He spoke highly of Palkhivala and his decision to withdraw from the PM's case. "This was a courageous decision by Palkhivala. I hope he will not be put to any difficulty because of this," JP said touchingly.

Our conversation turned to the up coming monsoon session of Parliament scheduled for 21 July. JP said it was necessary because Emergency cannot continue for more than two months without being ratified by parliament. "But what difference does it make? She has a brute majority in the House and can get anything done," he agonized. Then, with a deep sigh, he said, "at least for the present, democracy is dead in the country." Nevertheless, in view of these happenings, he expressed a desire to get the newspapers back, which was discontinued at his insistence a day earlier. This was duly complied with.

On my return to office, Mohinder Singh put up the daily report concerning JP and Chandra Shekar. The report said that Chandra Shekar was complaining of pain in the back and leg. I immediately instructed Dr B R Verma, joint principal medical officer to go and check up Chandra Shekar, along with Mohinder Singh and give a report.

At the Crisis Group meeting, Mathur said that there was hardly any possibility of JP being shifted from Chandigarh. He may have to continue in the PGI itself indefinitely as the GoI was reluctant even to shift him to the newly prepared room in the sub- jail. However, his effort to shift Chandra Shekhar to Patiala was bearing fruit. The GoI had cleared it but it was being delayed since Giani Zail Singh, Chief Minister of Punjab, was away in Srinagar and nobody else was capable of taking any decision. I informed the Crisis Group that the validity of the detention order of JP and Chandra Shekhar was only up to midnight 12 July and the Delhi administration had not sent any fresh order as yet. On this, Mathur got in touch with Khurana, the Union Home Secretary who was not aware of the situation. Gupta was asked to talk to the chief secretary, Delhi administration, so as to avoid any complication.

Discussion then turned on to the wireless message received from the MHA, GoI giving guidelines for interviews with detainees under MISA. The guidelines were both violative of the jail manual and the Indian Evidence Act. The "guidelines" imposed a blanket ban on the interview of detainees with friends. Relatives were to be allowed interview only on extreme humanitarian grounds when the detainee was seriously ill and advocates were allowed interview only within the hearing of an official, nominated by a competent authority. For GoI, it was a piece of paper and for them the job was done. But the field officers were put to extremely embarrassing situation of denying a facility to the detainee, given by established rules just on the basis of some guideline from the GoI.

Next morning, R D Sharma handed over to me a letter from Chandra Shekhar addressed to me. In the letter, he asked me why I did not allow all those who came to meet him to see him. He had stated that I should at least have allowed his brother to see him. How would he know that even for allowing the kids, I had to circumvent the Crisis Group! It was natural for Chandra Shekhar to be upset. After all, his relatives had come from a far-off place. But for the stringent GoI guidelines, all of them could have met him.

Early morning on Sunday (13 July), Mathur called me on the RAX and sounded excited. The message was that the Delhi administration had sent the orders for the transfer of Chandra Shekhar to Patiala Central Jail and I should take action to shift him immediately. I got to work and with Bhanot's help, lined up the arrangements for transport and escort. I called up Inderjit Singh Bindra, DC, Patiala, to tell him so. Chandra Shekhar would be arriving at the Patiala Central Jail in the forenoon and asked him to do the needful. I also rang up the Inspector General of Prisons, Punjab. He confirmed that instructions had already been issued to the Patiala jail authorities. Chandra Shekhar left with a police escort at about 11a.m. to be exiled into virtual 'solitary confinement' till the Emergency was lifted.

Bhanot reported that JP had not eaten the previous night because the food was bad. Since the university was reopening the next day, the Crisis Group met to review the situation with Dr Chuttani in attendance. Shifting of JP to the sub-jail was on top of the agenda and Mathur got in touch with Om Mehta at Delhi to seek clearance. Om Mehta said he would consult the Prime Minister and give a reply. Om Mehta telephoned Mathur in the afternoon to say that there was no question of shifting JP to the sub jail and he would continue in the PGI. The ostensible reason was international opinion.

But this reasoning fell flat when GoI vetoed the various alternatives that we suggested to take JP out of the PGI and to put him up in an open and more conducive atmosphere, as per his repeated requests and security considerations. We had conveyed intelligence reports that the university campus was rife with the news of JP. Everyone knew where JP was put up, and that was the coffee house talk. The PGI employees and people in the university campus now knew the whole ward as the JP ward. According to information, some student elements were likely to make an attempt to contact JP in the next few days.

Now that JP was normal health-wise, he should be made to live under normal surroundings, we argued. The alternatives suggested were the Union Territory guesthouse and some spacious bungalows in Sector 5, either lying vacant or occupied by re-employed bureaucrats. In the last few days, JP had developed nausea and had felt weak after his 15-minute morning walk because he had not been able to enjoy openness and fresh air. This was telling on the general health of the old man. Despite this, the GoI refused to budge and insisted that JP would be confined only within the PGI. I did not understand the logic at that time. Was there a link between this and the over-hyped 'death drill'? I wondered. By the time I understood the game, it was a bit too late.

Indira Links Emergency to JP Movement

On 21 July, Government of India, Ministry of Home Affairs brought out a booklet titled *Why Emergency?* purported to be a review document of the declaration of Emergency and the causes leading to it. This 'white paper', which read more as Indira Gandhi's manifesto than a government document, depicted JP as the villain of the piece and put the entire blame for declaration of Emergency on the movement led by him. The document opened with these gems of words, which can rival those of Goebles of Nazi Germany:

"The declaration of Emergency and the various actions taken by the Government to restore discipline, order and stability in the country have been welcomed by people from various strata of Indian society. The Prime Minister has said that the attempt of the Government is to put democracy 'back on the rails' and to ensure that the activities of an organised anti-democratic minority did not lead to the end of the very institutions of representative Government which the nation had evolved over the years."

The 'sermonising' to the nation contained in the epilogue of this document is worth reproducing:

"The Constitution of India has embodied in it a parliamentary system. The most abiding characteristic of this system is responsible government through an elected Parliament. Parliamentary government, as is well-known, works by the interaction of four essential factors: the principle of majority rule; the willingness of the minority for the time being to accept the decisions of the majority; the existence of great political parties divided by broad issues of policy rather than by sectional interests; and finally the existence of a mobile body of political opinion, owing no allegiance to any political party and, therefore, able, by its instinctive reaction against extravagant movements on one side or the other, to keep the vessel on an even keel." *(Source-Joint Parliamentary Committee on Indian Constitutional Reform).* It is through our firm adherence to this system that India has gained political stability, and her unity and integrity not only safeguarded but also strengthened.

The events in Gujarat in early 1974, the Bihar agitation that followed Gujarat, the concerted efforts by certain Opposition parties under the inspiration and leadership of Shri Jayaprakash Narayan to spread the movement to other parts of the country, the plans and programmes of the National Coordination Committee of People's Struggle culminating in the decisions taken by them in their Delhi meetings of June 1975, were all deliberately aimed at undermining the Constitution and destroying the very institutions through whose instrumentality democracy can flourish. They expose in all their nakedness the deep and widespread conspiracy, which has been brewing against the Prime Minister and the Government, led by her. In the name of democracy, it has been sought to negate the very functioning of democracy. Duly chosen governments were not allowed to function, and force was used to compel members to resign in order to dissolve duly elected Legislative Assemblies. A systematic campaign of hatred, vilification and calumny had been let loose by these Opposition parties to spread disaffection among the people and disrupt law and order throughout the country on a wide scale. The actions of a few were endangering the rights of a vast majority.

"A situation has arisen where these Opposition parties have forgotten basic precepts and democratic functioning. If they are allowed to go on, the result will be sapping the confidence of the nation in its cherished institutions; and instead of 'democracy' we will have chaos and anarchy. No Government worth the name could stand by all this and allow the country's security, stability and economy to be imperiled. The nation's interests demanded firm and decisive action."

The concluding paragraphs of the document describing the run up to the Emergency were more specific:

"The National Coordination Committee at a meeting held in Delhi on April 14, 1975 under the chairmanship of Jayaprakash Narayan considered a Socialist Party proposal for launching a massive civil disobedience movement in different parts of the country.

At a meeting on June 21, 1975, Shri Biju Patnaik (BLD) said that he considered the present moment opportune and called for swift action to ensure victory.

On June 21, the discussions mainly centered on the issue of the Federal Party and whether there should be an outright merger or an arrangement on the lines of Janata Morcha set up on the eve of the Gujarat elections.

On June 23, Jayaprakash Narayan said that a programme of action should be decided upon and put into effect by the political parties participating in the proceedings. He also suggested that other parties like CPM, RSP, and DMK etc. should be associated in due course. He emphasized that the demand for the Prime Minister's resignation was an issue in which the Opposition could effectively mobilize public opinion that tilt the scale against the Congress Party.

On June 24, in a meeting held at Shri Morarji Desai's residence, a resolution was adopted on behalf of the Joint Executive Committee of the five Opposition parties, namely, Congress (O), BJS, BLD, Socialist Party and Shiromani Akali Dal welcoming the Supreme Court's Order on Shrimati Indira Gandhi's stay application. The resolution reiterated that Indira Gandhi should step down from the office of Prime Minister and went on to say that if she failed to resign, they (the Opposition parties) would undertake a countywide movement, including *Satyagraha*, demanding her resignation. It also announced that Opposition parties would organize a mass rally on June 25 at 6 pm at Ramlila Grounds.

Jayaprakash Narayan who was to have left Delhi on the morning of June 24, agreed to extend his stay for this purpose.

On June 25, 1975, in the evening, a rally was held at Ramlila Grounds, Delhi, under the auspices of Janata Morcha and was presided over by Morarji Desai. In his address to the rally, Jayaprakash Narayan said that a 'grave situation' had arisen. He referred to the programme outlined by Nanaji Deshmukh earlier and said: "Nanaji has given a call on behalf of the five parties. It has my support and I am also a party to it. I have traveled throughout the country in search of the struggle. Now that the struggle has presented itself, how can I keep out of it? My regret is that except in Bihar and Uttar Pradesh, there is no struggle taking place anywhere else."

Continuing he said: "Friends, this civil disobedience will be of varied types. A time may come, when, if these people do not listen, it may be necessary to de-recognise the government. They have no moral, legal or constitutional right to govern; therefore we would de-recognise them; we would not cooperate with them; not a paise of tax shall be given to them."

He (JP) warned the country against the 'threat of fascism posed by Shrimati Gandhi's actions'.

He called upon the Army, the police and government employees not to obey any order, which they considered wrong: 'You have not sold your conscience and honour for the sake of your bread'. Challenging the Home Minister to try him for treason, he said, 'I am prepared for a treason trial'.

JP urged upon Chief Justice Ray not to sit on the Bench to hear the Prime Minister's appeal as he was 'obliged to the Prime Minister for appointing him', thereby holding the entire judiciary to contempt.

The Congress (O) leader Morarji Desai who presided, moved an oral resolution at the end of the rally, seeking the approval of the audience to the agitational programme.

And thus, these Opposition parties had irrevocably embarked upon the path of chaos and anarchy and were soon to set about executing their grand design without regard to the incalculable harm it will do to the country at a vulnerable moment of economic difficulties!

Under all forms of government, forcible resistance to the legitimately constituted authorities is a criminal act, and may properly be met with ordinary police action. However, the degree and extent of resistance is often such that normal police measures are inadequate to ensure the prompt restoration of public order. Under these circumstances, the propriety of emergency action is universally recognized in modern Constitutions including those, which are federal in character. The true justification for the present Proclamation of Emergency under article 352 of the Constitution is the preservation of the social interest in peace and order and the promotion of the public good."

Even before the publication of this booklet, from my conversations with JP, particularly the one on July 8, I could sense that he was carrying the guilt of being accused as the main cause for the 'Proclamation of Emergency' that was destroying a vibrant democracy and making it into a tin-pot dictatorship. He was unable to contain the 'guilt' within himself and wanted desperately to share it. This opportunity came on Tuesday, July 15, when our conversation covered many aspects that contributed to the proclamation of Emergency. It started with JP asking about interviews with him for relatives, advocates and friends. I told him about the latest GoI guidelines in this respect, which put a blanket ban on interviews with friends and stringent restrictions on interviews with relatives and advocates. JP wondered why. He said even under British rule, detention was not so harsh. Interviews were allowed even to political detainees under the provision of the jail manual. These guidelines were in his opinion further proof of dictatorial trend. "Why is she so severe? Why is she taking so much precaution? Who and what is she afraid of", he mused.

This anguish made JP open up and reveal many important things. According to him, the root cause for such a draconian act as the Emergency was Indira Gandhi's deep sense of insecurity and habit of drift in everything she did. From the time Indira became Prime Minister, she had felt insecure. She had no faith in her colleagues, especially Jagjivan Ram and Y B Chavan. She did not believe anyone. She had some confidence in Swaran Singh but he was an ineffective person. Kamaraj, who made her Prime Minister, was still repenting. Her top advisors were Sanjay Gandhi and his friends and sycophants from the services and outside. Mostly, it was a coterie of Kashmiri officers of mediocre caliber. He specifically mentioned the name of Mr Kaw of the RAW. Intellectuals like P N Haskar were not her advisers any more. Haksar had cautioned the PM about Sanjay Gandhi bringing a bad name to her in the Maruti affair. So Haksar was not in their good books these days. He had some difference of opinion with the Prime Minister on planning matters also.

The conversations shifted to the violent death of L N Mishra that was a pointer to Indira Gandhi's style of functioning. JP said that the Opposition had no enmity with L N Mishra. He was criticized only for his corruption. Though corrupt, Mishra was a good person and had a kind heart. He used to give donations liberally. Why should the Opposition have enmity with him just because he was corrupt? After all, he was only collecting money on behalf of Indira and the Congress party. Most of the collections went to these two sources. Opposition had nothing to gain by the death of Mishra. He (JP) had never criticized him by name. According to JP, the death of Mishra was the outcome of high-level conspiracy. Indira Gandhi had subconsciously exposed herself when she stated during the condolence meeting, "even if I am killed the Opposition will say that it was a conspiracy hatched by me." Even the grenade attack on Chief Justice A N Ray was a stage-managed affair. It was a dud bomb and the thrower knew it. Nothing was going to come out of the enquiries and investigations into these two affairs. These would also fizzle out like the Nagarwalla case, wherein he and the investigating police officer were killed to hush up the entire matter. People had a lurking suspicion of Indira Gandhi's hand in all these affairs. She had lost credibility through her acts of commission and omission.

JP said that the Opposition had no plan to indulge in violence or create any law and order situation. Even after the Allahabad High Court's judgment, if Indira Gandhi had kept quiet and just clung to her office, "we would have done nothing expect passing resolutions for her resignation." Instead of taking the High Court verdict gracefully, Indira went to the street and got solidarity rallies organized through her henchmen and sycophants. Factories were closed down and people brought to her residence in government transport for holding rallies and beseeching her not to resign. Indira addressed these rallies and abused the Opposition and criticized the judiciary. Forced with this severe distortion of the democratic process, "we had to act to show there is substantial public opinion in favour of her resignation. If we had not done so, we would have failed in our democratic duties", JP said.

JP was of the opinion that if the Supreme Court honestly delivered its judgment on Indira Gandhi's appeal, it could not set aside the High Court verdict because it was quite tight and to the point. According to him, Chief Justice A N Ray should not have been on the bench deciding the appeal. He was under great personal obligation to Indira for appointing him as Chief Justice of India, superseding other judges. As such, he could not be expected to be impartial. Even if he delivered a judgment purely on merit, it would be doubted and suspected.

JP went on to say that the Opposition movement was very peaceful. In fact, it was more peaceful than the movement of Mahatma Gandhi for achieving independence. The Lok Sangarsh movement was confined by and large to Bihar only, and certain sparks in UP. The other movement, asking for Indira's resignation, was only a peaceful satyagraha. He repeated there was no intention for violence and there was no occasion for such a drastic action such as scuttling democracy.

Even his call to the Army and police personnel not to obey illegal orders (touted as the immediate provocation for proclaiming Emergency) was issued only after consulting leading lawyers on the subject. He contended that what he said was already provided for in the Army Act and Police acts. He had only reiterated them. In his opinion, the loyalty of the military and police is to the Constitution and the government and not to any particular person, especially when that person has been convicted for corrupt practices by a High Court. He had challenged the Union Home Minister to try him for treason if his speech constituted an offence. But instead of doing that, why all this drama being enacted, JP wondered. In any case if he had committed an act of treason, he should be dealt with according to the law. Instead of that, why this extreme step of imposing Emergency and arresting all the Opposition leaders?

With a deep sigh, he said, "Where was Pandit Nehru and where is his daughter Indira? How ironic it is that the saplings of democracy so fondly planted and nurtured by stalwarts of the Nehru family should be uprooted by their very offsprings? " JP went on, "How it was in the Gandhian era. What dreams we had for this country. What has it all come to? Well, I should not even take the names of Mahatma Gandhi and Indira Gandhi in the same breath." I could sense that he was speaking in great agony.

JP went on to say that Indira, who had been bloated to the sky by her "yes-men" and sycophants, felt irritated by her failures and adverse criticism she was facing. She was not like this in the beginning, not even in her initial tenure as prime minister. But the *garibi hatao* election of 1971 and her massive victory changed all that. Since then she had become arrogant, autocratic and intolerant to even sincere advise and mild criticism. The relationship between JP and Indira had been very warm and cordial in the beginning. Over a period of time, Indira's intolerant nature and autocratic mindset changed all that and now it was one of head-on confrontation.

B N Tandon, a distinguished civil servant, who worked with Indira in the Prime Minister's Office from 1969 to 1976 and has kept track of the correspondence between her and JP, corroborates this. According to him, despite political differences, JP and Jawaharlal Nehru had a close personal relationship. The closeness was even more between Kamala Nehru and Prabhavati Devi, JP's wife. Therefore the affection which JP had for Indira was natural. This comes out in JP's letter to Indira on January 20, 1966, soon after she became Prime Minister for the first time:

> "In your hour of trial and tension my heart is with you. From my side I may assure you of complete support-whatever be its cost. Whatever you do for the peace and happiness of the people of this country you will find me on your side."

JP was always willing to support Indira Gandhi and participate in any task in the national interest. He was also not lacking in affection. At the same time, he would not spare her for her wrong and unethical acts. This was reflected in his letter of March 13, 1971, which inter alia said:

"I am not writing this letter to the prime minister but to Indu. First of all, please accept Prabha's and my congratulations. This electoral victory is an extraordinary event in the history of our democracy for which the entire credit goes to you...You have been given an unique opportunity for the service of the people of this country. I hope you will face the challenge of today with courage and humility after deep thinking.

I did not like your conduct at the time of the Presidential election (when she behaved in a dishonest manner by putting up Sanjeeva Reddy as the official candidate, and sabotaging it by supporting V.V.Giri) though I am aware at that time it was politically a question of life and death for you. Now that you have been given uncontested power, my prayer to God is that he may keep you thinking pure."

Indira Gandhi could not tolerate this mild rebuke even from a person who was like her father. She wrote an arrogant reply to JP:

"You did not like my conduct during the election of President but you have accepted that it was critical to my political life. I was unhappy to read this and to realize how little do you know or understand me. I have never bothered about political or any other kind of identity for myself. At that time the question was not of my future but that of the Congress party and therefore the country itself. I have no ambition of any kind for myself which could make me stray from my principles."

Even then Indira suffered from the illusion of herself and the country being synonymous. That was the cause for declaring Emergency.

JP wrote a very civilized but severe reply:

"You have put an entirely wrong construction to my statement. I have never believed that your conduct was necessary for your political life. That was not my view. When I do not regard a conduct to be appropriate, how can I consider it necessary? My meaning was abso-

> lutely the opposite, which was that even though I was aware that the moment was of great significance for your political life, I did not like your conduct.
>
> It is true that I know very little about you as a political leader, I have known you only in a personal way and even today I see you only in that capacity and feel happy at your success. But my experience in politics has also been a long one and even after distancing myself from politics I have been trying to understand in an objective manner all that is going on. I have experience of party splits too. It is on that basis I dare to say that whenever there is split in a party the claim made by leaders of both sides is that the conflict was one of ideology and principle, nobody says the quarrel was about personal power or position. In every split there can be an element of difference of opinion, but, at the same time, it is to a large extent a fight for leadership and position.
>
> And in the end I would like to say that until now on many occasions I have not liked your political behaviour, but I have never commented on it publicly. I am not writing all this in order to please you or because I expect some thing for myself from you but because I feel that you too know me very little."

This was the beginning of the rift and hardening of relationship between Indira Gandhi and JP, which eventually led to the confrontation resulting in the declaration of Emergency. Yet JP was the quintessential gentleman to the core. While he and his wife were in the USA, Kamala Nehru had written 39 letters to his (JP's) wife. The letters do not speak well of Indira's early life. Kamala had a poor opinion of her daughter Indira. The integrity of JP was evident from the fact that before he came out openly against Indira Gandhi politically, he called on her and returned all the 39 letters containing damaging material, to prevent the same from falling into wrong hands and used to blackmail her.

Be that as it may, JP had not read the Government handout – 'Why Emergency'- circulated to Members of Parliament, which was brought by Rajeshwar Prasad when he came to meet JP on July 24. I too read it only on that day. Obviously, JP had anticipated the tirades and canards contained in the document. His response during his conversation with me was clear and convincing. It was indeed unfortunate that I was not allowed to give this handout to JP to read and respond to the outside world with factual position. Though it was within my powers to give the booklet to JP, I wanted to test the 'democratic spirit' of the Emergency masters. As expected, they turned out to be small men who were afraid of their own shadow.

The undisputed leader of these small men (and women) was Prime Minister Indira Gandhi who, in the garb of Emergency, had clothed herself with intimidating powers and had built around her a solid fortress. According to Nayantara Sahgal, despite all these powers and security and "in a situation where no voice but her own could be heard, now that debate and dissent had been silenced, and there were no enemies at large, real or illusory, to react to, Indira's utterances continued to lay bare a complaining naiveté."

She was also totally unconvincing and irrational in explaining the reasons for declaring Emergency. In an interview with NBC Indira had said that she imposed Emergency to 'remove confusion in the minds of the people' about the dangers facing the nation! What a justification for extinguishing democracy?

Storm Erupts: JP Dares Indira

Along side our deliberations on Emergency and other matters, JP was composed and has been penning an elaborate letter to Prime Minister Indira Gandhi, contents of which he was keeping close to his chest. On 21 July it poured out both in the form of the first entry in 'JP's Prison Diary' and the epistle he penned to Indira.

These are the opening words of the 'Prison Diary' a full three weeks after JP's arrival in Chandigarh: "My world lies in a shambles all around me. I am afraid I shall not see it put together again in my lifetime. May be my nephew and nieces will see that. May be." Gushing flood of words continued:

"Here was I, trying to widen the horizons of our democracy. Trying to do it mainly by involving the people more intimately and continuously in the process of democracy. This in two ways. One, by creating some kind of machinery through which there could be a measure of consultation with the people in the setting up of candidates. Two, by providing a machinery–the same machinery as in One above would have done–through which the people could keep a watch on their representatives and demand good and honest performance from them. These were the two drops of essence that I wanted to distill out of all the clang and clamour of the Bihar movement. And here I am ending up with the death of democracy."

21 July was like any other day but turned out to be very eventful. I went to JP at about 10 a.m. Unusually, he was lying in the bed. For a moment I was concerned whether he was ill. He got up as I went into the room. He said he was quite healthy but felt a little weak. He had not gone for the usual morning walk inside the corridor itself. But I could discern a considerable easing of the tension of the past few days and he looked quite composed. He thanked me for allowing his brother-in-law to meet him the day before. He said he was surprised and distressed to find that his brother-in-law had not received the letter he had written to him on the 7th. He wondered why the government felt reluctant in sending letters, which were purely private in nature. I told him that the Delhi administration had sent the letters to the GoI. He just smiled and did not say anything. He said he had completed the letter to Indira and would be giving it to me.

Conversation then drifted to the Parliament session starting that day. He said the session would be a tutored affair and nothing would come out of it. Government would circulate a handout and the session would be stage managed just to ratify the Emergency and the various amendments. In this climate of terror, nothing better could be expected to happen. I asked him what about Gujarat State. He said that the government of that State perforce had to toe the line of the Center, lest it be dismissed and President's Rule imposed. It seemed as if Indira would stop at nothing. As if in a reverie he said, "I am not concerned what is going to happen to me. But what will happen to the nation?" He repeated this twice with a sigh. I asked him about the newspapers and he said that he would be reading them in the afternoon.

There was a feeling of contentment in him. I could clearly see that JP felt a heavy weight had been taken off his mind. When I got up to take his leave he went to the writing table and took out the letter he had written to the Prime Minister. It was a 15-page, closely written document. He handed over the letter to me saying, "Mr Devasahayam, most probably I will be punished for writing this letter. But it is all right. I have done my duty."

I received the letter and asked for a blank paper to cover it. He tore a blank sheet of paper from his letter pad and gave that to me. I could see his hands were a little shaky. He was visibly moved. I took possession of the letter and after saying *'namaste'*, quickly left the room.

Outside the room, I was informed by Kishen Lal, DSP (CID) that Dr Chuttani was keen to see me. I went to Chuttani's office and had some discussion. Chuttani told me that since he would be away for 3-4 days, he wanted to see me before going. He said JP was quite allright and in his absence doctors Aikat and Mehra would look after the old man.

Coming back to my office, I read the letter. At times, I was overwhelmed at the force and thrust of JP's language. I was pleasantly surprised to know that the old man had so much grit in him. Indeed, I felt as if I was holding a historical document in my hands.

The letter was the outcome of JP's reaction to the totally unexpected turn of events in the last few weeks. Even in his wildest imagination, JP would not have anticipated the 'destruction of democracy' by its very creatures. Indira Gandhi, daughter of Pandit Jawaharlal Nehru, doing it was some thing incomprehensible for JP. For the fiery revolutionary of the freedom movement, this was something he could not stomach. If there had been a storm outside he would have resisted it with his customary grit. This was a storm from within and JP just did not have the 'gall' to challenge it. But there was a deep sense of anger and feeling of utter helplessness that needed to be expressed in some manner.

Hence the flood of words. The letter was, in fact, JP's way of defiance, bidding farewell to Indira Gandhi and conveying a very powerful message - "I shall be content to die a prisoner under your regime"- that could rankle her for the rest of her life.

As Mathur was away, there was no Crisis Group meeting. Instead, I and Bhanot got together with Gupta in his room. I took the letter and gave it to Gupta saying that I have the epistle. He read through it and Bhanot listened to it intently. After reading through the letter, Gupta heaved a sigh and said that it was something like a flame and we should dispatch it to Delhi post-haste. But since Mathur was away, we had to wait. It was agreed that no copy of the letter was to be taken since it was an explosive matter and the lesser number of people who knew about the letter the better. Gupta and Bhanot both caught their ears and said that the letter was a dangerous thing.

Bhanot guessed as to what would be the reaction of Indira Gandhi on reading the letter. She would order his shifting to jail or a place far away from Delhi. I said that both these may not have any effect on JP. It was decided that I should keep the letter in secrecy till Mathur came back from Delhi. It was decided that a special messenger would take the letter to Delhi and I suggested that we send Mohinder Singh as the special messenger.

In the evening, I received two letters from M R Masani–one addressed to me and one to JP. In the letter to JP, he recalled his past association with JP, especially the days when JP was in Lahore fort.

I do not believe in dreams and premonitions. But my dream in the early hours of July 21st morning was indeed unique. In the dream I saw Pandit Jawaharlal Nehru in his natural grace and poise. But he looked sad. I asked him what he felt about the present happenings in the country. He said he wanted to talk to the people. A meeting was arranged of people belonging to all walks of life. He spoke and said that whatever was happening to the country was not good. He uttered in anger and sadness, "what is my daughter thinking she is doing to the country?" After this, the dream faded away. In the morning I felt a little tense, and told my wife about the dream.

There was delay in Mathur returning to Chandigarh due to a breakdown near Karnal and a relief car had to be sent all the way to fetch him. He reached at about 4.30 p.m. Gupta and I went to his residence at 5 p.m. He went through the letter. He kept interrupting the reading with his own reports about JP's Bihar movement and how it was all only a big confusion. He said JP had always been muddlehead and had contributed nothing. He also commented that JP went to Russia to sell the Bangladesh idea, but none of the top chaps in the Soviet Union met him. After finishing reading, he commented that it was a very well-worded letter. He said since this letter would be a top-secret document, it was necessary to take a copy. Accordingly, Bhardwaj (PA to CC) typed out a copy and the original was sealed and dispatched to the address of the Union Home Secretary, with a covering letter from Mathur. Mohinder Singh was the special messenger deputed to take the letter to Delhi.

Mathur briefly mentioned about his discussions at Delhi. He said the code word for JP would be *alpha* since he was the No.1 person in detention. He also said that JP was a special prisoner and he should be treated as such. About the letters written by JP, Mathur said that all of them except the one written to T. Abraham had been dispatched.

I showed Mathur the letters from Masani. He said there was absolutely nothing objectionable in the letter and asked me to give it to JP. After some time he changed his mind and asked me to wait till he got clearance from GoI. He asked me to ring him up the next morning regarding the letters.

I informed Mathur about JP's request to meet him. He was happy about the request. But he said he would like to play safe in this respect, especially in view of the fact that both he and JP were from the same caste. He asked me to send a note to him in this respect, so that he could think it over and take a decision.

Mathur echoed the views of JP when he said that the present advisers of Indira were not of high caliber. As such he should be careful in his steps to meet JP or other things concerning JP. The advisers, according to him, were not capable of mellowing or smoothening Indira. Whatever Indira was doing, she seemed to be doing out of an inner *shakthi*. Was it the *shakthi* to destroy democracy? I hoped not!

JP Ruminates: Why, Who and What!

Having taken the weight off his heavy heart, with his 'epistle' to Indira on 21 July, JP went into an introspective and questioning mode, evaluating himself, the movement, the 'disaster' it had brought and those he believed to be responsible for all this. He also wondered as to who would be behind Indira in this dangerous expedition. And he started putting his thoughts down in the form of a diary that he had stared maintaining from that very day.

The introspection started with himself: "Where have my calculations gone wrong?", he asked and explained that they went wrong because he made certain wrong assumptions. One, a Prime Minister in a democracy "would use all the normal and abnormal laws to defeat a peaceful democratic movement, but would not destroy democracy itself and substitute for it a totalitarian system". Two, even if the Prime Minister wanted to do it, her senior colleagues and her party, which had such high democratic traditions, would not permit it.

Unanswered questions that had been haunting him came out in a rush: "What can the people do, the youth do to fight against corruption, unemployment, poverty? Wait quietly for the next general election? But what if in the meantime the situation becomes intolerable? Then what are the people to do? Sit quietly and fold up their arms and silently bear their miseries? That would be Indira's image of democracy: 'silence of the grave'! And what if the elections themselves are neither free nor fair?"

JP gave his own answer: "I do not think in any democratic society the people have relied wholly and solely on elections to change their plight. Everywhere there have been strikes, protests, marches, sit-ins, sit-outs etc."

The outburst continued: "This Prime Minister has been accusing us time and again of wanting to destroy democracy and establish fascism. And here we see the same Prime Minister destroying democracy and establishing fascism herself in the name of the same democracy. She is saving democracy by murdering it with her own hands and burying the corpse deep down in the grave"

JP was categorical about the role of the Soviet Union and their agents in India in leading Indira down the path of fascism and dictatorship. The 22 July entry in his diary was very candid about this: "Quite a number of Congressmen are disguised Communists. They will go with Indira to the ultimate end. They have always been enemies of democracy. Behind them is the Right CPI and behind it is Soviet Russia. Russia has backed Indira to the hilt. Because the farther Indira advances on her present course, the more powerful an influence will Russia have over this country. A time may come when, having squeezed the juice out of Indira, the Russians through the CPI and their Trojan horses within the Congress will dump her on the garbage heap of history and install in her place their own man."

JP was sure that Indira, the disguised Communists in her party, the CPI and, behind the scene Soviet agents (KGB) must have prepared a detailed plan for substituting a totalitarian system for the democratic one that we had until 25 June. To all three of them – the PM, the Communist stooges in the Congress and the CPI – democracy was anathema and they were planning for long years the steps by which their goal could be reached: first 'social democracy' and then, naked Communist Party rule under carefully disguised Russian tutelage.

According to JP's understanding: "There must be two plans instead of one. One to which Indiraji is privy and is made to believe that it is her plan. In this plan Indiraji is always on the top till death intervenes. The other plan is a Soviet plan, which the CPI has been made to believe, has emerged from their own brilliant heads. Indiraji does not know this plan though she might have some private suspicions. It is also not known to the Communist stooges in the Congress, except a very few whom the Soviets trust and who by their outward actions have never shown any sympathy for the CPI or even the Soviets. They might even have appeared at times to be critical, if not hostile to the fatherland of socialism. This plan was to take effect at the point of transition from social democracy to undisguised Communist dictatorship. Many heads were then to roll, though in the social democratic period too head-rolling would not be such an outlandish matter."

JP then went on to question as to whether this or these plans would succeed. "I doubt very much" he answered himself. "But better not speculate about it now. In any case this country will go through hell for some time." (JP's 'Prison Diary'–26 July). JP was genuinely concerned about Indira's statement of bringing in social democracy in the country. He said this was the exact jargon used for the state of affairs in Hungary, Poland etc. just before the imposition of Russian hegemony. What they may be planning for India could be: "first 'social democracy' and then naked Communist Party rule under carefully disguised Russian tutelage." He only hoped that this terrible fate would not overtake India. That would be the point of no return.

JP had always suspected some understanding between the USA and Russia over India. In one of our conversations he had told me: "It is possible that they might have bargained over India and the USA had agreed to Russia holding hegemony over India as a part of international politics. In the event, it was quite possible that the KGB and the CIA were playing friendly games." In the context of the Bangladesh massacre on 15 August 1975, JP had noted in his diary: "The CIA and the KGB are both powerful and active everywhere in the world. In India the KGB seems to be doing better."

JP had led the most massive anti-corruption movement in the history of India because he believed that 'corruption (the phenomenon exploited by KGB) had become endemic under Indira Gandhi's regime'. He had also predicted: "India will arise from the grave, no matter how long it will take. I still think popular resistance will grow and gather strength. And the dictators will be defeated." As events unfolded later, though corruption could not be eliminated, Emergency was defeated and Indira did not sustain as India's first dictator as the Russians had planned.

In the midst of this in-depth introspection, JP's jail life was proceeding apace and our conversations were getting deeper. On 23 July, when I went to see JP, he was reading *Bhagavad Gita*. On my inquiry he said that his health was all right but these days, he felt more and more weak. Unlike before, he felt more tired after taking his daily walks. Otherwise he was in normal health.

I told him that a special messenger had left that morning with his letter addressed to the PM, to be delivered to the Union Home Secretary. JP did not say anything. I asked him what he thought would be the reaction when Indira read his letter. He said that she might use it for propaganda purpose. She could issue a statement that certain people (without disclosing JP's name) were accusing her of this and that and could come out with distorted versions. Alternatively she might order his transfer from Chandigarh to some secluded place and cut off all visits and communication with him. JP said that Indira was capable of taking the latter action since at times, she tended to be petty-minded. With a sigh he said that he had started worrying more and more about the nation. He was not concerned about his personal health but what would happen to the nation?

Our conversation turned to the Parliament session. He felt sad to read Jagjivan Ram's speech in the Lok Sabha. He was happy to know that some Opposition MPs had spoken in the Lok Sabha and Rajya Sabha against the proclamation of Emergency. JP said even during normal times Indira indulged in serious scandals such as the Nagarwalla affair, murder of L N Mishra and the Maruthi scandal. He wondered what she would do now, after assuming so much power and muffling the Opposition and the Press.

JP then revealed very confidential information about L N Mishra's death. When Indira visited Mrs Mishra to offer her condolences, Mrs. Mishra had told Indira in the Mythili dialect, "I had given my husband to serve you. If you found him inconvenient or did not need him, you could have removed him from the Cabinet and returned him to me. But instead of doing this, why did you remove him from this world?" I asked him how was it that Jagannath Mishra, brother of L N Mishra, was made Chief Minister of Bihar if Indira had a hand in the murder of L N Mishra? JP said that it was this huge bribe that kept Jagannath Mishra quiet. He said nothing would come out of the inquiries and investigations into the death of Mishra.

At the Crisis Group meeting, Mathur said that GoI had advised that since Masani was a political person, it would not be proper to allow him to communicate with JP. Accordingly I was advised to withhold Masani's letter to JP. Regarding Masani's request to meet JP, the decision was it should be turned down. The letter sent by Gulab Yadav to JP should be handed over to the old man. The matter regarding the shifting of JP to an open atmosphere also came up. I strongly pleaded for his shifting to the Sector 5 house, after taking necessary security steps. Mathur agreed in principle and said he would talk this over with H S Chinna, who was occupied the house.

In the afternoon Rajeshwar Prasad and Vimal Dave, junior lawyer of V M Tarkunde, came to see JP. Rajeshwar gave me the copies of letters written by Mr Masani to JP and the light reading sent by Masani. Rajeshwar was allowed an interview with JP from 4 p.m. to 5 p.m. in the presence of Mohinder Singh. This was followed by a meeting with Vimal Dave at the request of JP. Before departing, Rajeshwar gave me the GoI handout in the Parliament entitled, '*Why Emergency*' to be passed on to JP.

Mohinder Singh handed over two letters to me from JP, addressed to Ganga Babu and Kusum Deshpande. In the letter addressed to Kusum Deshpande, JP had paid compliments to the doctors, jail personnel and the policemen with special reference to my role. Very kind of JP indeed. But I thought that the 'great lady' might not be happy at the specific reference JP made of me as someone who was kind to him (JP). I asked

Mohinder Singh to delay the dispatch of the letter by a few days.

On 25 July, I went to the PGI to look up JP. He was lying on the bed and got up as soon as I went in. When I asked, he said that he did not feel very fit that day. His diabetic complication had surfaced again and he was taking suitable medicine. Missing heart beats were detected. Otherwise, he was alright. But he felt weaker. I could see that, with each passing day, JP was more and more depressed. He asked me whether there was any news about the Parliament session. I said that the Constitutional amendment to make the proclamation of Emergency non-justiciable had been passed by Parliament by a vote of 164-0. JP was distressed and said that there was hardly anything left of Indian democracy now. He never expected Indira to go so far. In fact, he confessed that the Opposition parties were taken by surprise by the speed and ruthlessness of Indira in bringing in her personal dictatorship by arresting all top Opposition leaders in one single sweep.

They never expected the daughter of Jawaharlal Nehru to act so swiftly in destroying democracy.

JP expressed concern at what the future of this country would be. According to him, India would more and more drift towards Russia and might end up as a mere satellite of that country, losing all self-respect and independence. Indira now had to rely more and more on the Russians and they were bound to take their pound of flesh. JP said that he was not sorry for his arrest and detention. He did try to organize a popular upheaval against Congress misrule. But why the others? He was particularly constrained about the arrest of Morarji Desai. He said Desai was such a mild person, he could never think of any violence. Indira was annoyed with him (Desai) because he had defeated her in the Gujarat elections. This was in spite of Indira's 11-day tour of Gujarat and spending millions of rupees to purchase votes, especially of the Harijans and tribals. He said if only Justice Sinha had given his verdict a day earlier, (on 11 June –the second day of the poll-instead of on the 12th). Congress would have been badly routed. In fact, Justice Sinha was very considerate to Indira. There was nothing that had stopped him from pronouncing his judgment on June 11.

In the Crisis Group meeting, Bhanot had interesting information to give. He showed a cyclostyled copy of a letter written by MO Mathai (Private Secretary to Jawaharlal Nehru for more than 15 years) to Miss Padmaja Naidu in 1967, when she was Governor of West Bengal. The copy was intercepted during the post-office censoring. According to Bhanot, the police had intercepted about 100 letters out of about 500 dispatched to various addressees. The contents of the letter was extremely damaging to Indira. It depicted her as a person given to easy and luxury living through corrupt practices. Bhanot said that the Supreme Court advocate P N Lekhi had brought the copy of the letter to Chandigarh from Delhi. There was a meeting in the High Court bar and quite a few advocates had decided to participate actively in the campaign (underground) to resist the present dictatorship. Bhanot also gave the intelligence report about the proposed Akali Dal plan to offer arrests and *satyagraha.*

On Sunday, 27 July, Dipinder Baxi, nephew of JP and his mother Chandra Kala Devi (sister of JP) came in the morning. I granted interview for both of them with JP. The old lady was a bit nervous. Baxi said he worked with the GEC. They had brought a few books and medicines to give to JP. I allowed the books and said there was no need to give the medicines because JP was in one of the top medical institutes of the country and medical experts were attending to him.

I met the old man in the morning of July 28. He looked quite fit. But he said that he was getting more and more tired, even after minor exertions like taking a bath etc. Doctors had advised him not to take the 15 minutes walk at a stretch. He was taking it in three laps of 5 minutes walk, 5 minutes rest…He now walked only in his room. He asked me what the news was. He did not read newspapers these days, though they were made available. I informed him there was nothing special, except that the Parliament session had been extended up to Monday.

When I told him that many RSS/Jan Sangh activists detained under MISA were tendering unconditional apology and were resigning from their party in order to get released, he said that they must be gutless and dishonest persons and whichever party they might join, they would only end up as traitors.

According to JP, Indira might stick to the election schedule because with this atmosphere of terror and with the top Opposition leaders in jail, her party had a very good chance of winning the elections. Government officials may intimidate the people to vote for the Congress, lest their name be noted and harassed later. She might take inspiration from the one-party rule of ZA Bhutto in Pakistan. I asked him who were the people taking decisions these days and he said he was not quite sure. Could it be Sanjay Gandhi? If so, God save the country, JP said because Sanjay was "just a spoilt boy and a merry maker".

JP asked me as to what happened to his representation for transfer sent to the Union Home Secretary. I told him we had not received any reply. He said he would represent again.

As I left JP that day, I had the distinct feeling that his introspection and his realisation of the terrible fate that had befallen free India had deeply distressed him and pushed him into a bout of depression he was trying hard to conceal. Physical illness will not be long in coming, I thought.

Indira's Neglect Makes JP Ill

My apprehensions turned out to be true as I went to see JP the next day. He was lying on the bed reading a book by John Masters. He got up as soon as I went into the room. He looked dull and disheveled. I asked him how he felt. He said that he had been experiencing severe to mild itching associated with diabetes for the last two days. Two days earlier, he had taken Pediactene tablet, to suppress the itching. He had been drowsy since then. He said he had practically slept the entire day yesterday and hardly slept last night because of frequent itching. He still felt heavy in the eyes but had felt comparatively better than yesterday. He had not taken the morning walk. At this stage, Dr. Mehra came into the room. I asked him about JP's complaint. He said that the medicine given to JP was quite a common one and was capable of causing drowsiness. The effect of drowsiness varied from person to person, depending upon the constitution. Since JP was old and generally felt weak, he felt drowsier. He would get over it in a couple of hours' time, the doctor said. I wished JP well and left.

Next day, in the absence of Mathur, Bhanot and I got together at Gupta's place. Bhanot said that when he had gone to the PGI to see JP he learnt that JP was scratching all over his body and was faltering in his speech. Bhanot had returned without seeing JP. He said he couldn't see the sight of the miserable old man. I was surprised. Bhanot was the senior-most police officer of the UT. It was basic courtesy that he should have met JP and found out how exactly he was feeling.

Since Bhanot's report was alarming, I immediately got in touch with Dr Chuttani. He said that JP was indeed in bad shape but there was nothing to worry. He had himself examined JP and the trouble appeared to be because of the drowsiness caused by the medicine. Normally, the drowsiness wears off within 24 hours maximum. But because JP had no resistance power, the drowsiness had prolonged. Dr Mehra too repeated the same explanation.

In the Crisis Group meeting, Bhanot said that he had prepared the preliminary draft of the 'Operation Medicine'. It was decided to consult Mathur before finalizing it. He should also be asked to talk to Chuttani as to the PGI involvement in the operation.

Feeling a bit worried about reports on JP's health, I went next morning to see him. As I went into the room, I saw JP lying on the bed and a doctor and a nurse at his side The duty doctor was taking his pulse. I could see that JP was really ill. I asked him what happened. He said he felt giddy, could not open his eyes and was feeling chilly. Even the fan in the room was not running. The doctor checked up the blood pressure and left, saying that they had to take an ECG. I asked the DSP on duty whether any senior doctor had seen JP. He said that Dr Mehra had seen him some time ago. I asked him to send for Mehra. On my asking, JP said that there was no improvement and, in fact, he felt quite bad. He pulled up the bed sheet, covering himself, saying that he felt chilly. He tried to keep his eyes open and talk to me. He found it difficult and his voice faltered. After about 5 minutes or so, another young doctor came with the ECG apparatus and started the test on JP.

As the ECG test was in progress, Mehra joined me. I asked him what the matter was and how the old man was feeling. Being an ENT specialist, Mehra was not very sure. He said that JP had vomited in the morning and felt quite unstable. He said that in order to counteract the effect of Pediactene drug, they had administered another drug to him the day before. But instead of counteracting it, that seemed to have added to the unstable conditions. He looked at the ECG and said it was absolutely normal. He said that he had sent a message to Dr Chuttani and he would be coming any time. JP was feeling uncomfortable lying down and tried to sit up. Mehra called in two nurses and got the bed lifted so that JP could sit comfortably. The old man was dozing off as we left the room.

Chuttani had just come and was sitting with the doctors in their cabin adjacent to JP's room and was going through the duty doctor's report on JP's condition. After going through the reports, Chuttani was of the opinion that JP's trouble could be due to over-medication and that they should stop all drugs for a while and observe the results.

After this preliminary review, Chuttani and other doctors walked into JP's room. I also went in with them. Chuttani himself did the check up now. First he checked the pulse, then BP. He tested the reflexes by asking JP to make certain movements. He also took the heartbeat. Chuttani asked the old man to take a few steps. JP got down from the bed and could not even stand up. His entire body trembled. With support, he took a few steps and got back to bed. Chuttani asked him what he had taken for breakfast. JP had just taken a glass of warm water with lemon. Chuttani advised him to take some toned and chilled milk and asked Mehra to do the needful. Chuttani asked JP whether he had felt like this ever before. JP said no. In fact, he had not taken so many drugs at any time before. The old man had no motion that morning. Chuttani cheered him up by saying that everything was alright. Pointing at me, Chuttani told JP that the 'big doctor is also here and is more worried than us.' JP weakly smiled and said, "naturally".

Back in the cabin, the doctors went into a conference. Chuttani wrote and gave me the day's medical report. He said there was nothing basically wrong and that all tests were positive. All his systems were functioning normally. The complication was due to the drugs and he would do something about it. After receiving the medical report, I left for the office. Back at the office, Gupta was anxious to know about JP's health and I briefed him.

In the afternoon, I gave the letter from Vimal Dave to Mohinder

Singh for handing it over to JP. The letter sought advice from JP regarding moving the court on his solitary confinement.

I went again to the PGI next day to look up JP. The nurse was changing his clothes. I sat in the DSP's room talking with him. He quoted JP as saying that, "though the doctors say I am well, I am not feeling better". The DSP was of the opinion that JP was undergoing mental strain. He said that JP mentioned to him about the doctors attending to him at the AIIMS. I asked him whether he was giving newspapers to JP. He said that JP had completely stopped reading newspapers for about a week now and as such, he no longer brought the newspapers to JP. I asked him about anyone trying to meet JP. He said not in his notice. Even the doctors and nurses were screened. Surprising, how the rumour about Kuldip Nayar meeting JP was floating around!

After about five minutes, I went into JP's room. He was sitting on the chair and was looking clean and better. He could sit upright and could talk. He faltered much less. He had eaten nothing the day before because of the vomiting sensation. This morning he had breakfast with toasts and hot coffee. He told me that though he was better, he did not feel healthy. He asked me about the news. I told him about Indira's written interview with the American magazine *Saturday Evening Review* herein she had said that Emergency would not be unduly prolonged. I also told him of a positive editorial in that day's *Hindustan Times*. JP felt that this was a deviation from Indira's earlier stand. His letter might have had some positive effect on the PM. He felt that even now, the situation could be retrieved and democracy saved. He said that he worried these days about the fate of the nation and not about his own health. He felt cheered after hearing the news and said he wanted to read the papers. I told him I would send the newspapers across as soon as I went to the office.

In order to pep him up further, I brought in some general discussion on future prospects. JP was of the view that Emergency might continue and Indira might go ahead with full force in implementing her 20-points programme. But freedom of the press and expression should be restored, he opined. He concurred with my opinion that judiciary needed streamlining and trimming so that they don't unnecessarily interfere with development activities of the Government on flimsy and false pretexts presented by litigants. He agreed with me that the standard and independence of High Court and Supreme Court judges have gone down. He also agreed with me that there should be an Indian Judicial Service in line with IAS and IPS so that the members of the superior judiciary could be free from political and communal pressures, which were very much prevalent these days.

In the Crisis Group meeting there wasn't much to discuss. Bhanot had intercepted a parcel addressed to JP, c/o deputy commissioner. It contained a report brought out by the Gandhi Peace Foundation. Mathur perused it and returned it to Bhanot. The police and Bhanot seemed to be getting overzealous. The parcel was addressed to me. The screening could have been done after I had received it. There was no need for the police to intercept it and screen it. Bhanot was indirectly told not to cross limits by Mathur and me. He looked apologetic.

JP's deteriorating health came up for discussion. I gave my view that it was more mental than physical. Besides the physical discomfort of staying within a ward, JP was upset about Indira's lack of response to his 'epistle' sent a week ego. This sense of neglect and helplessness had taken its toll on JP's health.

Emergency Gag Gets Tighter

In Chandigarh Union Territory, interviews with detainees was governed by Clause 14 of the Chandigarh Detainees (Conditions of Detention) Order 1971 issued under Maintenance of Internal Security Act (Central Act No 26 of 1971) which inter alia lays down: "Every detainee irrespective of the class shall be allowed to interview his relatives once a week. A maximum of five persons not counting children below the age of 12 years shall be permitted during each interview." Clause 2 (c) defines 'Relatives' which includes "father, mother, wife, husband, children, uncle, aunt, brother, sister, father-in-law, mother-in-law, son-in-law and daughter-in-law of the detainee." Clause 15 (2) dealing with letters permits a detainee to write four letters a week and receive any number of letters per week. Regarding censorship all that was provided for was that, "the jail authorities should ensure that the letters delivered or transmitted contain nothing which is prejudicial."

These were reasonable provisions and most of the detainees and their relatives were satisfied with these facilities. But the 'Delhi Durbar' was not amused. They wanted the top political leadership of the country confined in jails to really enjoy their version of 'freedom'. So came a confidential wireless directive from MHA, Government of India on 9 July 1975 with following guidelines:

- Interview with friends should not be granted
- Interview with family members should not be granted except in an extreme situation on humanitarian grounds like serious illness of detenu
- Interview with lawyers for professional consultation in the presence and hearing of officer nominated by Detaining Authority or Government (earlier it was in the presence but outside the hearing)

This communiqué had caused consternation vis-a-vis Chandra Shekhar that we saw in the earlier chapter. This was soon followed by the directive on 27 July prohibiting letters to friends and political leaders. All other letters had to be strictly censored. Considering the status and health of JP, and the fact that he had a small circle of relatives living far away, I had been ignoring these directives and granting interviews and allowing letters, using my discretionary powers as District Magistrate.

Then came the hammer blow on 4 August, through a wireless crash message restricting interviews with family members to only once a month, limited to just two members. What was worse 'family' was redefined to include only parents, husband, wife and children.

JP had none of these 'relatives' and the 'guidelines' if implemented, would result in the old man rotting in 'solitary confinement' without any contact with the outside world for the rest of his detention period. Emergency minions had crossed the limits and I decided to defy this draconian directive. So on 6 August, I shot off a strong letter to the Government, virtually accusing the Centre of targeting JP in order to isolate him and seeking an urgent clarification.

I did not wait for the clarification though, and in defiance of the directive, allowed interviews with JP's close relatives–brother-in-law, nephew, sister's grand son and brother–as they came in the following days. GoI soon amended the definition of family to include brother, sister and brother-in-law but the restriction of only one interview per month continued. I did not comply with this directive either and allowed interviews as and when JP's relatives came travelling long distances. In each of the case, I recorded speaking orders mentioning 'humanitarian considerations' in support of the decision.

These draconian and distressing directives could have been challenged in the courts of law and JP could have obtained some relief. Given to myself I would have gladly facilitated this because I was not in favour of these missives in the first place. But with higher officials showing signs of fear and panic it could not be done effectively. This was evident on Sunday, 3 August when Vimal Dave, Advocate, Supreme Court came to interview JP and get certain documents signed by him. After the interview, Mohinder Singh sought my instruction to attest the affidavit signed by JP and other papers. The papers contained a writ petition to be filed in the Delhi High Court, an affidavit from JP and copies of representation made to Lt Governor of Delhi by R Prasad and Vimal Dave. The instruction of GoI and Delhi Administration regarding interview and communication with MISA detainees was silent as to the procedure to be adopted regarding the filing of writ petition and documents signed by detainees.

I called Mathur on RAX and briefed him about the papers and told him that in the normal process we cannot prevent this document from being taken by the advocate to file a writ petition in the high court. Mathur agreed with me and said that permission can be given for attestation as well as the transmission of the document. Accordingly I advised Mohinder Singh and he and Dave proceeded to the office to do the attestation. Before leaving Dave gave me an unsigned copy of the documents.

But all of a sudden Mathur developed cold feet and what followed was a charade of panic and prevarication. As Dave was leaving the bus station with the attested documents, he was intercepted and brought back to my residence. I explained to him that after carefully going through the documents we were of the opinion that they contained certain details which are not in the interest of the state and which are really not necessary to achieve the purpose in view. After a fair amount of argument he handed over the original and two copies of the documents signed by JP for scrutiny. After rounds of consultation I asked Dave to leave the documents with me since they are going out from JP in detention I, as District Magistrate was duty bound to scrutinize them carefully and see that nothing injurious to the interest of the state is contained therein because once filed these would become public documents.

Dave consulted VM Tarkunde over telephone and then put me on to him. Tarkunde was quite hesitant and he argued with me for a while. When I told him my decision he said it wouldn't be proper to interfere with the writ matter in a High Court. I told him clearly that the matter had nothing to do with the High Court. The papers till they were signed by JP had no significance. Once signed by JP these have become documents of national as well as international importance. As such it was my duty as DM to see that nothing objectionable, which may be injurious to the interest of the state, goes out without proper scrutiny.

Tarkunde agreed with my contention and instructed Dave to hand over the documents to me. Tarkunde again talked to me and said that the documents should be returned by tomorrow or else they will file the writ on somebody else's behalf. Dave handed over the original and two copies signed by JP and left for Delhi.

I will die before democracy is dead: JP

JP was deeply disappointed by Indira Gandhi's lack of response to his impassionate 'epistle' of 21 July in which he had poured out his heart to the 'darling daughter of Pundit Nehru' and 'the girl who grew up in Prabha's laps'. He felt slighted and humiliated. Besides, he had been reading heavily censored newspapers containing news of intellectuals and groups of people 'hailing' Emergency and the 'decisive' leadership of Indira as the best thing to have happened to the country. He was particularly upset about his mentor Vinobha Bhave describing Emergency rule as *'anushasan parava'* [era of discipline]. These had tremendous psychological impact on JP and it looked as if he was giving up all hopes for the restoration of democracy.

It was under these circumstances that my crucial meeting with JP took place on Wednesday, 6 August. As I walked in, he was reading the *Upanishad*. He looked normal. He also told me that he felt well. He had a 16-17-minute walk just with the support of his walking stick. His bowels moved normally. He was also cheerful.

JP asked me what the date was. I told him it was 6 August. He told himself that the hearing of the PM's appeal in the Supreme Court was on the 11th. He asked me what was the report about the case. He also asked me as to what was happening in Parliament. I could not mislead him by saying that there was nothing special. Hence I told him about the amendments to the Representation of the People Act by Parliament the day before and reported in today's papers. He was upset as I narrated one by one the six amendments that had been made. The most prominent was the amendment granting immunity to the PM's election from being challenged in a court of law. He looked sad and said with a deep sigh that, "there was no hope now. Everything is finished. She will be there forever."

I also informed him of the convening of the assemblies on 8 and 9 August and also the likely amendment of the Constitution rendering the elections of President, Vice President, Prime Minister and Speaker of the Lok Sabha non-justiciable. He was more upset now. He said in a very sad tone: "Democracy is finished completely," and after a pause, "at least for the present." He said that his only hope was in the Supreme Court and that too had been shattered. "Now there is nothing to hope for and nothing to live for. This lady has demolished the very edifice so painfully constructed by her father and myriad others." I was touched by his sentiments and the way he expressed it. I told him that this was inevitable and one could see it coming.

Our conversation drifted on to the role of the Opposition. I told him about the rift in the Janata Front in Gujarat due to a dispute over Rajya Sabha nominations. He was sad to hear it. He hoped that the first experiment of an alternative to the Congress should not end in failure. He was of the opinion that since this was for the first time that Opposition was in power in Gujarat, it might have happened and might pass off well. I told JP that Opposition was as much responsible for the present state of affairs. They had no unity among themselves and every one was a leader unto himself. There was no spirit of sacrifice but only greed and selfishness. Democracy cannot be guarded and a nation cannot be built without sacrifices, I told him. He agreed with me.

Sunday, 10 August was among the most eventful days during JP's detention in Chandigarh. S N Prasad, JP's brother-in-law had come from Calcutta along with his wife and 3-year old grandson to see JP. The new guidelines received four days earlier allowed interview for only parents, husband/wife and children. Strictly speaking, I could not have allowed the interview. But since they had come all the way from Calcutta and that I had given permission over telephone last Sunday (before the new guidelines came), I allowed the interview for one hour and Mohinder Singh took them to JP.

B P Sinha, Bhupinder Singh Jauhar and S P Malik had come to see me. We were having a chat when Mohinder Singh came back at about 1.30 p.m. and gave me a letter from JP, addressed to the Prime Minister with a copy to me. I was shocked to read the contents. It was a brief letter (just over a page) in which JP wrote that he was dismayed at the way in which the PM had amended the Representation of the People Act and Constitution of India to suit her personal dictatorship. How she was completely destroying democracy and he felt completely helpless. If he were free he could have taken some action to prevent the destruction of democracy. In bondage he could do only one thing – resist with his life. As such, he declared that commencing from 25 August he would start a fast-unto-death unless Emergency was revoked and all detainees released within two weeks. He would not take anything except water, sour lemon and medicine meant only for ill health.

I asked Mohinder Singh what had happened. He said that JP was calm and composed when the interview with Prasad started. But toward the end, JP suddenly felt upset and exploded. JP said that democracy was finished in the country and he felt helpless. He could not tolerate this state of affairs any more. As such he would go on a hunger strike. He asked Prasad to tell this to everyone. JP then took the copies of the letter from under his pillow and gave them to Mohinder Singh. After giving the letters to Mohinder Singh, he took back the original to check up whether he had written with best wishes. He had not and he inserted these words in the letter and gave it back to Mohinder Singh.

I excused myself from the guests and rushed to the PGI along with Mohinder Singh. In the car, my mind raced ahead. In the event of JP going ahead with the fast unto death, there could be only two outcomes. Using the power of censorship, news of JP's fast would be totally blacked out and implementing the 'death drill' under 'Operation Medicine' we would be able to rush through the funeral and hush up the whole thing. By the time people came to know of the death, it would be too late and the brute force of the state could take care of reactions if any. That way JP would have passed into history unseen and unsung, with the nation slipping into slavery, perhaps forever. On the other extreme, news of JP's fast could leak out to the outside world, building up passions. And in the event of his death, violence of severe magnitude bordering on civil war could break out, endangering the very existence of India as a nation. Both the eventualities were extremely dangerous and should be averted at all cost, I decided.

On reaching the JP ward, I asked Mohinder Singh to wait outside and went in. JP was sitting in the chair, his chin on his hand in a pensive and contemplating mood. A napkin was still lying on his lap. He was a bit surprised to see me at the lunch hour. I asked him about his interview with S N Prasad. He was grateful. He asked me whether I had received the letters from Mohinder Singh. I told him that is precisely why I had come now and asked him why he had made such a drastic decision. He said he had no other option. He felt helpless. Constitution was being ravaged and Indira's personal dictatorship was being established through apparently legal means, without a whimper from Parliament. All top Opposition leaders were in jail, without recourse to the outside world. It was impossible for him to watch all this, in a pathetic manner, without being able to do any thing. Indira thought that the country was her personal property. She thought that she could do anything she felt like. At least, if Morarji Desai was free, he could have done something. Now everyone, including him, was helpless and he had no other means left except to offer the 'supreme sacrifice'.

The firmness of his words put me off but I did not give up. Then started an hour of arguments and counter arguments, during which I virtually called JP a coward unable to face harsh realities. I tried to explain to him that the amendments were not of such serious nature as to warrant his fast-unto-death. I explained two or three amendments in some detail. I also pleaded with him that 45 days was too short a period to judge the trend. He should observe things for some more time and then take a decision. For this purpose, he should read newspapers and form an opinion. JP refused to relent and said that his decision was irrevocable because in his opinion, Indira would only bring more destructive measures now that 'intellectuals' had totally buckled and there was no resistance whatsoever. Even the RSS/Jan Sangh, the political cadre he had considered as his 'hardcore soldiers', were tendering apologies and getting themselves released in droves.

This gave me an opening and I argued that all intellectuals did not buckle and there were many willing to follow JP. I mentioned Bhimsen Sachar and his distinguished 'freedom fighter' colleagues who at their advanced age, had decided to dare the Prime Minister and commence a public campaign against Emergency from that very day. I said people were in a daze and only now the enormity of the situation had begun to sink in. As of now, state power had held absolute sway but before long they were bound to slip and people would regroup. Also international opinion was bound to turn against Indira soon, making it difficult for her to sustain this artificial situation. In the event, people across the nation as well as the globe would need a JP to lead the largest democracy in the world back to liberty and freedom. I ended this passionate plea by saying that JP was not just an individual but also a 'mass movement' on which hopes of millions depended. As such, he had no right to end his life, which belonged to the people of this nation.

JP looked at me with sad and piercing eyes. He thanked me for the compliment, which as of now was empty in content. The situation was hopeless and bound to get worse. "I do not want to live to see the death of democracy before my very eyes. The least I could do would be to deny me that unparalleled agony and die before democracy is dead", he said with finality.

I was getting panicky and as a last resort, I brought in a personal angle. I told JP that since he did not read newspapers these days, his letter and threat of fast would be taken as a direct sequel to my conversation with him on 6 August. This could have serious and embarrassing implications, I said. He paused for a few moments, thought over what I said, and then relented. He said he was the last person to put me to any kind of embarrassment since I had been very kind and indeed like a son to him. Therefore, he would reconsider his decision and defer the fast for the present. He took the original letter from me and tore it off. I, however, retrieved the pieces and put them in my pocket.

After a few moments, JP said his decision as to the fast was irrevocable and he was not going to change it. He was only delaying it by a few days and putting it across in a different way, just because of me. He would read the newspapers and take a further decision in a few days. I again requested him to watch for some more time, deliberate further and take a decision. He was too great a person to take such a hasty decision. JP said that my advice sounded reasonable and he would deliberate the matter further before taking a decision. He asked me to instruct S N Prasad that he had given up the idea of fasting for the present, and that Prasad should not say anything about the matter to anyone. I left saying that I was positive that things would get better very soon. In the meantime JP should not concede defeat since it would demoralize the whole nation.

I came out of the room greatly relieved and told Mohinder Singh to locate S N Prasad and instruct him as desired by JP. I also instructed him to give newspapers (*Tribune* and *Hindustan Times*) to JP regularly. I came back home and had a late lunch alone, the guests having left after a long wait.

The intensity of JP's thought and soul searching that had preceded his decision to offer the 'supreme sacrifice' could be seen from the entries in his diary. On 6 August, he wrote: "The expected has happened. Indira has insured herself against a possible adverse judgment of the Supreme Court by amendments to the Representation of the People Act. A drastic Constitutional amendment is also expected. All this is to complete the dictatorship of the self-appointed saviour of the country. All this is said to be done according to the Constitution. Hitler too used the democratic process to establish his fateful dictatorship. Will India also have to go through hell to emerge again from this darkness? But the price India will have paid will be crippling. May God help her."

The entry on 7 August was very poignant:

"Total revolution is our slogan; Future history belongs to us"

"Will this now remain an irony of history? All *jee-huzoors*, cowards and sycophants must be laughing at us. 'They dared to get at the stars but descended into hell', this is how they may be ridiculing us. But only those who sought to get at the stars have achieved anything in the world, may be at the cost of their lives.

Instead of total revolution, we find today the dark clouds of total counter-revolution encircling us. It is a feast day for the owls and jackals whose hoots and growls we hear on all sides. But, howsoever dark the night may be, the dawn is bound to follow.

But will the dawn follow all by itself? And shall we simply wait, arms crossed? If social revolution were just to follow the revolution of nature, there would have been no place for human effort for social progress and change. What then are we to do? The answer is: 'They who raised the slogan and sang that song must offer to sacrifice themselves. And the first to kiss the altar must be the one who was their leader'. Doubts have been set at rest; the decision has been taken.

Last night while offering prayers to goddess Bhagwati I had asked for a way out of this darkness, and I got it this morning. My mind is now calm and composed" JP's mind may have been calm and composed. But his decision had certainly put my mind in torment and turmoil. It would have done the same to every freedom-loving person in the country. But thankfully it was averted.

Writing on this episode, Minoo Masani gave this account in his book:

In his diary entry on 11 August, Jayaprakash had referred cryptically to a letter to the Prime Minister which was not dispatched and which he said he had destroyed. The entry ran: 'My earlier decision stands. The letter was not sent–I destroyed it. I will wait for the proper time and see how the situation develops.'

The letter to which JP refers was the one he had written out in hand and handed over to M G Devasahayam, who was then District Commissioner of Chandigarh, and thus JP's caretaker. JP tore up his copy of the letter, but the original survived with Devasahayam.

It seems that Devasahayam, who was a competent and patriotic young officer, went and pleaded with JP not to risk his life and give up the idea of his fast. After a lot of persuasion, he was able to make JP change his mind. This certainly shows that JP treated him like a friend– there was no other friend who could possibly advise him in those days–and that Devasahayam had by his behaviour towards his distinguished prisoner earned his confidence. This little incident also shows that not all officials of Government had lost their values and their decent instincts during the Emergency."

International Opinion Turns Anti-Indira

Indira Gandhi was obsessed with International opinion and that was turning strongly and sharply against her and the Emergency. The most significant sign was a long investigative article titled *"Ruler of 600 million and alone – Indira Gandhi is unmaking a democracy 'to save it' and looking to exchange moral authority for bread"* in the TIME magazine of 11 August, written by Claire Sterling, regular columnist for *Atlantic Monthly, Washington Post* and *International Herald Tribune*, who had recently visited India. The article was scathing in its attack on the Emergency and Indira: "Her decline from popular grace began long before the Allahabad High Court ordered her to resign. If she had dumped Constitutional government rather than obey the order, it isn't because she was 'indispensable to India' as her Congress Party claimed, but because too many Indians seemed all too ready to dispense with her."

This is what the article had to say about JP: "Bihar's jails were literally overflowing (into schools, parks, zoos) with 70,000 political prisoners. About half were left-wing Naxalite terrorists; the rest were peaceful followers of Indira's implacable adversary, Jayaprakash Narayan, a saintly 72-year old intellectual who in recent years had become the principal articulator of the country's desperation and the first real threat to Indira's power. He is now among those jailed."

The concluding paragraphs of the article were highly damaging and foreboding:

"Indira Gandhi is perhaps more powerful than ever before, but she is also more alone. There is no one left to share with her the blame of the regime's failings, no one of any stature to partake with her the task of running her vast benighted nation.

So desperately isolated has she become, so driven into new repressions that cut off her line of retreat, that the dynamics of staying on top may well push her into becoming a real dictator. And, though she is not the woman to make India anyone's satellite if she can help it, her increasing dependence on Moscow and the Communists could send the country lurching into the Soviet orbit. Neither development is likely to leave the Indian Army unmoved. And that is perhaps the crux of the situation.

India's standing Army of nearly a million men has been resolutely non-political since Independence. But it is also sensitive to the smallest slight to its honour, dignity and military independence, not to mention the nation's sovereignty; and it is steeped in loyalty to constitutional principles. It was altogether her Army when she enjoyed unquestioned legitimacy of constitutional rule. It may not be should its ranking officers conclude that she has become something else. More than ever now her fate hangs on the Army's loyalty."

Taking a direct hit at Indira, the author concluded: "Someone once told me, as I was traveling around India, that the one thing worse than trying to govern the country by democratic persuasion would be trying to govern it by force. Yet that is how Indira is trying to do it now. Depending on how fast and how far she goes in changing from a traditional Prime Minister to the one-woman ruler of a police state, the Indian Army–the one group with the power to stop the process – could intervene. If it were to do so, it would almost certainly be not to replace her with a military dictator, but to restore the institutions it has been drilled into defending since birth."

Unaware of the Sunday's turmoil, at the next day's Crisis Group meeting, Bhanot reported that JP was much better and composed.

Chuttani's report was also the same. No one, except to a certain extent Mohinder Singh, knew about the commotion and how I had narrowly averted a possible disaster to the nation! Bhanot also reported about the threatened black-flag demonstration against the Emergency during the Independence Day function.

I went to see JP in the evening. He had just taken his evening walk. He looked cheerful. He asked me whether yesterday's efforts went smoothly. I told him yes. I also told him that I had been about to go for lunch yesterday, when Mohinder Singh gave me his letter. I was so upset that I had come to see him immediately. JP said that Mohinder Singh had told him so and he was really sorry. I told him that the period of one-and-a-half months was too short a period to have an idea as to the future. He said that he had pondered over my advice and was in agreement with me. He would not take any drastic decision now and would wait and observe for some more time.

In order to cheer him up, I told him that things were likely to return to normal soon, though that concept of normalcy might be different. In a vast country like ours, it was not easy to run a totalitarian rule. India was a great nation.

JP suspected some understanding between the USA and Soviet Union over India. It was possible that they might have bargained over India and agreed to Russia holding hegemony over India as a part of international politics. Taking advantage of the subject of America, I told JP about the TIME article and its main message. JP liked what he heard and I could see a glimmer of hope in his eyes.

From the BBC news bulletin I came to know of the Supreme Court orders on PM's election petition. The court had refused Indira's counsel's plea to dismiss the writ as infructuous in view of the amendments of the Representation of the People Act and the Constitution. Instead the court had given two weeks time to Shanti Bhushan, the counsel of Raj Narain to prepare the case for challenging the validity of these amendments. Both BBC and Voice of America saw this as a head on confrontation between the Supreme Court and PM.

Supreme Court ruling, Bhimsen Sachar's defiance and TIME article were all positive pointers to the limits of emergency and the extent to which Delhi Durbar would go in destroying democracy. Perhaps I could use these three instances as catalyst for putting JP back on track enabling him to recoup some of his lost fire.

So I spent the better part of my meeting with JP next day to discuss the Supreme Court decision and its impact. I told him that the amendment granting immunity to the PM's election from being challenged in a court of law was discriminatory as well as absurd. In our system Prime Minister was not elected directly by the people. Only Members of Parliament gets elected who in turn elect the PM. How can the election of a particular MP who happens to become PM be immune from legal challenge? In my view Supreme Court would throw out this amendment. But the issue was: Will the Supreme Court deliver a free and fair judgment? Under the prevailing atmosphere of terror and fear the chances are dim. There seem to be hardly any Supreme Court judge who has guts and grits. Yet there was hope and hope was the best healer.

I could see that my efforts to apply the balm and heal the old man were working and JP was taking my views and opinions seriously. His confidence level and hope in the restoration of democracy was also getting revived. These could be seen from his diary note of August 13 elaborating on the Supreme Court decision and amendment to grant 'immunity' to PM's election:

"Indira's appeal and Raj Narain's cross-appeal were taken up on the 11th. The case was postponed to 25th. Shanti Bhushan argued that the recent amendments to the Law and the Constitution affected the basic structure of the Constitution, which the Court had earlier held was not within Parliament's power. Mr Shanti Bhushan is undoubtedly a great lawyer. Niren De, Attorney General, conceded that if it was shown that the Constitution's basic structure has been affected, the matter could be gone into. This is a remarkable development. There still seems to be hope. Some vitality still remains in our democracy. De has asked the Court to define the 'basic structure'. That is good. To the layman with some understanding of our Constitution and of Parliamentary democracy, there is no doubt that the recent amendments, the Emergency proclamation etc. have not only affected the basic structure of the Constitution, but also destroyed it.

When I wrote earlier about the amendments, a very important point had escaped me. This was brought to my attention today. According to our Constitution, there is no direct election of the Prime Minister. Only members of the Lok Sabha are elected. And no one knows beforehand which party or parties will win and who will be subsequently elected as leader of the party or parties. This means all MPs are elected alike and law applies to them equally. Now, when one of them becomes PM, how can his or her election be not challenged as that of any other MP? He or she has not been elected directly as PM–there is no such provision in the Constitution. Therefore this particular amendment is stupid. Gokhale (Union Law Minister) and other members of the Cabinet seem to be mesmerized by the PM as a rabbit by the python. Apart from being stupid, which under the law is not illegal, to exclude the PM's election which takes place after the general election from the jurisdiction of election law is a piece of discrimination as between one MP and another, which is highly illegal and improper".

A ray of hope had dawned on JP and now was the time to strategies my move for reconciliation and proceed in a cautious manner, I mused. Perforce I have to adopt a 'split personality', a loyal implementer of the Emergency regime on the outside and a sincere interlocutor for the return of democracy from the inside!

Who Can Stop Sanjay Gandhi from Becoming PM?

Did Indira proclaim Emergency to save India and the polity or to protect herself and son Sanjay Gandhi? The answer – as provided by B N Tandon, then Joint Secretary to the Prime Minister and one of Indira's confidants– is that it was the latter and not the former. This is what he had to say: "A personal problem was also responsible for the deterioration of PMS (Prime Minister's Secretariat)–the Prime Minister's younger son Sanjay. His interference in administration and government started with his Maruti project. He needed the help of different organs of the Government. The manner in which his mother allowed him to misuse her office and power has been recorded in the Gupta Commission's report. Sanjay clearly told the officers working under Law Minister H R Gokhale, that there was no law above him. He wanted his wishes to be fulfilled immediately and without question. To help him, the Prime Minister attached one of her assistants to him and Sanjay's order and wishes were conveyed to different ministries and officers through this assistant.... All this had begun before the Emergency. Indira Gandhi used to send her ministers and senior officials to Sanjay for orders. The result was that a (coterie was formed) and a durbar was held in the PM's house in the Prime Minister's absence where senior officials reported their actions to this coterie and sought its orders. What was even worse was the fact that those officials who did not obey the coterie in the PM's house found that they were being investigated by the CBI, police, the income-tax authorities etc*."Indeed, the tidings of unaccounted autocracy, the hallmark of Emergency!

The Sanjay durbar had been going on unabated and peaked in the run up to the Emergency. Tandon narrates: "From the beginning of 1975 the situation began to deteriorate rapidly. Long established decision-making processes were beginning to be set aside. The earlier practice was to put up files, papers and correspondence etc. for the PM's orders after a thorough examination. Normally Indira Gandhi did not take very long to give her decisions but now all the papers began to be entrusted to Sanjay for his opinion. In most of the cases, no decisions were taken without his instruction. This new process began to cause long delays in the disposal of papers. In spite of being told about this many times, the Prime Minister's answer generally used to be that she had made sure that nothing was delayed at her residence."

Tandon's disturbing narration continued. In order to strengthen the new way of functioning the Prime Minister's home began to be set against the Prime Minister's Secretariat and its senior officials. The Prime Minister's mind was poisoned by the 'loyalty' mantra. Over a period of time, even the Prime Minister's Secretary was denied any role in the selection and appointment of key officials in the government, banks and public sector undertaking. Sanjay Gandhi ruled by proxy.

One such proxy was Navin Chawla, an ambitious IAS officer. This is what V Sundaram, an IAS colleague of his, wrote later: "In Indian bureaucracy while all bureaucrats of similar seniority are equal on paper, yet some chosen few are more equal than others. Chawla belongs to the latter category. Navin Chawla was very close to Sanjay Gandhi and wielded unprecedented power in his official capacity as Secretary to the Lt Governor of the Union Territory of Delhi, Kishan Chand, during the Emergency in 1975-77. He functioned as the de-facto Governor of Delhi and several bureaucrats who happened to interact with him

---

* (PMO Diary-1, Prelude to the Emergency- Konark-pages xxiv & xxv)

during this period have confirmed the fact that he was known for his unabashed authoritarianism. His controversial role as Secretary to the Lt Governor of Delhi was noted by the Shah Commission, which went into the Emergency excesses. Chawla did not cover himself with glory when the Constitution of India was subverted with impunity during the Emergency. As one who occupied a vantage position during that period, he was charged with arbitrary exercise of authority."

The Shah Commission did not mince words when it wrote about Sanjay Gandhi: "In the view of the Commission, the manner in which Shri Sanjay Gandhi functioned, in the public affairs of Delhi in particular, is the single greatest act of excess committed during the period of the Emergency for which there is no parallel, nor any justification for such assumption of authority or power in the history of Independent India... If this country is to be rendered safe for future generations, the people owe it to themselves to ensure that an irresponsible and unconstitutional centre of power like the one which revolved around Shri Sanjay Gandhi during the Emergency is not allowed to come up ever again in any form or shape or under any guise."

Such was the man who was being catapulted to be the prime minister of India, just because he belonged to a dynasty being benefited by the name 'Gandhi'. On Sunday 14 September, I had the occasion to get a feel of the outside world, particularly senior bureaucrats and their views of the state of affairs as well as the shenanigans going on in New Delhi. In the evening, I went to Sundaram's place, as it was his daughter's birthday. Rashpal, Balakrishnan, Bansal, and Manivannan were also there. The conversation, as usual, was on the state of the nation, the ongoing Supreme Court case and the 20-point programme. No one present spoke in favour of Indira or her government.

The prospect of Sanjay Gandhi becoming the prime minister was discussed. Under the circumstances prevalent at that time, there was no stopping the youngster from becoming the PM in the near future. Indira herself would like to groom him some more, before abdicating in his favour. But she might do so earlier in the event of the Supreme Court verdict going against her, it was said.

India being a democracy, such abdication was not possible in an arbitrary manner. The change over had to take place through a democratic process. This could be only through the elections–with the Congress Party winning a majority and electing Sanjay Gandhi as leader of the House. In anticipation thereof, Indira was grooming Sanjay as an extra-constitutional authority, vested with vast powers without any accountability.

Left to Sanjay Gandhi, he had no patience for the electoral process, nor did he have any respect for democratic institutions. With his wrench-like hold over what was left of the Congress Party, and his vice-like grip over his mother, Sanjay could bulldoze his way through and take over the high office. With the Opposition in total disarray and their senior leadership all behind bars under MISA, there would not be any hurdle facing Sanjay Gandhi in his efforts to become the PM. But only if the change over took place outside the democratic process.

Indira did not want it to happen this way. Not that she was unduly worried about the public opinion in the country or the Opposition. She was more concerned about the international opinion and approval that was necessary for her Emergency regime or the succession by Sanjay Gandhi to gain legitimacy. For this, the change-over had to take place only through the democratic process of election.

Sanjay Gandhi and his coterie consisting of Bansi Lal, Om Mehta, and R K Dhawan, though in favor of succession outside the democratic process, were not much bothered about the prospects of holding elections. They were sure of the Congress party winning hands down. Even before the Emergency, Opposition parties were woefully fragmented. The Emergency and its rigors had badly battered and bruised them. In such an event, and given the state of the people's mind gripped with fear and foreboding, the Congress was sure of a cakewalk in the election due in early 1976 and Sanjay Gandhi could then crown himself as the prime minister of the largest democracy in the world.

But one solid hurdle remained between their plans and ambitions and its actual achievement. That was in the form of a 73-year old recluse, by the name of Jayaprakash Narayan, currently in detention under MISA at Chandigarh. In Sanjay and his coterie's calculation, the only person who had the capacity and credibility to bring the Opposition parties together and rally the people in the event of an election was JP. And he, like other Opposition leaders, had to be released if elections were to have any meaning. With his indomitable courage and tenacity of purpose, JP was bound to give his all to see that the dictatorial Congress was defeated and their designs destroyed by the collective will of the people. So the major obstacle for young Sanjay Gandhi to become the prime minister of this massive country, while still in his early thirties had become the old man JP, more than double his age.

This analysis was agreed upon by all present at the birthday party and the consensus was that Sanjay had a fair chance of becoming India's PM, provided JP could be "put out of harm's way". Sundaram confirmed that at Delhi also, knowledgeable circles were talking on these lines. And I made a strong mental note of this very important piece of information, particularly the comment 'putting JP out of harm's way'.

On Monday 15 September 15, JP gave two letters–one addressed to the Union Home Secretary and the other one to his advocate Tarkunde – attaching a copy of the letter to the Home Secretary. Reading through his letters revealed that it was a complaint that letters written by JP to his friends and relatives did not reach them. He was unable to understand as to why he was being treated in this way and why were things so bad. I had already informed JP that within 24 hours of his handing over the letter to us, it was sent to the Union Home Ministry or Delhi administration for onward dispatch to the addressees, after censoring. I had also begun to wonder as to why 19 out of the 20 letters had not been delivered, as JP had complained. JP was in a melancholic and disturbed mood when I met him that day. He said he was drafting a letter to the PM and would hand it over the next day. He said that he no longer needed parole. "What is the use now? Let Indira feel happy," he said in disgust. "The worst is over and I don't want any mercy from her. All I wanted was to be of some help. Indira did not have this much of grace", he lamented. JP said that in his letter he would raise political matters also and demand elections on time.

With JP mentioning elections, I told him of the conversation at the party the evening before and what people said about the happenings at Delhi. When I mentioned that there was every likelihood of Sanjay Gandhi becoming the PM, JP had a hearty laugh. He could not even comprehend the possibility. But his attitude changed when I mentioned about the talk in knowledgeable circles and the way Sanjay was being projected. Otherwise, what was the *locus standi* of this youngster, not even a Member of Parliament, to inspect flood-affected areas of Bihar by plane, accompanied by the Chief Minister of Bihar and the PCC president?

All eyes were on the Supreme Court proceedings, I continued. It could go either way. If it went against Indira, she had to resign. In the event, what was the alternative? There was hardly anyone with any caliber or following to succeed Indira. The two names being mentioned - Swaran Singh and S S Ray – were lightweights and not acceptable to Congressmen. Over the years, Congressmen had become nothing more than vassals and servile sycophants of the Nehru-Gandhi family since they felt that was the only way to survive. Under the circumstances, Indira would find no difficulty in nominating Sanjay as her successor and abdicating in his favour, in the event of an adverse Supreme Court ruling. Handing over the prime ministership to Sanjay could allow her to return to power after sorting out the Supreme Court and other matters. Even if this did not happen, she would have ensured dynastic succession, which she always wanted to do.

JP was now intently listening and I told him that Sanjay had a powerful coterie supporting him and the projection being made was that it was time the youth took charge. I made particular mention of Priyaranjan Das Munshi. JP said that he was all for youth power and he would have been happy if only these young people trying to capture power were good and sincere. According to JP, they were not. Sanjay was a happy-go-lucky boy who was neither steady nor mature. He had flashy ideas and rammed them through, without proper thinking. Priyaranjan Das Munshi was also no good.

JP now appreciated the seriousness of the situation. He said that taking into consideration the various factors, the possibility of Sanjay

Gandhi becoming PM in this manner couldn't be ruled out. There was no question of his ever-becoming PM through the normal democratic process of elections. The only way was for Indira to abdicate in his favor following an adverse Supreme Court ruling. In the event of this happening, there was no hope of normalcy being restored. Democracy would be buried deep and India would pass under dictatorship for a long time to come.

JP suddenly stirred, raised his voice a few decibels and said, "even if I get half a chance and get out of prison alive I will fight this possibility with all my might. But alas, will I ever get a chance?" he asked in desperation. The fire in his eyes and the fervent plea I saw in it touched a chord deep within me and I solemnly promised to myself that I would strive my every nerve to give him that chance, come what may.

Floodgate Closes but Sluice Gate Opens

Wednesday 27 August was another eventful day. I could not go to JP in the morning due to some engagements. In the afternoon RD Sharma came to my residence and gave me two letters from JP. One was a message addressed to the PM and the other a letter to me asking for the message to be conveyed to PM with the utmost urgency. The message expressed grave distress at the Bihar and Patna floods. In the message JP had requested for parole for a month so that he could go and organize relief operations. I contacted Mathur and told him the contents of the message and it was decided to send the communication to Delhi immediately by special messenger. It was done accordingly and the message was sent out that very evening.

Soon after arranging for the dispatch of the message, I went to see JP. He was reclining on the bed reading a book of short stories. Got up and sat in the chair as I went in. He looked quite distressed at the flood situation in Bihar, especially Patna. He was unable to understand as to how so much water could come inside Patna. I told him about the breach of the bund in River Sone which was reported in the papers that day. It was due to the fault of engineers. JP was very much pained. He told me that Patna was a city with 5-lakh population. Old Patna is already miserable with very narrow streets and knee-deep water even in normal rains. If buildings at high places like the Secretariat, Raj Bhavan etc have been affected what would be the fate of low-lying areas? He wondered how the State Government would handle the situation. He felt that the present government was incapable of managing such a great disaster.

JP was in genuine anguish. He said that Bihar has been cursed with frequent floods and drought. This flood was one of the worst. This year there was a good kharif crop prospect. Now it is shattered. He said that whenever there was such natural calamity, inspections were done, meetings held, speeches made, reports prepared and certain decisions taken. But hardly any follow up or tangible action is ever taken to prevent such catastrophe in future. In a voice choked with pain and anguish JP said that in Bihar there is reeking corruption in almost all sections of government. This was more so among engineers and lower level revenue and administrative officials. Most of the politicians are hand in glove with these corrupt officials. By and large politicians were protecting and safeguarding corrupt and dishonest officials. They were also instrumental in harassing and humiliating good and honest officials at the instance of vested and corrupt interests. JP said that Biharis, except some people belonging to scheduled castes and tribes, are hard working. Politicians in Bihar practise and perpetuate too much of casteism and seem to thrive on that. Casteism coupled with rampant corruption among the politicians and in the government was responsible for the very slow pace of development in Bihar in spite of rich natural resources.

Now JP was in a pensive and reflective mood. He talked of relief work he did during the devastating drought of 1966-67, when he headed the Bihar Relief Committee. He said that out of the various agencies involved in relief work, CARITAS was about the best. A Protestant relief agency, the name of which he could not remember, also did good work. He fondly remembered the work done by Mother Teresa and her Missionaries of Charity. Though this was not in their line of work, they did commendable service, he remarked.

Indira had just then become the PM. At that time she was under heavy attack both inside and outside Parliament especially on the mink coat affair. JP, his wife Prabhavati, Ram Manohar Lohia and Indira were travelling by air from Delhi to Patna in order to inspect the drought situation. Indira wept while pleading with JP to persuade Raj Narain and others from attacking and criticizing her in a slanderous manner. She also wept like a child when told of the miseries and afflictions of the drought-affected people. That was Indira then. Now she had changed a lot. She used to be delicate, soft and tender. Now she is haughty and arrogant. A sense of insecurity seems to be haunting her. Hence she overreacts to a particular situation.

Our conversation turned back to the flood situation. When told about the Press report that Jagjivan Ram's helicopter trip could not materialize since the chopper could not land, JP commented that he was not in favour of VIPs hovering around in helicopters while the afflicted people suffer in anguish. He asked me about his message to the PM. I told him that it has been dispatched through a special messenger. As I left I told him that as soon as the GoI took any decision on his message I would inform him accordingly. JP was not very hopeful that the PM would accede to his request.

When I went to JP next morning he was taking a stroll in the corridor accompanied by R D Sharma. On seeing me, he returned to his room. First thing he asked me was the response to the message to the PM. I told him that it has already reached Delhi and I had also talked to Mathur who is in Delhi. I will convey the response of GoI as soon as it is known. I told JP that his message was very crisp and was not even dated. He told me that he wrote the message in a hurry. It was not meant to be a letter, only a message.

He then paused and said that he had slipped up in not writing that he would not indulge in anything except relief work during his parole. He will not talk politics at all. In any case he felt that this was not the time to talk politics in Bihar when the people are undergoing such misery. In fact, doing so would be treacherous. The only thing needed and to be done was to organize and provide maximum relief. He asked my advice whether he should write a detailed letter to the PM in this respect. I said that it would certainly be good if JP writes a letter to

PM containing the assurance, which may enable Indira to come to an early positive decision. But I advised him that PM should not get the impression that he was over anxious for his release and read motives in his genuine request. I also told him that the latest report was that the Raj Bhavan and the CM's residence at Patna has been marooned. The situation has been handed over to the armed forces.

It was not for nothing that JP is known as Lok Nayak. Within the confines of the PGI ward under detention, his heart wept sincerely and genuinely for those suffering under the onslaught of one of Bihar's worst floods. His entire being shook and he was willing to go to great lengths even to compromise with Indira to get out of the confinement and be with his people in their hour of trial and suffering and to give them whatever succor he was capable of. I remember someone mentioning sometime ago that for many people in Bihar JP was a demi-god and they nearly worship him. After watching JP today–his affection and love for his people - I could understand that statement in full measure.

When I went to see JP in the morning of Sunday 31 August, he had just returned from his morning stroll on the corridors. Immediately on seeing me he asked, "What is the news?" I told him the message received from Mathur on telephone from Delhi. He paused for a moment. I could see trace of disappointment on his face. He said that the matter was of extreme urgency, "I had written everything needed. I would work in co-operation with state government. I am prepared to give in writing that I will not talk politics. It will be mocking and insulting to the people to talk politics at this hour." After a long deliberation, he continued, "Indira may be thinking of asking for an undertaking. But it is a downgrading word. Without calling it an undertaking, I am willing to give one. I have asked for parole only for a month. They may or may not give me an extension. After the specified period, I would surrender myself to the government. In any case I would be only around Patna and can be taken into custody again." On his own he continued, "I hope she may come herself or send someone to talk it over with me. Though the floods are receding there will be a mammoth task to be done. The devastation would be too large. Many areas in Patna have been severely damaged."

When I got up to leave JP hinted indirectly that I might take the initiative for his release on parole. For that purpose he was willing to give some undertaking if necessary. True to his words JP sent a letter to me that was delivered by Sharma that night about 9 pm. It was a request to me to convey to the PM his assurance that he will confine himself only to relief work and will not even talk of politics in the event of his being released on parole. He wanted this clarification to reach the PM before she took a decision on his request for parole.

The letter was sent to Delhi haste-post-haste through Office Superintendent SR Chopra in the night itself with instructions to hand over the same personally to the Union Home Secretary. Before going home I told Sharma to inform JP next morning that his letter has already been dispatched to Delhi.

Unfortunately all these efforts to have JP to go on parole to serve his people of Bihar were in vain because of the mean mentality displayed by Indira Gandhi. Prof P N Dhar, Principal Secretary to the Prime Minister was a man with his heart at the right place, a rarity in the heartless emergency regime. This is what he writes on JP's parole petition and how Indira handled it.*

"Having decided to stay on (he had toyed with the idea of resigning earlier but was talked out of it by P N Haksar, his illustrious predecessor), I had to chalk out my priorities. One of the top priorities, which I set for myself, was to explore the possibility of reconciliation between Indira Gandhi and JP.

The first opportunity in this endeavour came in late August 1975, when the PM received a message from JP in which he expressed grave concern about the Bihar floods and asked for a month's release on parole so that he might mobilize people's help and organize popular relief in co-operation with the central and state governments.

The PM did not want to respond directly; she was still feeling the sting of the letter JP had sent her a month earlier in which he had bit-

---

* *Indira Gandhi, the 'Emergency' and Indian Democracy* — Oxford University Press

terly criticized her. What had hurt her most was his remark that 'nine years is not a short period of time for the people who are gifted with a sixth sense, to have found you out'. She looked upon JP's suggestion as a political ploy. She told me that JP was probably trying to upstage the government. I disagreed with that interpretation and told her that in my opinion JP was offering an olive branch.

In the meanwhile, JP sent another message in which he emphasised that he would not exploit the period of freedom for political purposes. Finally, it was decided that some knowledgeable person should go and reassure JP that all possible arrangements were being made to help the victims of the floods in Bihar."

Accordingly, on Wednesday 3 September, BB Vohra (Additional Secretary in the Ministry of Agriculture, Government of India) came and met with JP to brief him about the Bihar and Patna floods as well as the relief measures being taken in the wake of such unprecedented floods. As far as JP's request for parole was concerned it never materialized.

Despite JP's bitterness over Indira's meanness in denying him parole, I felt that with JP in this conciliatory frame of mind, the process of reconciliation could start leading to restoration of normalcy and re-railing of democracy. This, provided Indira is keen on going back to the democratic style of functioning.

Though Indira spurned the flood-gate of reconciliation opened by JP, by denying him parole, the devastating Bihar floods did open up a sluice-gate of opportunity for bringing about reconciliation between the two hard-core adversaries that could probably end the sordid saga of Emergency.

Sowing Seeds of Reconciliation

On Wednesday 17 September, when I went to see JP, I was a bit weighed down because our deliberations today could have far-reaching consequences. He was expecting me, he said. He was looking better and the swelling in his feet was only local. It had nothing to do with his heart, he said.

He was still drafting the letter to the PM. The deadline of my advice to JP had expired the day before. I could not hold him further from finalising the letter and give to us for dispatch. If he took a hard-line in the letter, that could not be helped and he could not be blamed. We had conveyed all his overtures, undertakings to me in writing and willingness to negotiate and reconcile for a political settlement, to Delhi promptly. Enlarging JP on parole would have created a conducive atmosphere for reconciliation and a normalisation process. But there had been no response whatsoever from the powers-that-be regarding the parole request. It was but natural for JP to feel insulted and withdraw the parole request in a huff, using some harsh words. But this would be falling into the trap of the autocrat and her progeny, who would like nothing better. So, I counselled him not to withdraw the parole request. We discussed the pros and cons of it in some detail. I was of the view that it may be a good idea for JP to take advantage of the adversity and the fact that Indira had been put on the defensive for not conceding his request for parole. A harsh letter condemning the Prime Minister for not granting parole and withdrawing it in protest would not achieve anything under the circumstances. It could only create more bitterness, whereas our objective was to create a conducive atmosphere for a possible reconciliation. At the same time, JP could put his mind to what Indira should do, now that the country had returned to normalcy, as per her own claim.

JP listened attentively and agreed with my contention. He said that, instead of withdrawing the parole request, he was going to insist on it in the wake of the new floods, as reported in the media. He was going to remind Indira that she herself knew about his capacity for organizing relief work. He was also going to categorically demand that the PM makes a commitment by October to hold elections on schedule. It should not be difficult for Indira to concede to his demand as she herself was claiming that there was near-normalcy in the country. Then why the Emergency and why all the detention, he asked.

Our conversation turned to the Emergency and its aftermath, particularly efforts towards legitimizing it. In JP's view, Indira was trying to justify the Emergency on the economic plank and that was the objective behind the 20-point programme, which was just gimmickry. Everybody was talking about it in a mechanical manner, without really understanding what they are talking. These programmes were fast becoming empty slogans like *garibi hatao*. Vital matters like health, family planning and education were not in the 20-point programme. There was nothing new in it–only some material for political propaganda. These kinds of point-programmes had the danger of programming the government servants like robots, where they didn't see or hear anything outside these programmes. A farce like this became a *Bible* for them, controlling and conditioning their thoughts and actions in the manner of autocratic regimes. The irony of it all was that even the RSS/Jan Sangh activists, seeking release from detention by giving apology letters, swore allegiance to the 20-point programme, as if it was a sacred document like the *Bhagavad Gita*!

Trying to amend the Constitution and enact new laws in order to implement these point-programmes was another fraud on the people. As it was, this wretched nation was overburdened with all conceivable laws, which merely remained on paper. It was atrocious to even think that the fundamental right of speech and expression should be taken away in order to implement the point-programmes. There was also no need to incorporate the fundamental right to property, because for the poor and the un-entitled this would be totally superfluous.

The Supreme Court's verdict on Indira's election petition was expected to have far reaching impact on the future of India's democracy. If the decision was in favour of Indira, she might adopt more stringent measures to consolidate power and strengthen her hold on the country. Were she to lose, then she might be in a tamed frame of mind and try to seek reconciliation. She might also adopt a ploy of stepping down, thereby paving the way for Sanjay to be made the PM.

Despite many pointers, JP just could not bring himself to believe that Sanjay could become the prime minister. I pointed out that it was a distinct possibility and not a matter to be brushed aside. There was a powerful and resourceful group of insiders in Delhi scheming and maneuvering things toward this end. JP understood the seriousness of my contention and said in that case, it would be farewell to democracy in India. Collecting himself, he said, "I have faith in the people and they would reject any such move violently. There would be revulsion in the minds of the people. In fact this should happen at least for a brief while for the people to understand the actual motive behind the Eemergency and its autocratic aftermath."

There was some consolation in JP when I told him that Justices Mathew and Justice Khanna of the Supreme Court had been asking searching and probing questions to the government advocates in Indira's case.

There was no Crisis Group meeting. But as had become his trade mark, Mathur, running scared or for some mysterious reason, created quite a scene which took some efforts to sort out. At about 1 p.m. that day he telephoned me to announce that shifting JP to the guesthouse had been cleared. As if it was a matter of great achievement, he had sent a formal note to the Home Secretary of Chandigarh administration and

I was asked to consult him and take steps to shift JP. I wondered as to what was there to consult. In any case, I knew that the guesthouse was not yet ready for occupation by JP and Bhanot had confirmed this when I had talked to him a little earlier. Bhanot had said that the camp work was still in progress and it would take at least another 24 hours before he could make the necessary security arrangements. I had agreed with him. But Mathur had already set the flap rolling. He had separately telephoned Chuttani, asking him to inform JP about the shifting, which was to be done that evening itself. Dr Mehra telephoned and informed me about this. I told him that the shifting today was not possible and Dr Chuttani should bring this to JP's notice. At about 5 p.m. Mathur rang up, as if in panic. He wanted to know why JP could not be shifted that day itself. I gave him the reasons. He got worked up and said I must talk to Bhanot and see to it that JP was shifted pronto. He wanted me and Bhanot to inspect the cottage and talk the matter over with Dr Chuttani.

I went to guesthouse along with Mohinder Singh. Bhanot was already there. His reasons were convincing and the camping work was still in progress. I agreed with Bhanot and we went over to Dr Chuttani to explain the position. He was perturbed since he had already informed JP, who might be upset in the event of any delay since he had been anxiously waiting for this change. I said we will handle it and went to see JP. He was in the midst of his letter to the PM. He was a bit taken aback, seeing both Bhanot and me, together. He thought we had brought some important news about his release or parole. We explained the matter to him and told him of the difficulties in shifting him today and that positively, he would be shifted by the morrow. He did not show any signs of being upset and readily agreed to our request. We left saying that we would be back at 9 p.m. next day for the shifting.

Hardly had I reached home, there was a telephone call from Mathur. He wanted to know as to what had happened and what JP's reaction was. He obviously heaved a sigh of relief when I told him about JP's pleasant reaction. It was indeed intriguing why such a senior officer as Mathur got rattled and panicked on such minor matters. This only deepened my suspicion of the sinister Delhi agenda. As events later turned out, this suspicion was well-founded.

JP did stick to my advice and on Thursday 18 September 1975 gave the letter addressed to the PM. I went through it, discussed it with Mathur, and dispatched it to the Union Home Secretary immediately. The content of the letter, which did not have rancour or bitterness, was mainly an expression of deep concern at the Bihar floods, which was devastating particularly because of the breach of the right embankment of main Kosi canal. Mathur, being a Bihar cadre officer, could appreciate the seriousness of this breach and said that it was a very serious matter and the loss would be tremendous. He explained it on a diagram. But he was cynical about JP's capability in organizing relief. In the last couple of days, I had been observing Mathur. For no rhyme or reason, he denigrates JP. It could not be from his heart, because basically Mathur was a good and decent man. Obviously, he was doing this for some one else's sake. It might be that he suspected one of us as possibly carrying tales. I took the opportunity to discuss JP's frame of mind and the moment being opportune for a political dialogue between Indira and JP, so that the process of reconciliation could be initiated. Bhanot's response was typical of a policeman. He asked, why should there be a political dialogue? Indira wielded absolute power and there was no challenge to her authority. JP was of no consequence now. In the event why should Indira talk to anyone, least of all to JP who was a spent force?

Though I refused to get provoked, Mathur could not contain himself. He said, Bhanot, how long do you think police raj can run the country? There is a need for political dialogue. The question is with whom, and when. Mathur then turned to me and asked as to what our advice to the GoI should be regarding JP's parole request. I was candid in my view. Unless we were aware of the considerations that went into a decision by the GoI, we would not be able to give much of an advice. According to me the matter was simple. If the powers-that-be wanted the current autocratic trend to continue, then there was no question of granting parole to JP. But if the GoI and, particularly PM, were interested in initiating the process of reconciliation, then the first step should be taken to release JP on parole.

Bhanot butted in and said: "We are giving too much importance to JP, who is basically a cowardly and timid man. He thinks that he has a national and international stature. Will break but not bend. He cannot sustain a long battle. We don't have to worry about this man much."

This time Mathur ignored him and asked me as to what were the irritants bothering JP. I listed them as:

- Curtailment of interviews and making it strictly for close relatives only. As of now, none of his friends and well-wishers had a chance to meet him.
- Non-delivery of most of the letters written by JP to his relatives and friends.
- Lack of companionship and feeling of solitary confinement
- Inability to experience open sky and fresh air

Mathur said that he was going to Delhi and would talk the matter over with Khurana. Gupta intervened, saying that nothing much could be achieved by talking to Khurana. Instead, Mathur must talk to Om Mehta, Minister of State for Home Affairs. With contempt in his voice, Mathur retorted, "I don't want to talk to politicians". I once again stressed the point that JP was in a proper frame of mind for a political dialogue and if the PM was interested in the process of reconciliation, this was the opportune time to send an emissary to mediate with JP and open up a dialogue with him. Tarkunde telephoned from Delhi saying that he wanted to come over on Saturday to meet JP. Received some letters–one of them from the USA–addressed to JP and a book *Roses in December* by M C Chagla. Asked Mohinder Singh to deliver them to JP. I went to JP along with Bhanot at about 8.45 p.m. He was just finishing his meal. Proceeded to the cottage within the campus. As we came out of the ward, JP remarked with a deep sigh, "open air after 2½ months". He then said that this would be his fifth abode since his arrest. JP was happy to see the cottage and the facilities, particularly the openness. He wanted a writing table, which was provided. He was told that he could use the entire cottage, including the drawing and dining rooms. He was very happy. When we left, I borrowed his book *Footsteps into the Future* by Rajni Kothari.

JP Writes to Sheikh Abdullah

Having lodged JP in an open ambience with fresh air, as he had demanded, I felt greatly relieved. Besides reducing JP's physical stress, it would also soothe his mind and create a facilitating frame for possible reconciliation parleys in the coming days. With this at the back of my mind, I decided to step up my efforts to put the pieces together.

I was not happy at Mathur's response to my request for sounding Delhi to initiate the process of reconciliation through political dialogue with JP. In any case, there were severe limitations for Mathur. Firstly, he was a civil servant who was not supposed to meddle in political matters. Secondly, he was a Kayastha from the Bihar cadre, known to JP and, therefore a suspect in the eyes of the Delhi Durbar. So, if Mathur took up the subject of political dialogue with someone in Delhi, it would most certainly be misconstrued. Bansi Lal, who was already upset with him, would pounce on him. The Sanjay coterie, which would certainly be opposed to any reconciliation and normalisation, would make life miserable for Mathur. Yes, I could understand Mathur's predicament.

Yet, I was passionately consumed with the idea of initiating the process of reconciliation. I felt bottled up, without any avenue for articulating this necessity. I had no direct access to the powers-that-be in Delhi. My closest contact was with Bansi Lal who would be the first one to sabotage any reconciliation move between JP and Indira. I could go to his archrival Giani Zail Singh, the Punjab CM, for his intervention and take up the matter. But I had only casual acquaintance with the Giani and no personal equation. I was not sure of Zail Singh's reaction or his bona fide. Rashpal was another source, but he had opined the other day that the time was not ripe for such an effort. I felt distressed and disappointed that I could not even get this message across to the powers-that-be in Delhi effectively, particularly as JP was willing and keen for a dialogue leading towards reconciliation and possible restoration of democracy. I racked my brain for one whole night and the next morning as to how to find a way and mediate. It was then that I suddenly remembered Rashpal's statement that Giani Zail Singh had approached Sheikh Abdullah to take the initiative for starting a dialogue with JP. Rashpal had also mentioned that this effort of the Giani had Indira's blessing. I remembered JP's fond mention of the Shiekh and their personal relationship. In a moment, things fell into place and I knew what my next move should be in the process of initiating a dialogue.

On Friday, 19 September, as soon as I finished my office chores, I went to meet JP. He was sitting in the rear verandah of the cottage looking relaxed and cheerful. He was obviously feeling happy in the open surroundings of the green lawn and the trees. We talked about lawns, gardens, and trees. He listened intently when I explained the concept of greening Chandigarh, the contribution of Dr M S Randhawa and the unique rose garden the city had. He was deeply impressed when I explained about the vastness and exquisite nature of the rose garden, considered to be the largest in Asia. He was happy to know that my residence was just across this rose garden and I take my occasional strolls there on days I do not play tennis.

Our conversations shifted to Indira's case in the Supreme Court. He was of the view that the Supreme Court had to really stretch hard if it had to decide in favour of Indira. A lot of things hinged on the judgment, which would decide as to whether the country would be condemned to head towards dictatorship or would have a chance to get democracy back. He wondered as to whether the Supreme Court judges had the courage and integrity to pronounce on merits in the face of ruthless power and dictatorial trend. I felt the time ripe to broach the subject of reconciliation and political dialogue and said that the Supreme Court judgment notwithstanding, the issue whether India would drift toward dictatorship or return to democracy depended largely on Indira and JP. If the confrontation continued, this appeared bleak. The only hope for democracy was reconciliation between JP and Indira, the process for which had to be initiated, I insisted. JP said he was willing but did not know how to go about it. He wondered through whom should he initiate the move, and then carry out the dialogue.

When I mentioned Sheikh Abdullah's name, his face brightened. He said: "Yes, the most apt person, no doubt. Sheikh has very good equation with Indira also." Taking advantage of JP's favourable response, I suggested that JP could write a letter to Sheikh Abdullah and indicate his mind. This might work out, since Giani Zail Singh was already in touch with the Sheikh, with the blessing of Indira. JP was happy to know about this development and Indira's interest in initiating a political dialogue. He said he would seriously consider my suggestion of writing to Sheikh Abdullah in the next couple of days.

I informed JP that Tarkunde would be coming over the next day. He was glad that I had told him, so that he could prepare and keep notes on various points to be discussed with Tarkunde.

As I left, JP held my hands and said he was glad to be in open surroundings and thanked me for that. He also said that he felt greatly relieved, whenever I visited and talked to him. He was particularly thankful for the idea of writing to Sheikh Abdullah. I was glad to notice the warmth and cheer in JP. As I drove back home, my heart felt light in the hope that a reconciliation between JP and Indira could be effected soon and the dark days of dictatorship might be over.

In the evening, I had a fruitful chat with Rashpal and told him about my discussions with and how I had prepared JP to initiate the reconciliation process by writing to Sheikh Abdullah. But it would be better if the initiative came from Sheikh Abdullah, so that JP could respond appropriately, thereby getting the process going. Could Rashpal get this done through Giani Zail Singh or any other source? Rashpal said that he would put his best foot forward and give it all he had.

Tarkunde came in the morning of Saturday, September 20. I sent him to JP along with Mohinder Singh. I could not converse with Tarkunde, as I was busy in a meeting connected with Chandigarh Lawn Tennis Association, of which I was Founder-President, and the exhibition tennis match in which Ramanathan Krishnan and probably Vijay Amritraj would participate. Obviously things had moved fast and the newspapers of Monday 22 September, brought encouraging news. There was a PTI report in *The Tribune* from Srinagar, stating, "Sheikh favours conciliation at all-India level." The report went on to say that Sheikh Abdullah, the Chief Minister of Jammu and Kashmir, had stated that he was at the disposal of the Prime Minister for any mediatory efforts to resolve the situation prevailing in the country "in a spirit of conciliation". He was also reported to have stated "everyone would like normalcy to be restored" and the "Prime Minister is more than keen to end the Emergency, depending on the overall situation."

This news report looked like a manifestation of divine will and the timing was most opportune. The idea of writing to the Sheikh had already been planted in the mind of JP and this news story would go a long way in facilitating a positive communication.

Now that JP had started reading the newspapers, I was confident that he would have read the report and started thinking on these lines. I did not want to rush to him and put pressure to write a letter responding to the statement of the Sheikh. It would be prudent to let things take their own course and JP should have enough time to make up his mind. Mathur had come back from Delhi and we had our routine meeting in the morning. He was not very enthusiastic about his meetings in Delhi. He had taken up the matter of non-delivery of JP's letters with S L Khurana and C V Narasimhan and they promised to look into the matter. He did not talk to anyone regarding a political dialogue or initiating the process of reconciliation. According to him, this would have brought no response. Suddenly, in his typical style, he asked, "Is JP a person worth talking to? Does he represent the people any longer?" I retorted by saying, "of course yes". Not long before, JP had rallied millions of people against corruption and misrule and he still represented the conscience of the nation.

When I mentioned about the reported remarks of Sheikh Abdullah and Zail Singh's efforts to get him to mediate, Mathur just nodded, without making any comments. I went to see JP the next evening. He was having a stroll with R D Sharma on the lawns. One seeing me, he came back and we sat in the verandah.

Before I could open any conversation, JP himself mentioned about the press reports on Sheikh Abdullah's statement on reconciliation and was sure it was due to my efforts. He said that this report had come when he was considering my suggestion of writing to the Sheikh. Since yesterday, he had been drafting a letter to the Sheikh and had to do it twice. He had finalized the letter now and would be giving it to me.

While feeling encouraged by Sheikh Abdullah's statement, particularly about the PM being interested in normalisation and ending of the Emergency, JP was nevertheless quite apprehensive. He was, in fact, extremely distressed by the reported statement of Indira in a conference of "Educators in Secularism, Socialism, and Democracy" which was in very bad taste, according to him. Reports said:

"The Prime Minister, irked by the vocal concern of the western press over the eclipse of Indian democracy asked hysterically, 'would this country be considered more democratic had a large number of people been killed after June 29, if myself, my family, and the chief ministers and others who support me had been annihilated?"

"What does she think? If she is thinking that she can manage to create hatred and venom against the Opposition by these lies, she is sorely mistaken," JP said in bitterness. "With the PM having this kind of attitude, continuing with such gross lies and distortions, there is no point in my persisting with my request. I am going to withdraw my request for parole." After this outburst, JP calmed down but turned his anger against K L Shrimali, who had presided over the educators conference. "It is indeed surprising that this K L Shrimali has no sense of shame or self respect. Does he not know as how he was sacked as

Union Education Minister by Jawaharlal Nehru at the instance of his daughter Indira?" JP asked and went on to give the details: "Shrimali was Education Minister in Nehru's cabinet and was removed under the Kamaraj plan. Since Shrimali was not a professional politician, the Kamaraj plan was not applicable to him. Yet he was sacked unceremoniously and Shrimali had himself complained to me about this. The reason was that Indira wanted Shrimali to release substantial grants to the yoga ashram of Dhinendra Brahmachari, her yoga instructor. Shrimali told her that the yoga ashram had not utilized the earlier grants properly and had not furnished utilization certificate. Under the circumstances it was not possible to release further grants due to audit objections. On this, Indira got annoyed and had Shrimali sacked by her father." Despite this humiliation, Shrimali is now sitting smugly, listening to this entire tirade by Indira and paying court. "Don't these people have any sense of self-respect?" JP wondered.

We talked again about the letter to the Sheikh. JP said that the letter was ready. In the process of writing the letter, he had torn off two drafts and thrown them in the waste paper basket. I advised him not to do this because I did not want papers written by him to fall into undesirable hands. He agreed, went to his bedroom, took out all the pieces from the waste bin put them in the toilet and flushed it down. Then he gave me the fair copy of the letter addressed to Sheikh Abdullah.

I glanced though the letter and was struck by his intensity of feeling and sincerity to restore normalcy. In his letter, he offered his full cooperation toward conciliation efforts and requested the Sheikh to come over for a discussion. However, he concluded the letter with a caveat:

"You have said that the PM is more than keen to end the Emergency. Well, the first test of her keenness will be whether this letter is allowed to be delivered to you and whether you are permitted to see me."

We briefly discussed the Supreme Court case. JP was of the opinion that there was no idea in taking up the main case before deciding on the validity of the Constitutional amendment, which was before the SC.

In view of the importance of the letter and my own anxiety, the same was sent to Delhi by courier in the night itself.

Indira Explores Reconciliation

Though we did not know each other, there appeared to have some telepathy between Prof Dhar and me. Having established reconciliation between JP and Indira as a priority, Dhar's first move was to send Vohra to JP to make a small opening. This is what he records in his book on the report given by Vohra on his meeting with JP:

"He (JP) also asked Vohra to convey a message to the Government of India, which Vohra jotted down. The highlights of what JP told him were:

> 'A great deal of work needs to be done...I am keen to serve my people...confident I shall be able to rally popular support...Even though I am not in touch with them I am confident that all opposition leaders in Bihar will listen to me...It would be wrong...absolutely improper and morally wrong...for me to take political advantage of the present situation in Bihar...I have no intention of making even a mention of political matters...The British government released political workers in 1934 (the reference was to the release of Rajendra Prasad and others at the time of the Bihar earthquake that year); the present tragedy calls for a review of the situation for similar means...If I am released the whole agitation can be called off...a proper atmosphere would have been created.
>
> — B B Vohra, 5/9/75'

JP had also asked Vohra to tell me verbally that 'this was a good time to review the entire policy that had been followed in the name of the Emergency'. These messages convinced me that JP's stance had changed from one of belligerence and confrontation, that he was now ready to negotiate. Indira Gandhi did not agree with my view. She thought I was too optimistic, but she was not discouraging either. In spite of her strong reservations, she agreed that it would be desirable to establish some contact with but was not sure who could be entrusted with that delicate job. She mentioned the names of two well-known politicians who had earlier undertaken similar missions but failed. When she gave me details of those efforts I felt that those gentlemen had been more interested in augmenting their own political capital than in closing the gulf between her and JP. In view of the earlier experience, she felt there was now a need for a low-profile person who was not an active politician and who JP would trust.

The only person who I thought fulfilled these conditions was Sugata Dasgupta, whom JP had appointed as Director of the Gandhian Institute of Studies at Varanasi. I had known Dasgupta for some time and had faith in his integrity and competence. After securing Indira Gandhi's approval I talked to him; Dasgupta was very happy to undertake the mission. He was to meet JP on 25 September 1975, but just before his departure for Chandigarh we received a letter from JP addressed to Sheikh Mohammed Abdullah with the request that it be transmitted to the addressee. The letter shed some more light on the way JP's mind was working....

Since JP was in a mood to explore the possibility of reconciliation with Indira Gandhi, I thought Sugata Dasgupta's visit was well timed...."

At about 7 pm on Wednesday, September 24, Mathur telephoned saying that he wanted to discuss certain urgent and confidential matters with me and I should go over to his place at 9 pm. Rather intrigued I went over. There was nobody else–only Mathur and me. He said that he had received telephone call from Khurana stating that one Dasgupta is coming to Chandigarh by tomorrow morning flight. He was coming at the instance of PN Dhar in order to meet JP. Dasgupta's visit was to be kept a total secret and nobody should know about it. He is to be picked up from the airport and his meeting arranged with JP in absolute confidence. I was to handle the matter personally with nobody else associated. Mathur had already booked a room for Dasgupta in the UT guesthouse as his guest. No name was to be entered in any register.

Mathur was not clear as to who Dasgupta was and what his mission was. Since he was not a known political figure we were wondering as to whether his visit has any thing to do with the initiation of a political dialogue. However we agreed that since he was coming as an emissary of Dhar there must be come importance attached to it. Mathur advised me to keep my eyes and ears open to find out what was Dasgupta up to.

On my drive back to my house I was wondering as to the timing and coincidence of this visit. JP's letter to Sheikh Abdullah must have been handed over at the Home Ministry in the forenoon. And there was this message in the evening. In my mind I felt that this development must have something to do with JP's letter to the Sheikh. I decided to find out tomorrow.

I sent for driver Kushal Singh and instructed him to quietly pick up Dasgupta at the airport and take him to the UT guesthouse and report back

Next morning after picking up Dasgupta from the airport and lodging him in the UT guesthouse, Kushal Singh reported at about 8 am I got ready and went to the guesthouse at 10 am, met Dasgupta, shook hands and introduced myself. Dasgupta introduced himself as a friend of Prof PN Dhar and has come to see JP on his behalf. JP knows him well he being the Director of the Varanasi based Gandhian Institute of Studies of which JP was Chairman. We proceeded to PGI in my car. In the car, Dasgupta told me that the main purpose of his visit was to find out first hand about JP's health, state of mind and willingness to initiate the process of reconciliation. I did not probe him any further sine I did not want him to get suspect about my intentions.

JP was in the room and was very much surprised to see Dasgupta with me. Dasgupta touched JP's feet, folded his hands and stood deferentially. Addressing Dasgupta by his first name Sugata, JP said, "How happy I am to see you!" and embraced him. Dasgupta understanding the question mark in JP's eyes gave an explanation to his sudden and unannounced visit, "JP, I met Prof Dhar a few days ago at the UGC meeting. I expressed a desire to see you. He gave permission and also requested me to have a detailed chat with you on various matters." Neither JP nor I were convinced as we exchanged glances. Obviously, Dasgupta's visit was an exploratory mission prior to a possible commencement of political dialogue in the wake of JP's letter to Sheikh Abdullah and the other communications sent by us.

Dasgupta and JP briefly talked about the Gandhian Institute. Dasgupta said that the functioning of the institute was not satisfactory. In the absence of JP an acting chairman has been nominated. Directors were not taking interest and some reorganization and streamlining needs to be done. Their conversation then shifted to Bihar floods. JP mentioned about his request for parole to the Prime Minister, letter to me on 31 August giving an undertaking that he will not indulge in any political activity during parole, visit of BB Vohra and the fact that there has been no response. JP said that now that the dangerous flood situation is over there was no need to go on parole. He had made the parole request thinking that our own 'democratic' regime could not be worse than that of the British who had released Dr Rajendra Prasad from jail during the Bihar earthquake in 1933. Dasgupta remained silent. Since JP needed an answer to his question I said that consideration and stakes were quite different now than it was for the British in 1933.

JP turned to Dasgupta and asked as to what exactly was happening in Delhi. Dasgupta hesitated for a moment and said: "Nothing is clear. Things may get clear after the Supreme Court verdict. It could go either way." JP mentioned about Tarkunde's opinion that it was futile to deal with Gandhi's case before the SC decided on the validity of constitutional amendment itself.

The conversation turned to the general state of affairs in the country. Dasgupta said that intellectuals at many places are staging volte-face. Even those who criticised Indira earlier are now vying with each other in showering praise on her. There is near total sycophancy among the intellectual circles. He particularly mentioned discussions among the lawyers and teaching community. How much slavish and cowardly could our people become? JP asked in deep anguish. He also expressed his bitterness about Indira trying to spread canard about opposition planning to annihilate her and her family. It doesn't behoove a prime minister to tell such blatant lies, JP remarked.

Subtly but swiftly, Dasgupta shifted the conversation toward the JP Movement. Hesitantly, he asked as to whether the Movement was relevant any more. "What is more important is the presence of JP outside which itself will have sobering effect on the state of affairs. Once this is achieved other things could follow," observed Dasgupta. A rather clever way of drawing out JP and feel his pulse, I thought.

JP responded in a rather general manner. He said that the Movement had a purpose and had emanated from various factors. The Movement was active only in Bihar and some parts of UP. The Movement was directed against corruption and misrule and was not to be indiscriminately spread. No doubt certain elements had used the Movement for achieving narrow political and personal ends. That does not mean that the Movement has lost relevance.

As for himself 'being outside', JP said that Indira and the GoI have indeed missed an opportunity wherein the continuation of the Movement could have been reviewed. JP had given such an opportunity by requesting for parole in the wake of the Bihar floods and giving an undertaking that he will not indulge in political activity. Even at the height of their hegemony Britishers made use of such an opportunity during the Bihar earthquake in 1933-34. They used this calamity, released Rajendra Prasad and arranged the visit of Gandhiji and Nehru to the affected areas. This led to the meeting of the AICC and temporary withdrawal of the freedom movement. Indira had failed to utilize such an opportunity offered by Bihar floods and his request for parole. The hint was obvious.

Dasgupta had no answer and was at a loss to give an explanation. The atmosphere was tense. I intervened and said that Emergency was too recent a phenomenon and the rulers are not properly equipped to handle situations and opportunities. Further the stakes and the standards were different now than those obtaining in 1933. Since I didn't want the discussions to turn very serious in the first meeting itself since JP had no warning and opportunity to prepare, I suggested that JP may take some rest and we could meet later. This was readily agreed to.

Dasgupta and I went back to the UT guesthouse and spent some time in conversation. Within an hour or so we had established a fair rapport. I asked him as to what precisely his brief was and what he wanted to achieve now. Dasgupta was candid. His mission was to find out the state of mind and state of health of JP. More particularly his state of mind. Is he the old revolutionary self or has he mellowed down? Is he in a mood for confrontation or compromise? Has the three-month imprisonment broken him in any way? What are his views on Emergency and the direction in which the country is going etc. He was to gather these and report to Prof Dhar to enable him to chalk out future course of action.

Since Dasgupta was keen to gather as much insight and information about JP, he asked me for my opinion. I spoke in vague terms and said that if Delhi is expecting a broken JP they are mistaken. It was for Dasgupta to find out himself. I played my cards carefully so as not to create any doubt in the mind of Dasgupta.

We returned to JP in the evening at 6 pm, JP had a paper in his hands wherein he had noted down some points. He said he was taken by surprise this morning. Now he had thought out things and is more prepared. Before Dasgupta could open up conversation JP asked pointedly, do the people blame me for all that has happened? What is the general feeling and reaction in the country? Dasgupta said that people are by and large happy at the decline in prices and the general sense of discipline prevailing. Nobody is blaming JP. Some people in fact are giving credit to him.

JP then pointed out about non-dispatch of his letters to friends and relatives, stringent rules regarding interviews, definition of family etc. He also hinted about his transfer to a place nearer Delhi or Patna.

Dasgupta promised to take up these matters with Prof Dhar.

Dasgupta haltingly returned to the subject of the JP Movement again. He said the movement has achieved what it should and is more relevant. Compared to the various movements launched in pre Independence days, JP Movement was broader based and enduring. And now...he hesitated to proceed further. As previously agreed between Dasgupta, and me I intervened and said that in my view also the JP Movement has achieved its primary objective–that of stirring the dormant conscience of the people against corruption and misrule. Now the task was to consolidate through cooperation and mutual understanding so that normalcy is restored. A climate has to be created for the purpose and JP's cooperation was needed to create this climate.

The point made by me appeared to have gone home and Dasgupta was looking at JP eagerly. After a brief pause JP said that he was satisfied with what the Movement has achieved. Now if election is announced and opposition leaders released there is no question of any Movement. And JP came out clearly and categorically now. He announced that he was willing to formally withdraw the Movement, if necessary, provided:

a. Elections are announced as per schedule.
b. He and all other political prisoners are released.
c. Freedom of speech and Press are restored.

Significantly, JP did not make withdrawal of Emergency as a precondition. He had good reasons for this. He said that he is more than willing to cooperate in the process of reconciliation and that is why he had written to Sheikh Abdullah. He told Dasgupta about his letter to the Sheikh and its contents. All the same he was not sure as to whether the letter will be delivered at all. He asked Dasgupta repeatedly to write to Sheikh conveying his desire to meet him at the earliest.

In his effort to move away from the subject, Dasgupta mentioned that he and people in Delhi were happy when JP gave up the idea of fast unto death at the instance of Devasahayam. JP reacted by saying that it was only a temporary measure. He may have to choose the extreme step of personal sacrifice if elections are not announced. Dasgupta said that JP should not resort to such an extreme step. JP was emphatic that if he felt that there was no other way he would certainly resort to fast unto death. Dasgupta said that it would be a waste since nobody will know. JP retorted saying that it doesn't matter, at least his conscience would be clear. With this note we ended the meeting well past 8 pm. Dasgupta took leave of JP and promised to convey everything to Prof Dhar and through him to the PM. He hoped that something positive might turn up the next few days. If need be he will make more visits.

We drove back to UT guesthouse. Dasgupta left for Dehi by the Kalka Mail leaving around midnight.

When I met JP on 29 September, I asked him as to what he felt about Dasgupta's visit. Nothing much, was the reply. "Dasgupta happened to meet Dhar. And so he came." Dasgupta is well known to him, JP said, "He is the son of SN Dasgupta, the famous author of *History of Indian Philosophy: An In-depth Analysis*. His books are even better than those by S Radhakrishnan. Dasgupta will now report to Dhar. JP didn't think anything much was going to come out of it. He was however glad that some steps towards possible reconciliation has been inititiated.

Kamaraj Dies a Sad Man

It is irony of fate that Kumaraswami Kamaraj, the most democratic among Congressmen, was instrumental in making autocrat Indira the Prime Minister of India. He played a leading role in shaping India's destiny, from the time of passing away of Jawaharlal Nehru to the Congress split in 1969. He was born humble and poor in a backward area of Tamilnadu on 15 July 1903. He was a Nadar, one of the most depressed castes of Hindu society, during his time. His schooling lasted only six years. At twelve, he was a shop assistant. He was barely 15 when he heard of the Jallianwala Bagh massacre, which was the turning point in his life. Two years later, when Kamaraj saw Gandhiji at Madurai, his path was chosen. He became a member of the Indian National Congress.

Bachelor Kamaraj was forty-four when India became free. He was elected president of the Tamilnad Congress Committee in February 1940. He held that post till 1954. He was in the Working Committee of the AICC from 1947 till the Congress split in 1969, either as a member or as a special invitee. Kamaraj was elected to the Madras Legislative Assembly in 1937 unopposed. He was again elected to it in 1946. He was also elected to the Constituent Assembly of India in 1946, and later to Parliament in 1952. He became Chief Minister of Madras in 1954. He was perhaps the first non-English knowing Chief

Minister in India. But it was during the nine years of his administration that Tamilnadu came to be known as one of the best administered states in the country.

In 1963, he suggested to Nehru that senior Congress leaders should leave ministerial posts to take up organisational work. This suggestion came to be known as the 'Kamaraj Plan', which was designed primarily to dispel from the minds of Congressmen the lure for power, creating in its place a dedicated attachment to the objectives and policies of the organisation. The plan was approved by the Congress Working Committee and was implemented within two months. Six Chief Ministers and six Union Ministers resigned under the Plan. Kamaraj was elected president, Indian National Congress, on 9 October 1963. Twice he played a leading role in choosing the Prime Minister of India.

On the death of Nehru in May 1964, Lal Bahadur Shastri was made the Prime Minister. It is believed that Shastri's elevation to prime ministership may have been a ploy by the Congress bosses to create an opportunity to groom Nehru's politically inexperienced daughter, Indira, for eventual leadership of the party and the nation. Though the 'Kamaraj plan' was supposed to reinvigorate the Congress Party with new blood, some senior people like finance minister Morarji Desai feared – not unreasonably – that it was a ploy to allow Indira to bypass more deserving and experienced politicians on the path to becoming the next prime minister. Morarji Desai argued that he had been edged out of the political inner circle in order to clear a path for Indira.

When Lal Bhadur Shastri died in Tashkent in January 1966, the tussle for the prime ministership was between Morarji Desai and Indira Gandhi. Within the Congress Party, Desai represented the conservative old guard. He was among the elder leaders who, like Nehru, had risen to prominence in the nationalist movement. Indira, on the other hand, represented the left-leaning socialist wing of the party and was popular among younger and sycophantic politicians without substance, who depended on the Nehru dynastic hegemony for their survival.

Kamaraj had enough power in the party to swing the election in favor of whichever candidate he chose. Indira seemed to be a more malleable choice than Desai. He thought that she would allow him to continue to manipulate party politics and maintain his control over patronage. Besides, he had the typical 'Madrasi' mindset of subservience to the Nehru clan, which persists even today. Kamaraj met with senior Congress leaders from different states and convinced them to unanimously back Indira. She subsequently won the backing of the majority of the party's representatives in Parliament and became one of the world's first elected female heads of state.

It did not take long for Kamaraj to realize his folly. Indira Gandhi revealed her true character when during the 1969 Presidential election, after nominating Sanjeeva Reddy as the official candidate, she went behind his back to mobilize support for the rival Independent candidate V V Giri. This led to Indira's expulsion from the Congress and the split in the party. Kamaraj never forgave himself the grievous error of judgment, promoting dynastic succession instead of political merit.

Kamaraj died on 2 October, the Gandhi Jayanti Day. There was much in common between Mahatma Gandhi, Jayaprakash Narayan and Kamaraj Nadar, the most prominent being their simplicity. It is said: "Greatest of ideas are the simplest." After knowing Gandhi, JP and Kamaraj we can confidently say, "so are the greatest of men."

Indeed, these three were among the greatest of men to walk this land, but for whom freedom would have been a distant dream for India. JP and Kamaraj were closer to each other, both in age and political philosophy. In fact, they were born only a few months from each other. Adherence to the noble principles of truth, honesty, integrity, sincerity and simplicity had drawn them together.

When I went to JP the next morning, he was reading the newspaper. With a deep sigh he put the paper down and said that we have lost Kamaraj at this critical juncture, "fate seems to be harsh on India."

JP said Kamaraj was a good man, simple and sincere. He played a key role in bringing Indira Gandhi to power and he repented it many times, later. I told him about his reaction after the 1969 Congress split. The day after the split, lying alone on a barren cot without any hangers on, Kamaraj had told two visitors that Indira Gandhi was a *'pithalattak-*

kari' (a female fraud) who has betrayed the party and the country for which he felt sorry. He had been a sad person since then.

I told JP about the reported reaction of Kamaraj in the wake of the proclamation of Emergency and Indira becoming a dictator. Kamaraj had wept bitterly and said, "*yellam pochu, yen thappu*" (all is finished, my blunder). Perhaps this agony had led to his early end. JP agreed and said that one of the sentinels of freedom and an honest statesman was gone and the country was poorer for that.

Next day, JP went on to record his thoughts on Kamaraj in his diary, which was a candid and a clear analysis of Tamilnadu politics:

"Kamaraj died yesterday in Madras of a massive heart attack. A great and even heroic figure of Indian politics is no more. His life's work was not complete yet. The last time he met me in Delhi, he said some thing like this: 'what you are doing is the only hope for the country.' But when I toured Tamilnadu later, he was not pleased with my speeches. I could not condemn the DMK and call for a struggle against the Tamilnadu government. The reason was that Karunanidhi, unlike the Congress chief ministers, offered to meet the Opposition and discuss with them their criticism of the DMK government. He said he was prepared even for an impartial enquiry into their faults, charges of corruption or of any other kind. In fact, he mentioned that in one case, he had actually appointed a High Court judge as a commission of enquiry. He also pointed to the Public Men's Conduct of Enquiry Act he had already enacted and expressed his preparedness to discuss either with me or Opposition leaders any faults that the Act might be found to possess, such as the deterrent punishment provided in it for anyone whom the due process of law, as laid down in the Act, found to have willfully made false charges. Under these circumstances, a responsible Opposition was expected to take the DMK leader at his word and make a serious attempt to take the obvious steps. I, in fact, in one of my speeches in Tamilnadu, urged Kamaraj to take up this therapeutic line and clean up the murky political climate in the State.

I am not suggesting that whatever Rajaram and Sezhian told me in Madras or Delhi had to be taken at face value, or I took it that way.

But in the absence of any response from Kamaraj and the Opposition it did not seem fair, at least for me, to attack the DMK government and give a call for a people's movement against it. A people's movement could still be developed (because, as I have endeavoured to show, it need not in every case be against the government; the latter may honestly cooperate with the movement because its objectives are far wider: a total revolution) but naturally Opposition leaders in Tamilnadu, including Kamaraj, were not interested in any movement unless at least its immediate political aim coincided with the Opposition aim.

For Kamaraj, the situation was made more difficult – as compared for instance with that of MGR – because (as he had told me at the Delhi meeting) he did not want to weaken the DMK as otherwise the ADMK would be correspondingly strengthened, for Kamaraj, the ADMK was even worse than DMK. Yet owing to the national policy of the Congress (O), he did not want to draw the Congress (I) nearer to him. Thus, unlike other States in India, the position of Kamaraj as a Congress (O) leader was a very uncomfortable and delicate one. As he told me he did not trust Indira and *vice versa*. But in the quadrangular politics of Tamilnadu, being openly opposed both to the DMK and the ADMK, he had little elbowroom to maneuver. He knew that an unscrupulous politician like Indira would have no qualms about joining hands with the ADMK and he dreaded this eventuality. So, tentatively, his position was to 'go it alone' at the next election. However he preferred to wait and see. But for his party's national policy, reinforced by the Bihar movement and its natural repercussions, he would have eventually thrown in his lot with Indira. His position and options open to him further complicated and narrowed down after the proclamation of Emergency and the consequent events.

However, death has settled the issue for him. His followers, I am afraid, will break up and disintegrate. Indira, by deciding to attend his funeral, has already dealt a severe blow to the Tamilnadu Congress (O)...

"Public figures cannot afford private life", Jawaharlal Nehru is reported to have lamented once. But Kamaraj was one who willingly merged his private life into his public life. A life-long bachelor, this freedom fighter had only aspired for his motherland's freedom from foreign rule and to serve its people afterwards. He was honest and selfless to the core. In his innocence he believed in Indira, who betrayed him.

Kamaraj's death came as a major setback for JP's Grand Alliance plan to defeat Indira Gandhi's Congress, as and when election came. JP had confided in me that he considered Kamaraj the most suitable person to head the united political party he was contemplating. According to him, it would be poetic justice since Kamaraj, who made Indira the PM, should be the one instrumental in removing her since she had turned an autocrat. But that was not to be!

JP's Blueprint to Defeat Indira

JP was making his own plans for the elections as and when it took place. Visit of Dasgupta and the preliminary parleys had brought some confidence and hope in JP that the end of the Emergency and restoration of democracy might be at hand. This pepped him up, both physically and mentally, and JP was gradually getting back to near normal and started thinking about the future. He was of the firm conviction that unless a viable and working political alternative to the Congress emerged and sustained, the ruling party would continue to revel in the 'There is no alternative' (TINA) syndrome and an Emergency kind of situation would get repeated. JP planned to devote whatever life left in him to accomplish this mission of uniting the Opposition.

This was the main subject of discussion when we met on 6 October. He was cheerful because relatives had told him of the release of certain persons and improvement in the Bihar flood situation. He asked me as to whether there was any news about elections. He felt there was no justification in delaying or postponing elections that were due next February. Indira Gandhi had herself said that things were absolutely normal. Then why not elections?

JP then went on to analyse the chances of the Opposition in the event of elections as per schedule. As of now, they were a divided house, he said. Would the trials and tribulations of the Emergency unite them? He wondered. Would a single, viable Opposition be formed? Once elections were announced and he was released, he would go all-out and do his best to defeat Indira at the husting, he said. He hoped the people wouldn't be fooled again. "This lady must be defeated. She has ruined the country enough", JP fumed.

I played the 'devil's advocate'. Was she not the hope of the minority–both linguistic and religious–and their champion? I also pointed out that minorities were the majority in this country. Would it not be very difficult to defeat her at the polls, I querried. The Jan Sangh had a communal image and non-Hindus did not feel comfortable with them because of the RSS. Most non-Hindi speaking people were suspicious about the Jan Sangh because of their linguistic fanaticism. Congress (O) was a divided house, and their leader, Morarji Desai was a suspect in South Indian eyes because of his perceived pro-Hindi views. His role prior to and during the 1965 Tamilnadu anti-Hindi agitation had antagonized the Tamil population. His rift with Kamaraj had led to the DMK coming to power. Because of the above reasons, South India would vote en bloc for Indira. This was particularly so since the Emergency, its harshness and perceived excesses were no issues in the South, because these were not felt in that part of the country.

Our conversation drifted to the anti-Hindi agitation of 1965 in Tamilnadu, which catapulted Dravidian parties to political prominence in the State. This was due to the unwise and arbitrary imposition of Hindi by certain fanatical elements. Hindi could have developed by itself because the language was popular and many people were learning it both within and outside the school system. But due to the perception of its forcible imposition, there was backlash, which became very violent in Tamilnadu. Even strong Hindi supporters, including Rajaji, had become opposed to its imposition. Tamil language and culture were much older and deeper than Hindi. Being a non-Hindi man, Desai had to champion the cause of Hindi to get a base in the North Indian belt. But he had lost the South in the process. Desai need not have gone to the extreme. Perhaps he had not studied South Indian psychology and had taken them for granted.

About the composition of the united party JP was contemplating, to take on the Congress (I), JP had only a broad framework in mind and details were to be thrashed out when the party would actually take shape. The framework would have Congress (O) with the socialist faction of Congress and the Bharatiya Lok Dal as core components. The Jan Sangh would provide the cadre base, which was essential for facing elections at short notice. Parties like the DMK in Tamilnadu and the Shiromani Akali Dal in Punjab would provide the much-needed regional base.

I was astonished and pointed out that JP's views on several occasions had been sharply critical of the Jan Sangh and its communal hue. I specifically quoted his article in a journal way back in 1968: "When, following Gandhiji's murder, the Rashtriya Swayam Sevak Sangh was under a shadow, there were many protestations made about its being entirely a cultural organisation. But apparently emboldened by the timidity of the secular forces, it has thrown its veil away and has emerged as the real force behind, and controller of, the Bharatiya Jana Sangh. The secular protestations of the Jana Sangh will never be taken seriously unless it cuts the bonds that tie it so firmly to the RSS machine. Nor can the RSS be treated as a cultural organisation as long as it remains the mentor and effective manipulator of a political party".

I asked JP that despite such a categorical disapproval, how he could associate this 'communal organisation' in his fight against the Emergency rule and its eventual overthrow. JP was candid in describing the causes, criteria and compulsions leading to the decision to associate the Jan Sangh with the united Opposition party. The main reasons were two. One was JP's unwillingness to opt for the alternative of associating with the Communists, the other cadre-based party, since according to him, "Communists were professional collaborators. They collaborated with the British and must now be collaborating with the Emergency coterie." Indeed they were! The second was the solemn pledge taken by top Jana Sangh and RSS leaders in his presence to totally give up communal politics in the event of coming to power at the Centre and JP had no reason to doubt their honour and integrity.

JP went on to say that the Jan Sangh was no longer communal and there had been lot of changes in the party outlook. According to him, the Jan Sangh could even emerge as a national party. As far as Desai was concerned, he also realized his mistakes. He used to be very rigid and egotistic. He told me last year: "JP, I have learnt more in five years in the Opposition than what I have learnt in 20 years in office".

JP was clear that the monolithic and servile Congress Party had to be defeated if democracy was to be revived in the country. There was finality in the voice of JP when he said: "These parties merging and providing a viable alternative is the only hope for our democracy". And I thought it prudent to leave it there.

Our conversation revealed that according to JP the only way out for Indira is to restore democracy by lifting Emergency, announcing elections and releasing political prisoners. There is no half or quarter way. Indira Gandhi has to go the full length if this nation is to survive as a sovereign country. For this one, she has to be serious and two, she has to be fully in charge of governance. "Is she really serious and is she in charge, I wonder", said JP. Besides, is she really serious about reconciliation? JP asked.

'Reconciliation' through Foreign Route

As if to respond to JP's question, things started moving on 22 October. At the office, Mathur called me over urgently. When I went to his room, he was fidgeting, holding a thick manila envelope and looked a bit nervous. He gave the envelope to me. It was addressed to 'JP Narayan, c/o Chandigarh Medical Hospital, Chandigarh, the Punjab, India'. The envelope bore the insignia of a lion and crown. I felt quite curious. With a voice a bit shaky, Mathur said: "These are the instructions about the letter from the Government of India. Only the Prime Minister has read the content of this letter and the envelope was sealed in her presence. The letter is to be delivered to JP without any one opening it."

I protested, saying that under the rules, no letter or communications could be given to a detainee without its content being known to the District Magistrate. Mathur overruled the objection. "These instructions are from the Prime Minister. She has personally seen the letter. It is our duty to obey instructions". Mathur then wrote the delivery instruction on the outer cover and I signed receipt on the cover itself. Mathur said that the envelope might contain historical documents. Gupta, who was present, was of the view that there might not be anything important. We guessed the content for some time and then I left.

I went straight to JP at 1.30 p.m. I had taken the envelope inside the book 'Constitution of India' so that duty policemen did not suspect the letter. JP was in the bathroom and I waited. After five minutes JP came out and he was only wearing pyjama and for the first time I saw his frail body. He put on a vest and kurta in my presence. He said his taking bath was delayed due to his sister's visit and hence, lunch was also delayed.

I gave him the envelope. He tried to open it but couldn't because the paper was thick and gave it back to me. I opened the envelope, took out the letter and gave to JP. On top of the cover containing the letter was again the insignia with the words 'Lord Brockway, MP'. JP said the letter was from Lord Fenner Brockway, eminent Labour MP of England. He was a member of the Cripp's Commission and they had been friends for long. JP read the letter carefully and smiled while going through the last paragraph. He said it was quite a sentimental letter and gave it to me to read. I told him about the Prime Minister's instructions and was hesitant to read the letter. JP said, "now that I have read the letter, it is my property and Prime Minister's instructions do not apply any more. Go ahead and read".

I reluctantly read the letter which recalled Lord Brockway's ties with India, particularly the freedom movement. The role of JP during the freedom struggle and later in the nation building was referred to. Then the letter touched upon the Emergency, the circumstances leading to it, detention of political leaders and the common objectives and goals being sought to be achieved. The letter expressed deep sadness about this damage to India's democracy, which was largely due to the deep division between Indira Gandhi and Jayaprakash Narayan. This crisis could be resolved only through cooperation between the two. JP, known for his humility and selflessness, should forgive the past and extend his full cooperation to Indira so that normalcy is brought back and democracy restored at the earliest. Since Indira was unable to put it in writing, Lord Brockway was expressing the feelings on her behalf and went to the extent of apologizing for the imposition of the Emergency and the subsequent events. Lord Brockway concluded the letter by saying that 'the ball was now in JP's court' and he was available to render any service, depending on JP's response to the letter.

I looked up to see JP smiling sadly. He lamented: "This is a good letter and Lord Brockway has the credentials to speak for India and Indira. Brockway has been an intimate friend of the Nehru family and has helped a lot in the achievement of India's independence. But what use? I have already given my mind in my letter to Sheikh Abdullah, that was not even delivered. Several meetings have been held with Indira Gandhi on electoral reforms. There is the Santhanam committee report. But Indira is not serious about any reforms". I referred to the point in the letter regarding common aim of doing away with corruption. JP said that while it was true that certain top leaders were not corrupt they depend on dishonest people in order to run the administration. Otherwise they felt that governments could not be stable. This was because the system of administration did not enable honest leaders to function independently.

JP clearly said that Indira Gandhi was not interested in changing the system and doing away with corruption. The irregular licenses, permits issued and other things done prior to the 1971 elections by Indira to collect money were without parallel. She was in favor of the corrupt system. She patronized corrupt people. Officers were forced to commit irregularities by ministers openly.

JP recollected Tarkunde telling him that there was talk in certain circles that he (JP) had weakened in spirit after the detention. "They may be referring to my request for parole and my letter to Sheikh Abdullah", JP said. To reassure himself that his spirit had not weakened, he read out the letter to Sheikh Abdullah. "Does it show any indication of weakness?, " he asked and continued: "The parole request was made with genuine intention to serve Bihar people in their worst catastrophe. Indira Gandhi should have shown grace and released me on parole. I could have talked things over and arrived at a settlement. How can I make an offer of active cooperation to Indira while in detention? People might take it as weakness and surrender". I thought it was time to intervene and said I didn't think that people would misunderstand since JP was not seeking power and people knew it. JP continued with his musings: "Before assurance of cooperation what about elections? Indira Gandhi may pull in a ruse and play a trick to hoodwink the Opposition. Why can't I be released before any cooperation is sought and any talks held on major issues?" I thought the questions were pertinent. However, I told him that the content of the Brockway letter was a virtual apology on behalf of Indira, and a request for cooperation. This could be a great opportunity to take the reconciliation efforts to fruition leading to the lifting of the Emergency. I requested JP to read the letter again and think over the matter for two, three days and draft a positive reply. He agreed. I went back to office and told Mathur and Gupta about the contents of the letter and JP's immediate reaction. Mathur asked if JP was that important for Indira Gandhi to seek a compromise. I said yes, otherwise why this letter, I remarked. I decided not to allow this opportunity to slip, because at the face of it, this was an initiative taken with the involvement of the Prime Minister herself. To understand this initiative and its importance, one has to digress a little and look at Lord Brockway as a person and his credential to speak for India and its democracy. Archibald Fenner Brockway (1888-1988), the journalist and politician, was vocal in his opposition to conscripted military service and acted as a prominent pacifist during the First World War, in which cause he was sent to prison.

Born in Calcutta in 1888, and educated at Blackheath in London from 1897-1905, Brockway developed an early fascination with politics, assisting the Liberals during the elections of 1905. He was a founder member of the Old Boys' Association in 1907, by now a committed socialist. He was an early member of the Independent Labour Party after a brief spell with the Social Democratic Foundation. Professionally, however, Brockway established a career as a journalist, initially at *Quiver*, a monthly journal, and at the *Daily News*. Nevertheless Brockway continued to meet with fellow prominent radicals in his role as interviewer for the weekly *Christian Commonwealth* newspaper, including George Bernard Shaw and H G Wells. In 1913, he was appointed editor of the *Labour Elector* - the newspaper of the Independent Labour Party.

After serving in prison for opposing the First World War, Brockway returned to political affairs with the India League, this time campaigning for India's independence. He also became chairman of the No More War organisation. In 1929 Brockway stood for and was elected to Parliament as a Labour Party member. In spite of his earlier formidable credentials as a confirmed pacifist, Brockway supported British participation during the Second World War, believing that the forces of fascism could only be dealt with by force: "I could no longer justify pacifism when there was a fascist threat," he later wrote.

With the end of the war, Brockway was returned to Parliament as a Labour MP for Eton and Slough in 1950. Once in Parliament, he allied with Bevan and Benn and joined the Left-leaning Tribune Group. In the late 1950s, he was a founder member of the Campaign for Nuclear Disarmament. Leaving Parliament in 1964, Brockway found his way back via a life peerage. As chairman of the Movement for Colonial Freedom, he continued to be politically active in spite of his advancing age. As late as 1980, Brockway served as chairman of the World Disarmament Campaign. A prolific author, Brockway penned four volumes of autobiography. He died in 1988, six months shy of his 100th birthday.

Two days later, on 24 October, when I went to JP in the morning at 9.30 am, he was at the breakfast table, heavily clothed with two sweaters, mufflers and a cap. I asked him why he was so late for breakfast and why was he so heavily clothed. He said he did not feel well and his stomach pain had reappeared. He had acute pain while passing stool and profuse sweating. The medicines given did not agree with him and he was waiting for Chuttani, who had gone to Delhi, to come back. He spoke about his *vaid* at Jaipur and asked me to talk to Chuttani. I said it would not be proper for me to do that, particularly because Chuttani considered ayurveda *hocus-pocus*. I also remembered Dr Shivpuri of the Delhi Chest Institute calling it 'Ayurvedic poision'. JP observed that allopathic doctors did not realize the value of the ayurvedic treasure that we had. They would appreciate it only if a foreigner wrote about it. He said that he never had this kind of stomach pain. For the last two weeks, he had hardly had any appetite. Dr Kalra, who was in the room, told him to drink boiled water and instructed the cook to boil the water, keep it in a pot with tulsi leaves and give to JP to drink.

JP had not completed the reply letter to Lord Brockway because of his indisposition. He had, however, started compiling his thoughts. What to write? He had considered what I had suggested. He would give a brief background, in mild language, for Brockway to appreciate. Then he asked: "How can I offer cooperation unilaterally? I am not the only person. I have to consult others like Desai and Ashok Mehta. All of them are in jail. And cooperation in what? Indira Gandhi has not changed her stand. She is as rigid as ever. What meaning if I just write I will cooperate, when Indira is not serious?" He asked.

Then JP briefly went down the memory lane and recounted an intense conversation. He had met Indira in 1973, after the Gujarat movement, and when the Bihar movement was accelerating. Indira had said: "*Jayaprakashji mein aapka madat chaahti hoon*" (I need your help). "I was taken aback. Why was she asking me for help? I told her, *tum* (I address her as *tum*) *meri madat chaahti ho? Kya madat? Kaisi madat?* (You need my help? What kind of help and why?). She immediately changed posture, *"Mein soch kar baad mein bataungi"* (I will think and tell you later). JP met her again in February-March 1974. On that occasion, Indira had said: *"JPji mein aapka madat maangi thi… ki yeh hai ki… mujhe* Opposition *ka cooperation chaahiye. Desh ki haalaat bahut kharaab hai. Aap hi Opposition leaders ko samjha sakte hain*" (JP, the help I wanted from you was to get the cooperation of the Opposition leaders. The state of the nation is very bad. You are the only person capable of convincing the Opposition leaders to cooperate).

JP had said that there was no doubt that the country's condition was very bad. He would try his best to bring together the Opposition leaders. But unfortunately, he fell ill. He was staying with Ramnath Goenka and sent for Atal Behari Vajpayee since Jan Sangh was the most boisterous opposition party. Vajpayee promised all cooperation, provided Indira Gandhi took them into confidence. Vajpayee also said that Indira asked for help and cooperation only when she was in trouble. "I told Vajpayee not to think that way. The country is in bad shape". Vajpayee agreed. "Country is more important than party. We are willing to cooperate. What are the plans of Indira Gandhi?," he had asked. There was a delay in giving this clarification to Vajpayee. JP gave the reason: "Indira Gandhi normally comes to see me if I am ill. She came to the Gandhi Peace Foundation earlier. She didn't come this time since she does not like Goenka. So, by chance, I couldn't meet her for a few days." In the meantime, Indira Gandhi made a statement at Bhubaneshwar that JP was corrupt and associated with corrupt people. "I don't know what went wrong with her. I made a strong repudiating statement that went well with the press." Indira regretted this statement later, and Dasgupta had confirmed it. The conversation went back to Brockway's letter. JP doubted whether the letter was at the instance of Indira Gandhi. It was possible that B K Nehru or someone else would have sounded him out. But in all probability, the initiative could be that of external forces, with Brockway in the lead, since he was born in Calcutta and had close association with many Indians. He took genuine interest in India and was a member of the Cabinet Committee on Indian Affairs. Once such a letter arrived, Indira grabbed the opportunity and pretended as if she was serious in pursuing reconciliation.

Nevertheless, JP said that Brockway deserved a response and he would complete the reply in 2-3 days. I advised that wording of the letter should be mild. Public opinion in England was very important, even more important than in the USA. He agreed and said that we had a love-hate relationship with England and we had got away with the hate part. As I was leaving, JP asked me about my office time. I said, a DM has no office time. Even mid-night is working time. He smiled and agreed. As I left, he said that he felt greatly relieved after talking to me.

At the office I told Mathur about JP's frame of mind. He tended to agree and said I could have brought in a successful negotiation since JP knew me as a sincere officer. JP could be brought around but Indira Gandhi was not serious. She should at least send seasoned people like G. Parthasarthy, who could handle the matter professionally. "But Indira has a different agenda", he said dejectedly. It was interesting to note that JP's and Mathur's understanding of Indira matched and she was not serious and sincere in pursuing reconciliation and ending the Emergency.

When I went to JP on 27 October, I was perturbed to see him lying in the bed quite disheveled and tired. His pain had increased and he had hardly eaten anything for the last few days. He had no appetite, was unable to walk and felt exhausted and tired. Dr Wahi and Dr Talwar had just checked him and Chuttani had done a detailed checking yesterday, with instruments. Nothing had come out and his ailment had not been diagnosed. The medicines being given to him did not suit him. JP was of the view that allopathy could not cure him. At this time, Wahi and Talwar came back to the room and Talwar did the check up again. He suggested only liquid diet and said that JP's liquid intake was less and he should take more soups, juice etc. Wahi said JP's heart was perfectly all right but they were unable to diagnose the cause of the pain. They would take an X-ray in the evening. Dr Kalra gave a hot water bag to JP. After Wahi and Talwar left, JP told me that he was feeling tired and had pain. I said it could be more of mental stress than physical pain. With a tired smile he acknowledged it. What was Indira Gandhi doing about elections? he asked. She would give only 33 days notice and try to hold an 'instant election' to ensure the victory of her party. He said he was in mental agony since people might blame him for all that had happened. I said there was no such blame. People may even give credit to him. JP said, if things go on like this, dictatorship may stabilize. I said things were in his hands now, and he should positively respond to Lord Brockway's letter. JP said he was unable to sit and write, but certainly, would try and do it as early as possible and the response would certainly be positive.

On the pretext of JP's deteriorating health and their inability to diagnose and cure him, the team of doctors decided to shift him back to the Hospital ward. So, on October 30, in the afternoon Chuttani telephoned to convey their decision to shift JP to the ward. I rang up Bhanot to put the arrangements in place and informed the Government of India. As soon as I got confirmation from Bhanot that arrangements were in place, I instructed Mohinder Singh along with Kishan Lal, DSP, to help the doctors shift JP from the cottage to the ward. This was promptly done and JP went back to the confines of the ward at 7 p.m. after 43 days in open surroundings.

Reconciliation Sabotaged! JP's Life in Danger

Though old in age and suffering from diabetes and mild heart problem, JP was by and large in fairly good health and was apparently being given the best of medical care at the PGI. Yet, major ailments kept afflicting JP right under the nose of some of the best doctors in the country. There was a strange coincidence between the ongoing reconciliation efforts and the appearance of these ailments. The first symptoms of some major ailment in JP appeared on 26 September, just a day after the first visit of Sugata Dasgupta and the commencement of preliminary efforts towards reconciliation, following JP's letter to Sheikh Abdullah.

When Dasgupta returned a second time, he brought back JP's letter to Sheikh Abdullah, which had not been delivered. Sheikh Abdullah was not that immature to issue a public statement offering his services for reconciliation between JP and Indira, without obtaining some kind of assurance from the latter. Yet, the letter containing a positive response from the former was returned in original. The excuse that the letter contained political matter was lame and unconvincing. What else would a letter on such an important political issue contain? Obviously, devious and dangerous forces, which were keen on 'putting JP out of harm's way', were at work with or without the knowledge of the Prime Minister. Was the Sanjay coterie playing its cards?

For about a month after 26 September, JP was okay. But on 24 October, the ailment [severe stomach ache and acute pain and sweat while passing tools] reappeared with more intensity, and was noticed by me when I visited him in the morning. Doctors had no explanation for this. This, again inexplicably, happened just two days after the delivery of a sealed letter from Lord Brockway to JP under direct orders from the Prime Minister. This letter, pleading for reconciliation, was a major step towards restoration of normalcy and for which, he was contemplating a positive response that could have altered the course of events. Because of the sudden reappearance of the ailment with high intensity, JP was unable to write a reply to Lord Brockway. These strange coincidences suddenly occurred to me and coupled with the return of JP's letter to Sheikh Abdullah, they caused me serious concern.

On 31 October, Bhanot and I jointly met JP in the ward to make an assessment. He looked and felt better. He felt it was better to stay in the ward. The stomach ache might have been due to contaminated water. JP's room was warmer and more pleasant. The adjoining room had been made into a dining-cum-drawing room. JP felt concerned about the delay in the Supreme Court judgment. He felt the court had been dilly-dallying and for the sake of the PM, even the Supreme Court was willing to twist rules and procedures.

Both Bhanot and I met Chuttani afterwards. Bhanot asked Chuttani to fix wire-mesh in the room adjoining that of JP. I asked Chuttani what exactly was ailing JP. The answer was evasive. Chuttani said nothing was clear and it seemed to be more related to the mind. I said, maybe JP was perturbed over the delay in his appeal in the Supreme Court, which was adjourned to 15 November. The court had asked for a medical report. It was possible that poor food intake and mental strain had led to this kind of trouble.

S N Prasad came to meet JP that morning. He brought some books and gave letters from Ganga Sharan Sinha and Mrityunji Prasad (Rajeshwar Prasad's son), requesting for interview with JP. Mrityunji Prasad was JP's wife's sister's husband.

I met Rashpal and Sundaram over dinner and Rashpal talked about efforts at reconciliation. Based on reports from Delhi, he said that the trend was changing. Indira was more in favour of reconciliation and had placed Sanjay Gandhi under check. Highly censored and pruned version of JP's letter had reached Sheikh Abdullah and he was upset over it. Dasgupta would be coming again in a few days and JP was likely to be taken to Goa soon. Rashpal had no clue about the letter from Lord Brockway. Obviously, Indira was playing this close to her chest.

Tarkunde had called from Delhi and left a message with my PA that he and Maharani Mohinder Kaur of Patiala would come to see JP on 3 November. Mohinder Kaur should be allowed an interview as a friend of JP as the Delhi High Court had struck down the restriction regarding interview with friends under the Government of India guidelines. I asked Rashpal about the Maharani and came to know that she was a Congress (O) leader, who was arrested after the Emergency and released within a couple of days at Indira Gandhi's instance. The Maharani's relatives were Indira's supporters. Rashpal was meeting her tomorrow and would talk to me after that.

The next day, the Maharani sent a copy of the Delhi High Court order regarding interviews with friends through advocate Kanwaljit Singh. I talked about this to LR and sent the judgment copy to him. When I asked Mathur for advice he was incoherent as usual. He said no Maharani was to be allowed to interview JP and even Tarkunde should not be allowed. I asked under what rules? Under 'Devasahayam rules', he retorted. This put me in an embarrassing position because under the rules, it was not possible to refuse an interview to Tarkunde. Mathur said he would talk to P P Nayyar. I booked a call to Ms Shailaja Chandra, Special Secretary, Home, Delhi administration and talked to her. She said the High Court ruling was there and the matter had been referred to the Government of India. I also talked to M K Miglani, DC, Gurgaon. He had not seen the copy of the judgement and suggested that I keep the matter pending. In between, Rashpal telephoned and the Maharani also spoke to me. I asked her to wait for a few more days so that this issue got clearance. She didn't want to embarrass me and withdrew her request for an interview.

3 November was Diwali day and Tarkunde came to meet JP. He

was a bit late because the Maharani of Patiala had gone to receive him at the airport and he had dropped in at her house.

He asked me about the 'interview with friends' and I said that we had asked for GoI clarification. Tarkunde said that JP's case in the Supreme Court had been adjourned to 15 November. He was taking up the plea of shifting JP to Delhi, Allahabad or Lucknow. Water in Chandigarh did not suit him and he had quoted me in support. If the plea was rejected, they would ask for company and suggest the names of two persons.

I met JP and greeted him with Diwali wishes. He had still not written the reply to Lord Brockway. He was unable to concentrate. He, however, talked about the Sangarsh Samiti's plan of token protest by fasting and Satyagraha all over the country, starting from 14 November. The idea was to keep the protest alive. They used to do it during the British days under Gandhiji's guidance. JP again expressed concern about Indira's silence on elections. I said elections were bound to be announced and this state of affairs could not continue for long. The economy would come under strain and break down in a couple of months. Indira needed a bogey to fool the people once again. She had won elections by stunts and was now pulling off the biggest of them all. All chances were there for her to succeed again. Even in the USA, Nixon had managed to fool people for seven years. In India, it could be double that time, I observed.

Why was Indira Gandhi so crazy for power? What was she going to do with this much power? Did she dream of being a Joan of Arc, the redeemer and the deliverer of this nation? How could a 'betrayer of democracy' redeem this nation? These were the torrent of questions coming from JP. A betrayer only believes in treachery. She practised it by sponsoring Sanjeeva Reddy for the Presidency and then stabbing him in the back by supporting V V Giri. She was undependable and could do anything for power. She kept repeating that she was calm and never lost her temper. This is far from true. She had been adamant and arrogant. Nehru used to say, "*Indu bahut ziddi ladki hai*" (Indira is an adamant girl). Nevertheless, he was very fond of her and wanted her to become the PM after him. JP said that Shastri once remarked to him: "If Panditji had told me of his wish, I would not have accepted the office of PM." Unfortunately, Shastri died so soon. He was a man of the people and had deep roots in the rural life of the country.

Nehru had no such roots. He was an intellectual and dreamer. He belonged to an affluent family and enjoyed luxuries. He was the son of well-to-do Motilal and studied in England. He came back to India and became leader mainly because of his family background. He did not go through the mill and had no grass roots exposure. He was a man of destiny and could have shaped the future of this country. But he failed because he did not know the real India as Mahatma Gandhi had. Indira had lesser grounding than Nehru. She floated in the air and thrived on manipulation and sycophancy.

I said Sardar Patel should have lived for a few more years. JP agreed and said that things would have been much different. "If only Patel had become the PM instead of Nehru, the destiny of India would have been different." JP then went on to say: "When Gandhiji was asked to choose between the two he said Nehru, because Patel was considered a Gandhi man, being a Gujarati." When Patel died, he was 79 and had been ailing for sometime.

JP confided that his own illness was more due to mental strain and agony as to what was going to happen to this country. "When all these bad things are happening, I can't do anything. I am feeling helpless. Having been in public life for such a long time, it is very difficult to keep quiet." JP added that he felt sad at the cowardice and meekness shown by intellectuals and the middle class, and they were the ones who shaped opinion. "Once they have become meek and cowards, what is the hope for this country? Perhaps they can't help it because of their dependence on the government's favour and pleasure." I refuted this contention and said that 90 per cent of the intelligentsia was against what was happening now. "It is futile for them to unnecessarily get entangled. Their feelings will surge out at the opportune moment."

I continued and said that Indira Gandhi's henchmen were basically playing on the illiteracy of the masses and sentiments. Our masses were gullible and were cult worshippers. They were easily taken in by gimmicks and stunts. It took time for them to realize the truth. Once they realized the truth, Indira's fall would be more pronounced. JP should have a positive attitude and should be available at the critical time to give leadership. He was cynical when he said that there was hardly anything positive in the country today. I said,

> "No, there is and it will come out at the correct time. It is not advisable to be in a hurry. India is a great nation. The present stress and strain is good for the country. People got freedom and democracy cheap and have taken them for granted. There was no bloodshed. There is necessity for bloodshed. Only blood can purify the system, water cannot. A shock treatment was necessary. What is now happening is a punch in the jaw."

JP agreed.

On the lunch table that day my three-year-old daughter Madona suddenly shouted "*inquilab zindabad*" (hail revolution) for the first time. I didn't know where she picked it up from. Who knows, may be this was a pointer. I went through the motions of Diwali, but my heart was not in it.

On 4 November, a meeting of the Crisis Group was held at my request and I sought clarification regarding interviews with friends. Mathur tried for P P Nayyar, who was out of station and talked to Vasudevan. He said they were appealing to the Supreme Court against the Delhi High Court verdict. Meanwhile, it was left to the discretion of the DM whether to allow interviews or not. Mathur put down the telephone and jokingly remarked, "Our DM may use the discretion wrong side up."

The Sangarsh Samiti move for a protest fast from 14 November was confirmed and JP might go on a token fast. Bhanot said that nothing much would happen at Chandigarh. Bhanot was of the view that JP was basically a coward, afraid of death and could not go on fast-till-death. Mathur said: "So what, if he dies. We have to cremate him here only. I don't think his death will cause any flutter now. He is out of the minds of the people and is a forgotten man." What a set of buffoons, I thought. *Deo volente,* they would soon see the real truth.

On 6 November, Rajeshwar called from Delhi saying that he wanted to visit the next day. He wanted permission for Ganga Sharan Sinha, MP, to see JP and he quoted the Delhi High Court order. I declined, saying that we were awaiting clarification from the GOI. He could talk to the Union Home Secretary or the Delhi administration if he wished.

JP's health was causing concern. There was a full barium enema test last night and four hours of X-ray.

On 7 November, there was a telephone call from Mathur, asking about JP's health and a medical report to be sent to the GOI. I telephoned RD Sharma, to bring the report immediately. He obtained the report from Dr Chuttani and brought it within an hour. This is what the report said:

> "Patient complaining of increased weakness, continued revulsion against food and also has pain in the lower abdomen. Puffiness of face and edema on legs has appeared, which is attributable to insufficient food intake. No change in cardiovascular status. Diabetes under control. Has been requested to try and take the diet prescribed (2000 calories + 80 G of protein). Has also been put on Nacton (Spasmolytic agent) and frusemide (diuretic)."
>
> — P N Chuttani, 7-11-1975

I took this to Mathur who called Chuttani and had a talk with him. Based on this talk he added a footnote to the report:

"Discussed with Dr Chuttani. Revealed as follows. Potential danger of the illness taking more serious shape. Further observation for 24 hours necessary for giving a more definite advice." With this footnote, the report was sent by wireless to the Union Home Secretary immediately.

After sending the message, Mathur said that the doctors had not been able to diagnose JP's ailment and his pain had persisted, with swelling of the face and feet. We have to be on our guard now, said Mathur. Chuttani felt that the main reason was psychological since JP was quite depressed and gloomy. What is your view? Mathur asked.

I said the pain had been there for over a month now and had not even been diagnosed. "No doubt, JP is depressed and under mental strain. He feels that intellectuals (middle class) have become cowards." Mathur winced and I could see anguish on Gupta's face. I continued, "JP feels that people have taken to the Emergency and taken in by IG's one-sided propaganda, blaming JP for the ills of the country." Mathur was briskly taking notes and was going to talk to Khurana. Should I talk to him in this manner? I told myself, why not? JP would be more depressed if he heard the Supreme Court judgment. It might be unanimous, by the way the Judges were rattling like schoolboys. Mathur asked me to see JP forthwith and give an assessment before he talked to Khurana.

I left the meeting and went straight to JP. There was a strange smell of incense in his room. I asked him what it was, and he said it was some spray. He was sitting in a chair with his legs on the teapoy, with a pillow. His face and legs were quite swollen and eyes were puffy. For the first time, I felt jittery and had a strange sense of sinking pain within. JP spoke with difficulty. He said he had no appetite and revulsion to food. He had not been eating anything for the last three days. He had severe pain the night before and had to take tranquilizers for going to sleep. His vision was blurred and he could not read newspapers properly. He was fiddling with the newspaper, and said that he could manage to read only the headlines. The bearer brought a glass of pomegranate juice and JP drank it.

I asked him about his likes and dislikes. JP said he did not want to take any solid food. Only juice and soup was acceptable. In fruits also, he said he would prefer apple, pomegranate, orange and black grapes. I asked him whether he was getting good fruit and he said, no. I said I would send some good fruit and pure apple jam also. On hearing this, the bearer said that Mr Paddha, chief nutritionist of the PGI, was waiting outside and I called him in. He was quite concerned at JP's poor intake of protein and insisted JP take juice/soup every hour. He had prepared a mixture of rice and spinach, and insisted that JP take it. Like a child, JP asked for an apple pie for the evening. Paddha said he had already prepared and kept the pie in the fridge. He said ice cream was also in the fridge and JP should take it, since his intake was quite low. He need not worry about the sugar in the ice cream. Paddha also suggested bread with apple jam, which was good.

After Paddha left, I asked JP whether he ever had this kind of swelling on the face. He said no. He felt that the trouble was more due to mental strain. I requested him not to be unnecessarily perturbed and that he should think positive. JP was fumbling with *The Tribune* newspaper, which had some news on Bangladesh. He was concerned about the happenings in Bangladesh. To soothe him, I said, at least here there was no killing, though you and other leaders have been jailed. It was indeed unfortunate for the people of Bangladesh who were dreaming of a '*Sonar Bangla*'. "I am perturbed at times," JP said and "I can't help it. The happenings in the country and the peevishness of the people do perturb me. I am also upset because being away from relatives and friends, it is difficult for them to come and see me. My brother said he would come yesterday, but has not come. I am upset." I told him that Rajeshwar would be coming today. He was to come at 11 a.m. but had not yet arrived. He would certainly come because he talked to me from Delhi. Ganga Sharan Sinha had also sought an interview and I was considering it, I told JP.

Fiddling with newspapers, JP saw the news item that the Supreme Court judgment on Indira's appeal was to be delivered on 7 November. He asked me if anything was known as yet. I told him of the Chief Justice of India's pronouncement upholding Indira's election because of the 39th amendment. He, however, had criticized clause IV of the amendment as violative of rule of law. JP said, "one has to be thankful for small mercies." The judgment was on expected lines and he had not been expecting much from the Supreme Court whose caliber had gone down since the time of Subba Rao and Hiddayatullah. But what about elections? Indira could not give any more excuses. But she could not be believed. She would come out with something to confuse the people. I took leave and came home for lunch.

On my way, I put my 'thinking cap' on. Behind all this talk of 'mental strain' being responsible for JP's deteriorating health, I had a deep suspicion that something was amiss. I was also increasingly getting uncomfortable with Dr Chuttani's standard response and snide remarks about JP's health. Given the way things were, I determined that it was not safe for JP to stay on in the PGI and something should be done to get him out.

Strategising JP's Release

At home, Rajeshwar was waiting. He had brought a letter from Masani and few books. Rajeshwar said that Masani wanted to come on December 4 to see JP. I said Masani should write to me and I would write back, since the matter was yet to be clarified by GOI. Rajeshwar asked me about JP's health and I told him briefly about my assessment. He asked, "cant some other doctor be brought in?" I suggested he should talk to Chuttani in this respect. I allowed an interview, with Sharma present as Mohinder Singh had to go to the airport that day to receive the visiting Commonwealth Parliamentary delegation. I asked Rajeshwar to see me before returning to Delhi.

I went back to office and reported to Mathur that JP was in bad shape and it was a matter for concern. I suggested that it would be better if JP were shifted to some other place, nearer his home, for some time. This place was alien to him and the water and climate did not seem to suit him. Chuttani and his team of top doctors had not diagnosed the illness for over a month. Was it not time to try another set of doctors? Besides, JP had been here for over 4 months and his life was getting stale because of inactivity and lack of company. A change would do him good. Though Chuttani had not suggested this due to an ego problem, we ought to take the initiative. If need be I could get a representation from JP, I suggested. Mathur said, "No, you should not do it. JP, though a confused and adamant man, is not a crook. He would tell this to Chuttani and it would be embarrassing to all of us. The fact is that JP can't be looked after anywhere else better than Chandigarh. It suits Indira politically and administratively to keep JP in Chandigarh." I said, this might be true but the reality was that JP was sinking and the doctors at the PGI looked on helplessly. If this situation continued, soon we may have to face the prospect of 'JP dying in jail'. "Please pose this before the powers-that-be in Delhi", I said emphatically.

As we came out, I told Gupta that I was jittery about JP for the first time. Bhanot, who joined us at Gupta's room, said that DSP Kishan Lal had seen JP today. Kishan Lal is an elderly person and he knew the signs - swelling on the face was disturbing, which indicated that JP's end was near. He might not live for more than 3-4 months, Bhanot stated.

By the time I went back to his room to read out Masani's letter and reiterate my stand on JP, Mathur had talked to Khurana, emphasizing the point of 'JP dying in jail' and the special medical report had been sent to Delhi with the remark adding that JP's health was critical and could take a turn for the worse any time. When I came back home in the evening, Rajeshwar was waiting for me after meeting JP. He felt very agitated and perturbed about JP's condition and feared that he might die if the situation continued. He was keen to take JP out of the PGI and, if possible, straight to Jaslok Hospital in Bombay, where he would be among friends and in very capable hands. I consoled him and said that I had a plan to take JP out of the PGI so that his family and friends could have him treated in a hospital with good ambience and better doctors. Rajeshwar could help the plan by sending a personal letter to the Prime Minister, which should end with the words 'if JP dies in jail'. He should stay at Delhi, draft the letter, keep it ready and await advice from me in the next couple of days. Rajeshwar promised to do the needful and left. Later, A C Sen, Special Assistant to the Union Home Minister, telephoned to find out about JP. I took the opportunity to repeat my earlier contention to Mathur, so that the message - 'if JP dies in jail' - went directly to the ears of the Home Minister.

I could not sleep well that night. I was confused and confounded. The poor state of JP's health was inexplicable. PGI had a team of eminent senior doctors in almost all fields of specialization – Medicine, Cardiology, Diabetology, Nephrology and others – experts related to the ailments that JP suffered from. If need be, specialists were available on call from Delhi and other places. Yet, for over a month, they had not been able to diagnose JP's problem, let alone cure him. Chuttani kept repeating that it was due to mental strain. To a layman like me, it seemed strange and unusual. It even passed my mind that this was intentional. The coincidence of sharp deterioration in JP's health with the progress of the reconciliation efforts could not be easily glossed over. Despite racking my brain, I could not find an answer. Hence the disturbed sleep.

I think on November 8, I found the answer, albeit indirectly. I went to the PGI in the morning and met Dr Mehra outside JP's room. He said that there had been some improvement - better intake of food and less swelling. The barium enema and X-ray had proved there was nothing wrong with the heart and his lungs were normal. Diabetes was also under control. Dr Mehra also repeated the Chuttani line of psychological strain

A messenger from Delhi had brought a sackful of greetings and telegrams to JP c/o IG and I had taken them with me. JP was sitting in the chair, with legs up on the side-table. Dr Kalra and Mrs Kalra were there, talking to JP about the food intake. Mrs Kalra was talking to JP, as if to a child. A nurse had brought new spectacles and a little while later, Dr Jain, the Ophthalmologist, also came. The glasses were for distance vision and were dark and fitted JP well. He looked better and the puffiness in the face and legs had reduced. Leg swelling was less. He had taken *kichdi* and spinach, along with the apple pie, thereby improving his protein intake. He had slept better last night. I told him about the sack full of greeting cards and letters. JP smiled, seeing the sack.

After the doctor crowd left, I talked about the Supreme Court judgment. The court had upheld the legislative competency of Parliament regarding the amendment of election laws, with retrospective effect. On that basis, the grounds of the Allahabad High Court disqualification were non-existent now. Hence Indira's appeal had succeeded. There was not much enthusiasm among the public regarding the Supreme Court judgment because it looked contrived. Indira might have gained, I said, but the prestige of the Supreme Court had gone down in the eyes of the public, except those belonging to the Congress.

After a while I asked about JP's reply to Lord Brockway's letter. I advised him to expedite the response. I said, why not write an interim reply, otherwise Brockway might take it amiss. JP said he would write now in a couple of days. Only his deteriorating health was the cause for the delay and Brockway knew reply to this kind of letters do take time. I asked him where the letter was, since I wanted to read it again. He said he had kept it in one of the books I had given him. He didn't remember exactly which one. He also did not remember how many days ago he had received the letter and what were the contents. I searched the room for a while but could not trace it. JP said he would search the room thoroughly and retrieve the letter. I told him it was a highly confidential letter, and should not be lost or misplaced.

I came back home and asked Mohinder Singh to search JP's room thoroughly and find Brockway's letter which was highly confidential. He promised to do the needful and get back to me.

Tandon telephoned in the evening to find out about JP. I said though there was concern, there was no need for immediate anxiety. It seemed to be more of mental strain. He felt that people were reconciled to the Emergency and he was useless. Tandon had asked for a written report from Mehra, who asked my advice and I had said no.

Next day, Mohinder Singh went to JP's room and thoroughly searched for Brockway's letter. He called me saying that he couldn't find the letter. He also reported that there was some improvement in JP's health. And he had taken solid food. I obtained a medical report from R D Sharma and passed it on to Mathur.

It was now evident that Brockway's letter has been taken out and thereby effectively preventing JP from favourably responding to it in order to help bring an end to the Emergency. No more proof was needed. I was now near-certain that reconciliation efforts were being sabotaged and there appeared to be a definite scheme in the sharp deterioration in JP's health. In the event, it might not be safe to keep JP in the PGI, where his life might be in danger. I must move and move fast, I thought to myself.

Mathur telephoned in the evening to say that Dasgupta was coming the next day to see JP and the same arrangements were to be made. There was need for a big push to get JP out of the PGI and I decided to utilize the occasion of Dasgupta's visit to strategise the push and make it work.

'If JP Dies in Jail' – The Pincer Assault

Given the series of events and disturbing coincidences of the past few days, on 10 November 1975, I was perfectly justified in harbouring dark and deep suspicion about the safety of JP in the PGI and the advisability of continuing his detention there. Besides, it would do a world of good to JP's frame of mind to move to a different atmosphere and ambience, where he could be freer, with family and friends. I decided to talk it out with Dasgupta.

He was picked up early morning and taken to the UT guesthouse. He wanted to get back to Delhi by the evening, so that he could meet Dhar who was going to Trivandrum the next day. I talked to Tandon and fixed up a ticket by the afternoon flight.

I received a telephone call from S N Prasad. He said he came to Delhi on 5 November and met Dhar. He went to Madras, came back on 8 November morning and again met Dhar the next day. Dhar had asked him to come to Chandigarh to meet JP. I said he was welcome.

I met Dasgupta at the guesthouse at 10 am. We exchanged information on JP's health and what was happening in Delhi. He said there had not been much progress. He reported to Dhar after the last meeting and he was keen to arrive at an early decision. Dasgupta said that debilitating indecision had set in at the top level. Even Dhar had to wait for two or three days to get time to talk to Indira and there was no clarity of thought. All decisions were centered in one person. Powers-that-be in Delhi now realized that the decision to clamp the Emergency and arrest political leaders was a hasty one and were finding it difficult to retrace the steps. They could not take a hasty decision to release political leaders now, as it would have a lot of repercussions. They had become prisoners of their own action. I said now that the SC verdict had come, Indira must feel very powerful since the state of uncertainty was over. Would she at least now take dispassionate decisions in the interest of the country?

I said JP's health was bad and caused a lot of concern on 7 November and a special medical report was sent to the Union Home Secretary. Dasgupta said that Dhar did not know about the 7 November report. I suggested that Dhar should call for the same and act quickly. God forbid, if anything happened to the old man, people would never forgive Indira . JP was pretty old and as days went by, he was getting more and more bitter, felt he was being slighted and nobody bothered about him. He also believed that intellectuals had turned cowards. Then we went on to review the situation. With hope of parole having been extinguished, JP was now harping on only one thing - elections. Why should people be denied their right, he asked. "Let her get the verdict of the people." Dasgupta said the Congress would sweep the polls. I said it doesn't matter: at least, the people would have decided and given their mandate to govern. We agreed that though there was apparent calm and quiet, things could burst any time.

Dasgupta spoke about the farce of the Delhi University students union resolution which supported the Emergency. When the resolution was moved, only three lecturers out of about 500 assembled participants had remained to vote and others had walked out. Intellectuals who refused to sign a statement for the foreign press criticising JP included K N Raj. Students had stopped pamphleting and started conspiring. This state of affairs was fraught with danger and could not continue for long. In elections, timing was the most important factor. It was important that elections were free and fair and there wase a level playing field. Opposition had to be given a chance. That was all JP had asked for and he would not bend down for this. Dasgupta had a proposal, which he wanted to sound me with. It was to release JP and others and hold elections on due date. There should emerge a consensus and a minimum programme. JP should support the minimum programme and cooperate with government, even if the Congress and Indira came back to power. He said Dhar liked the proposal and we should find out if it would be acceptable to JP. Even if JP agreed, would the Congress stick to it? This needed thinking.

But there was no clarity of thinking even at the top most level, Dasgupta said. No one was clear as to what was happening and what was to be done. Everyone was just drifting. Dasgupta had asked Dhar: "What is in Indira's mind, what do they want? I can't play any positive role and can't talk to JP with confidence if you don't give me a proper brief." Dhar came out with a cryptic and pungent comment: "The horror of the situation is that there is no horror".

We proceeded to the PGI and, in the car, I told Dasgupta that the instructions were that no one else was to be present during the talks. He said yes, but he wanted me to be present because he needed my valuable help during the talks. "JP has lot of confidence in you. My meeting with JP last time without you was a virtual flop. It would be better if you were present. Please don't worry about instructions. I would convince Dhar later." He asked whether there was any letter to JP from Sheikh Abdullah and I answered in the negative.

JP was sitting on a chair, with plates on a side table. He was about to start his breakfast. We asked the bearer to continue serving the breakfast, uninterrupted. JP looked dull, with a heavy-set face, and talked very quietly. The bearer brought some cornflakes with milk, in a bowl. JP's face brightened as he saw Dasgupta, who asked: "JP did you want to see me?" "Yes I did," JP replied. He wanted to know what had happened after the last meeting. Dasgupta said that he had reported to Dhar, and things were moving fairly fast. Dhar was keen to have an early sorting out of matters, but the system itself had become quite slow. All decisions were centralized. As of now, there was dialogue only with JP and no dialogue with Morarji Desai or anyone else. Ramkant Parikh, who kept meeting Desai, had told Dasgupta this. Om Mehta kept denying any dialogue. "When I asked Dhar about it, he said Om Mehta did not know of these meetings. It looks as if Bahmananda Reddy also does not know."

"Dhar wants these meetings to be kept absolute secret. There are factions opposed to a dialogue and reconciliation. If they come to know, they may put obstacles or might embarrass Indira Gandhi. As and when the reconciliation comes about, it should be an absolute surprise", Dasgupta said. He requested JP that whenever he wanted to see him (Dasgupta) he should tell me (DC) and not S N Prasad or anyone else. JP agreed to keep it a top secret.

Then Dasgupta gave a brief report about the state of the nation. Though there was apparent calm, things were only drifting on. There were divergent views among the intellectuals as to how to handle the Emergency. Ramesh Thapar and A K Dasgupta were violent. They felt that things would explode soon. Affairs must be sorted out as early as possible. According to them, time was the prime factor. It was impossible to believe that a dialogue with JP would fail. Ramesh Thapar had pulled up Dasgupta: "You had no brief for such an important meeting. You went without any brief and were extempore. You should have asked Dhar to prepare a brief if you were serious."

What about elections, JP asked. Indira kept dodging the question. Hardly much time was left now, Dasgupta said. He added that there were two opinions. Dhar felt there would be elections. Congress circles also felt the same way. But there was a chance of elections being postponed. What would be the pretext, JP asked. Emergency, said Dasgupta. Only Indira knew what was going to happen. I said elections were bound to be there, otherwise Congress would not even have a bogey, when things go bad, after a while.

The bearer brought two toasts and some scrambled egg. JP sprinkled some salt and pepper and was nibbling at that. Suddenly, he stirred and spoke: "Tell me one thing Sugata. Indira has all the powers, the entire government, lots of money and a huge party at her disposal.

What is she afraid of? Morarjibhai and me, two poor old men? Or is she afraid of her own shadow?" Dasgupta winced as JP continued, "If all her claims are true and she believed in them, what is preventing her from going in for elections and ensuring a free and fair one. As things are, probably she would win again. The election itself would function as a catharsis. Why should people be denied their basic right to choose their government?" Dasgupta didn't reply and JP continued, "Indira and her men keep saying a lot about the Emergency and the wonderful things it has done. They say this has been done to protect democracy. Even today, a sycophant (he was referring to G S Dhillon's speech at Jaipur) said that Emergency was a very nice way of protecting democracy. It is like some one saying that strangulating is the best way to save a child with illness!" Sugata winced again and I could hardly control my laughter.

JP applied some apple jam to a piece of toast and thanked me for sending the jam. JP changed the subject and asked Dasgupta about the institute? How were the finances? Was the same staff there or had there been changes? Dasgupta said everything was all right but the financial position was tight since government had not released the grant. JP asked as to what was Dhar doing about it? Dasgupta said that Dhar was understanding and was doing his best. But Nurul Hasan, the Chairman, was not taking a decision. He was trying to be more loyal than the king. Though Indira had clearly said that nonpolitical institutions associated with JP and Morarji were not to be touched, Nurul Hasan was waiting for word from above. He was not taking a negative decision also and was only dragging matters. This, in spite of Dhar's intervention. He was waiting for Indira's orders. Surprising such a minor thing should wait for the PM's decision. JP asked how could the administration of such a big country run with so much of centralization?

Dasgupta said that various people were expressing strange opinions. One ex-Congress MP from Haryana, who was now chairman of some commission, had met him at Ramesh Thapar's place. Since he was a staunch anti-JP man, they were not introduced to each other lest there might be a clash between them. That man was narrating the achievements of the Emergency, saying that Indira Gandhi had brought deliverance to the country. He wanted elections on schedule, since everything was going on well and the Congress would win hands down. He wanted all Opposition party leaders, except JP, to be released and elections to be held on due date. When Dasgupta asked as to why JP should not be released, he gave a curious reply–that JP was an incorrigible moralist who could not be convinced by anything except through the moral angle. Indira could do this, since there was hardly any morality left in the Congress Party. As far as the other leaders were concerned, they would fall for other things and could be managed.

Strange indeed, I thought to myself. The ex-MP was from Haryana and chairman of a commission and, therefore, a crony of Bansi Lal. We had already seen the thought process of Sanjay Gandhi and his coterie and their belief that JP was the only obstacle to Sanjay's ascendancy to absolute power. No wonder then that one of Bansi Lal's cronies was spreading the theory that elections should be held with JP behind bars. My apprehensions turned into premonition that there were deliberate attempts to 'put JP out of harm's way' and this added to my resolve to get JP out of the PGI without any further loss of time.

Dasgupta asked whether anyone had written from Britain. JP said only Fenner Brockway and no one else. It was about a month now, and he could not send a reply because of bad health. JP went on to say that Western intellectuals were taken in by Indira for two reasons–her extremely sensitive reaction to criticism in democratic countries and her repeated insistence that she was a democrat and was doing everything only within the provisions of the Constitution. Their attitude was not to force her too much to the corner, but to give her a chance to live up to her pronouncements. Dhar had told Dasgupta about Fenner Brockway's letter.

Dasgupta opined that India's democracy, as and when restored, might not be the original one or a blueprint of the British one. JP agreed and said all democracies need not be of the same design. It had to be working and virile as in the USA, though the pattern might be slightly different.

Is relaxation of pre-censorship any indication of normalcy returning, JP asked? I said, no, because in the place of pre-censorship, the government had given the newspapers elaborate guide lines and Editors could violate guidelines only if they were willing to risk arrest. Government was thinking of setting up a board consisting of representatives of government, industry, editors and working journalists. Ramesh Thapar's advice to the industry people was that they should preempt the government by appointing a board themselves. It should have the same composition but the persons should be different, i.e., they should have a B G Verghese instead of a Chalapathi Rau. But nobody was acting in the belief that they could escape the worse. They would do so until death came, commented Dasgupta wryly.

He also commented that thinking and reaction among people, especially intellectuals, was confusing. Indira herself had said that intellectuals and the press were with the Opposition, but the people were not. According to Indira's philosophy intelligentsia was of no consequence and only the voting illiterate masses were important. Only they could be fooled and won over by stunts and slogans. What could the intellectuals do? They could speak and write and both were banned. They were not taught to wrestle nor would they like to. Wrestlers were holding the field day. No wonder intellectuals were baffled and confused. JP should be out to guide them, lest they got frustrated and drifted away.

JP agreed and said that this system of crushing of ideas and opinions should not continue for long. In the absence of a natural vent, certain elements might take to the gun, which was dangerous. "There is no question of any movement if I go out now. I don't have a magic wand, which I will wield when I go back and the movement will get going. It takes time, years to organize the movement. During British rule it used to take a decade to organize protest movements. In any case, if elections are announced everyone will be busy with elections, nomination etc. and nobody will have any time for the movement."

"I will be a fool if I think that I will be running a movement after I go out" JP observed. For a number of politicians, political position is a matter of bread and butter. Well Indira Gandhi had enough money to lead a comfortable life even if she was out of power but not all other politicians. It is the bad politicians who were spoiling the show. Selfishness was mixed up with politics. Even a petty matter like transferring a patwari had become politics. This had to change.

Dasgupta said that certain people who were released (for instance Prashant of Patna) had to be rearrested since they insisted on holding meetings. Perhaps they were keen to keep the flag flying. JP had to be out to guide these elements and to channelise the initiatives and action of right thinking people. Dhar felt that way since the current developments did not point toward good things. JP had to play a great role in putting back things in proper shape.

For a while, JP was pensive and then opened up: "Since my detention, I have not been keeping good health. Only for about a month, I was well. The doctors here are good, the DC here is very kind, but due to lack of company and being away from relatives, I do not have the feeling of good health. It would be better if I were shifted to AIIMS in Delhi. The doctors there (Bhatia etc) are like family doctors. I have friends to talk to and would be feeling at home. Alternatively, I should have the company of Radhakrishnan and Dadaji". After a pause, he continued: "I am not casting any aspersions on the PGI. I have the best of treatment, but the lack of friends is telling on my health. There is only one person I have heard of in Chandigarh, i.e., C L Lakhanpal. The climate and water of Chandigarh also does not seem to suit me. If I am released now, it will take time for me to get back to my normal health. Most probably I would be staying at home at Patna for some time. There is no question of trying to revive the movement for the present."

After this personal note, JP went on to the public domain: "But this point must be emphasized over and over again that elections must be held in time. It is a natural catharsis. It can clean the system. Indira may not feel that way. Her supporters may not feel that way. But I am a democrat and would continue to be so. Only elections at the due date can put the wheels back. Please tell Dhar that JP feels strongly about it. Political parties will fight elections their way. Democracy without real Opposition is meaningless."

To our surprise, JP came out candidly about his political strategy to defeat Indira Gandhi's Congress at the polls that we had deliberated upon earlier: "I will try to unify the three parties–the Bharatiya Lok Dal, the Congress (O) and the Jan Sangh. Charan Singh of BLD is the most amiable of the whole lot and he is very keen on merger. He is willing to give up the name of his party and will ask for no position. Congress (O) will also come around. Jan Sangh is a problem. They were proud and were confident of taking over power from the Congress. Their pride would have got a beating now and they might be reasonable. The RSS people are outright reactionary if not fascist. JS would pounce on Muslims. I had to contain them saying what wrong have the Muslims done to us?"

As if possessed, JP went on: "The concept of development should change and we have to go back to the Gandhian methods basically. Building up of the rural base is of great urgency and Indira is hardly giving any attention to it because she has no rural rooting. One has to learn to live in villages. Indira has no humility and she keeps on talking about herself. She keeps comparing herself with various people, the latest being a Zen Buddhist". (*The Tribune*, November 1, 1975) He took out the paper and read it asking for more light. He was quite amused and remarked that it was a complete distortion of facts.

Dasgupta said Dhar was keen on the early release of JP. So kind of him, said JP. He said, he understood it might be difficult for Indira to take decisions. He being the culprit no.1, she would come under compulsion to release others, once he was released. In any case, JP was not interested in his release when others, especially Morarji would be still inside. JP then asked Dasgupta of news of his friends in Delhi. Dasgupta spoke about Ramesh Thapar and Ramkant Parikh. He could not meet Goenka because he lived in Calcutta. Most of the other friends were in jail. JP said Goenka owned only the *Indian Express* group of newspapers and as such, was not affected by the government decision to delink newspapers from industrial houses. To settle his son, he had bought a big jute mill in Calcutta. Since his son was not a good businessman, he himself had to manage it now. Hence his frequent trips to

Calcutta. Otherwise he was Madras based and spoke Tamil as fluently as any Tamil.

It was nearing Dasgupta's flight time. As we got up to leave, JP told Dasgupta in a no-nonsense tone: "Please remember one thing and tell Dhar, I do not want any mercy from Indira, I don't want any special treatment, let not Indira think that she will be doing an act of mercy by releasing me, I am content being in jail like anybody else." He asked Sugata to come and meet him as often as possible.

In the car I told Dasgupta that my assessment had come 99 per cent true. He agreed and said the meeting was very positive and thanked me for that. He said that the last meeting without me was negative. JP had pounced on him, saying, "I will fight elections and see how Indira Gandhi gets back to power." My presence had mellowed him , leading to positive results, he said.

Though the talk with JP was positive this time and Dasgupta could take back a 'minimum area of agreement', he was deeply distressed by the happenings at Delhi and he came out candidly in the car. Dhar had told him that though he was pursuing the reconciliation process with the tacit approval of the PM, there were very powerful forces opposed to it. The names mentioned were Sanjay Gandhi, Bansi Lal, Om Mehta and R K Dhawan. From the happenings in the last few days, Sugatha strongly suspected that reconciliation efforts were being sabotaged and even the life of JP could be in danger.

Dasgupta's statement gave me the opportunity to take up my most important agenda, that of implementing the plan to get JP out of the PGI immediately. I told him about my premonition and what I had done already. Then I unveiled my pincer strategy, with one common outcry – 'If JP dies in Jail'. Pincer is a maneuver in which an enemy force is attacked from two flanks and the front. In this case, the 'Delhi Durbar' was the enemy force and the maneuver would be:

- Frontal attack through official channels conveying this message to Delhi. This had already been done through the Chief Commissioner and the Union Home Secretary;
- Right-flank attack by Dasgupta who should put up a strong note

to Dhar describing the deteriorating condition of JP and ask the question 'If JP were to die in jail'. Dhar must ensure that the note is seen by Indira Gandhi without delay, if possible today itself;

- The left-flank onslaught would be by JP's brother Rajeshwar Prasad. As soon as he reached Delhi, Dasgupta should contact Rajeshwar Prasad and ask him to deliver the letter he is keeping ready, to the Prime Minister either today or early tomorrow. The letter would contain the outcry–'If JP dies in Jail'.

Dasgupta understood the plan and appreciated it. As he shook hands with me he said he would do his best and when we meet next it might be with the positive news of the release of JP.

Pincer Works: JP Released

The silent pincer assault to get JP released was working as per plan. The official report of the Chandigarh administration about the sharp deterioration in the health of JP conveyed through wireless message on 7 November had imparted a sense of urgency in the GoI circles. The personal appeal of Rajeshwar Prasad dated 9 November, addressed to the Prime Minister containing the message 'If JP dies in Jail' was delivered at the PMO on 10 November. Dasgupta's report conveying the same theme reached Dhar and the Prime Minister on 11 November.

The objective was to create a 'crisis mindset' in the decision makers in Delhi, but for which, nothing would have happened. The Prime Minister and others were given enough to mull over regarding the release of JP. The culmination of all these was that things moved and moved fast on 12 November, which was a day of sensational events.

At about 9 am, R D Sharma telephoned from Dr Mehra's office in the PGI to say that two doctors had come from Delhi and wanted to see JP. He asked for my permission. Mehra also talked to me, saying that the doctors J S Guleria, general physician and K K Malhotra, nephrologist, had come from the AIIMS to examine JP. I granted permission and telephoned Mathur to inform him of this development. He said he knew it and these doctors were to submit their special report to Dr Karan Singh, Union Health Minister, first thing in the morning. Mathur said that he had convened a conference to discuss the matter at 10.30 am and had asked Dr Aikat and Dr Wahi to attend, since Dr Chuttani was out of station. I should also go to the meeting. I asked him whether I should see JP before going to the meeting and he said no, not necessary

At 10.15 am, Sharma came with a message that JP wanted to see me urgently. I ignored what Mathur said and drove to the PGI straight and went to JP's room. He was reclining on the bed, trying to read newspapers. He had not shaved and the puffiness in the face had reappeared. He felt very weak and tired. He had taken no food in the last two days. He felt very sick and was convinced that he could not be cured at the PGI. He wanted to request the GOI to shift him to AIIMS, where there would be familiar doctors and friends would be nearer. He could not write because his hands trembled. Otherwise, he would have put the request in writing. I said he need not worry, I will reduce it in writing and convey it to the proper quarters. JP indeed looked bad and I was told that he had bouts of hiccups and vomiting last evening.

While rushing back to the office, I met Bhanot coming up the ramp and asked him to come to Mathur's room. Came back to office and quickly dictated a note regarding JP's request for shifting to the AIIMS. As the PA was typing the note, I rushed to Mathur's room where Dr Wahi and Dr Aikat were already present. Mathur was talking over the secraphone to Khurana, repeating the medical brief on JP given by the doctors:

"Lungs function normal–heart as usual–puffiness of the face –edema of the feet. Five disturbing symptoms: (1) complete aversion to food (2) hiccups and vomiting (3) puffiness of face and edema of feet (4) malignant pain in the lower abdomen and (5) clouding of memory. It is not explainable to the state of the kidney, which is functioning normally. Trouble is mainly due to a deep mental depression and a complete lack of will to fight and recover. JP can be put on the 'seriously ill' list. He has made a request to DM for transfer to AIIMS Delhi. No, he can't be moved now by road. No long journey by plane also. He can be moved up to Delhi by plane." The telephone got disconnected at this point.

As Mathur tried to reconnect to Khurana, my PA brought the typed note, which I quickly signed and gave to Mathur. Bhanot also joined the meeting. When the call got through, Mathur was told that Khurana had rushed to the Home Minister and Narasimhan was on the line. Mathur repeated certain portions of what he had already told Khurana and read out my note on JP, requesting for transfer to AIIMS Delhi. Narasimhan asked whether JP could go home straight, if released on parole. No, Mathur said, he had to remain in a good hospital for at least 15 days and if decision taken to transfer, a competent doctor of that hospital had to come and tie up matters before shifting. Mathur told Narasimhan to convey the entire message to Om Mehta also. He then tried to ring up Om Mehta, but he was not available. On his own, Mathur said that a message should be conveyed to only one person. If conveyed to more than one, there could be distortion and gave a short lecture on that. As the doctors went away, Gupta also walked in to the room.

Mathur was in an upbeat mood and said that the chaps in Delhi were bloody rattled. None of them had slept last night. "Indira Gandhi wanted information and action, ever since my telephone call last evening/night". He said that Indira, Om Mehta, Khurana and Rustomji did not sleep last night: "We have done our job and has put the matter across as forcibly as possible. Let us wait now." Bhanot said that nothing was going to happen and at best, JP might be shifted to the AIIMS. Now that things had settled down well in the country, Indira Gandhi would not spoil things by releasing this forgotten old man. None of them –Mathur, Gupta, Bhanot – knew about the pincer movement, which, in fact, had shaken Indira and this last night telephone call was the proverbial last straw on the camel's back. I did not open my mouth.

My pincer movement had providential support in what happened the previous (11 November) evening. Bhanot had gone to the PGI at about 5 pm. JP was hiccupping and vomiting, and the nurse was running around for doctors. JP was in miserable plight and Bhanot was shaken. Since I was unwell (down with conjunctivitis) he did not disturb me and instead went to Gupta's room and told him in strong words what he thought of JP's medicare. Both of them rushed to Mathur and stressed upon the seriousness of the matter. Mathur talked to Drs Wahi and Aikat. They were not clear, but reported JP's condition as 'serious'. Mathur called Gupta and the doctors at his residence at 8.30 p.m.. After being convinced as to the seriousness of the matter, he telephoned Khurana. Initially the message didn't register and to force the issue, Mathur asked Khurana for specific instructions in case of JP's death any moment: whether to be cremated in Chandigarh, whether relatives to be informed, etc. In that case, we had to wait for their arrival and JP's body had to be embalmed. What about autopsy etc? Now the seriousness of the situation registered and things got moving. There was a telephone call to Mathur from Om Mehta after a while and also from Rustomji.

In the absence of the two key persons – Dr Chuttani and me – who have been personally handling JP, the panic was complete. Gupta went to Bhanot's place at about 11.30 and asked him to put JP's 'death drill' in to operational mode. He had said that JP might die any time, and might not even live thru' the night. Bhanot had already requisitioned one company of CRP and one battalion of the BSF and both had already arrived and the commandants of these Units were waiting in his room. In short, Bhanot had put the 'Operation Medicine' in motion. Perhaps it was destined that this 'death drill' for JP should not remain merely on paper! If not anything else, this panic put some more pressure on the 'Delhi Durbar', leading to my basic objective being achieved.

Around noon, on 12 November, Sushil Kumar, DC, Delhi telephoned to ask if he could send Gulab Yadav to Chandigarh to stay with JP. I said I would find out JP's willingness and get back to him. When I mentioned this to Bhanot, he sarcastically said, "has the whole thing boiled down to this only – the mere arrival of a personal servant?"

I went back to JP after lunch at about 2.30 p.m.. He was sitting in the chair and looked slightly better because he had shaved and taken a bath. The swelling in the face was the same, and he had not yet taken lunch. He said they might bring him some lunch now, but he would not be able to eat since the very thought of food was revolting. He asked what had happened to his morning request for transfer to the AIIMS. I told him that we had put the matter forcibly through several channels and had succeeded in shaking Delhi a bit. What might happen could be much more than a mere transfer to AIIMS.

Have you shaken Delhi enough to order a release, he asked. "Possibly," I said, "quite possibly." JP smiled weakly. I told him that Indira Gandhi had not slept last night and had been worrying the Home Minister, who, in turn, had been pestering the civil servants. I asked him about Gulab. He was a little reluctant and said, "What use? He will also be a prisoner, and won't be able to move out. He would like to see the city and has no friends here." I told him these were minor matters that could be taken care of. Once in a while, Gulab could be allowed to go out, accompanied by someone. I felt better if Gulab stayed with JP, since he knew his habits and could talk to him. JP would feel more at home. After some more persuasion, JP agreed and asked what happened if he was shifted to Delhi? I said Gulab would also go with him. JP reiterated that it would be better if he were shifted to Delhi. "There will be a change in atmosphere and I would feel more at home. Will Indira take a positive decision? She is quite vindictive." I said, she had to take a positive decision because this state of affairs just could not continue for long.

I came back to office and informed the DC, Delhi that JP had agreed to Gulab staying with him. Sushil Kumar said that he would issue the necessary orders and I should locate Gulab. I booked a call to the DM Patna and tried to telephone Tarkunde. The Patna call came through in 15 minutes and I told the DM about what needed to be done. He promised to locate Gulab in a few hours and pack him off pronto to Chandigarh.

While I was wondering as to what was happening to our efforts to get JP released, came the telephone call from DC, Delhi at about 4.30 pm saying that that he and the Chief Secretary, Delhi, were taking off for Chandigarh by a special plane at 6 p.m. and would reach at about 7 p.m. I asked what the purpose of their visit was and he said that they would come and talk things over. He wanted me to organize some transport, which I promised to do.

I walked into Mathur's room, where Gupta was also sitting. I told them about the call from the DC, Delhi, and my impression that things had started moving. Mathur had not yet received any message. We felt that if the DM and CS, Delhi were coming together and that too by a special aircraft, it might be with some important and definite proposal, possibly for shifting JP to Delhi in the same aircraft. It could even be release. We decided to wait.

I came back to office and called Mohinder Singh over to brief him on the developments. I asked him to be available. Mathur called me to his office at 5.30 p.m. Gupta, Aikat, Wahi, and Bhanot were there. Khurana and Om Mehta had talked to Mathur and the message was that JP was to be released on parole but had to be kept at Chandigarh for few days. GoI is reluctant to face the risk of JP moving to Delhi immediately. They wanted to watch the reaction and further developments for a couple of days. We discussed how to do this. It was decided that Aikat and Wahi should meet JP and tell him that it would be risky for him to move for some days at the present rate of improvement, even if a decision was taken to move him to the AIIMS. The DC and the SSP would come in later and persuade JP to strictly go by the advise of the doctors, in the interest of his health. The doctors were to meet JP at once, at about 7 p.m., and the DC and SSP would meet him after the orders by the CS and the DM, Delhi had been served.

Bhanot had serious reservations. He said JP was an adamant man and he would like to move tomorrow itself and it would be difficult to contain him. Students and others would try to flock in as soon as the news went out that he was free. Why was the GoI forcing this on us? Could we not tell them otherwise? Mathur said he had tried his best to put forward the fragility and futility of this move by the GoI. JP was no fool. Delhi did not understand. Any way, a decision had already been taken at the top-most level and we had to adhere to it, since it would be futile to oppose it. As the doctors left, Mathur told them that they were not to mention anything about parole or release. They should just tender a medical advice.

I reached home at about 6.30 p.m. I had a wash and waited for news of the arrival of the CS and the DM Delhi. At 7.15 p.m., I telephoned the control tower and was told that the aircraft would touch down at 7.40 pm. At about 7.25 pm, there was a telephone call from Delhi. A girl's voice said that she was the receptionist at the Gandhi Peace Foundation and wanted to confirm the news of JP's release. She said that UNI had broken the news already. When I said I did not know, she virtually called me a liar and asked who else would know? I said I did not have the faintest idea and she was welcome to try. The girl put the phone down in a huff.

The telephone started ringing continuously now and I dodged almost all the callers. Mathur telephoned at about 7.40 p.m. and said that there was a message from Om Mehta to be conveyed to the CS and the DM, Delhi who are bringing two orders – Parole and Release. They should serve the parole order first, and if JP refused to accept it, they should come back and talk to Om Mehta and if he was not available, to RK Dhawan and get instruction about the Release order. I was astonished at this SOS from Om Mehta and the mystery of the 'two orders'. I had a lurking suspicion that there was something fishy and decided to grill the two emissaries from Delhi before advising JP.

As soon as I got the information that the aircraft had landed, I called up and asked Mittal to pick up LR and take him to the UT guesthouse. I walked over to Gupta's house and both went to the guesthouse in the staff car. The CS, Delhi, JK Kohli and the DC, Sushil Kumar had already arrived and Bhanot also had come. I had a good rapport with Kohli, since he was a Deputy Director in the National Academy of Administration, Mussoorie when I was a probationer there. He enquired briefly about my career in Haryana. We sat down over a cup of tea and both Kohli and Sushil Kumar wanted to have a background of the case and a brief on JP's mental state. . I gave a summary - his health, request for parole after the Patna floods, request for transfer to Delhi etc. I also told them about Om Mehta's message. We quickly finished tea and went to Mathur's residence.

Mathur repeated the message from Om Mehta and asked what the orders were. Kohli said that the first one was for release on parole for one month and the second one was for revocation of the detention order and release. Om Mehta called from Delhi and Mathur said that the officers had just arrived–there was slight delay in the flight–and are about to go to JP to serve the orders. Om Mehta reiterated the previous message, which Mathur repeated to Kohli and Sushil Kumar.

As we came out of Mathur's residence, I asked Kohli as to why there were two orders and why they had to take Om Mehta or Dhawan's clearance to serve the release order ?. He fumbled for words and gave a vague and evasive reply, which did not convince me. I could see that he was in a predicament. Then I asked a specific question. What was this parole order? Was it conditional or unconditional? Kohli now felt relieved and said it was an unconditional parole. And given our good rapport, he volunteered the information that though it was a parole order, in effect it was release and if JP did not indulge in objectionable political activities, his detention order could be revoked in the next few weeks. The release order they had brought was only a back up, and he did not know as to why they should consult Delhi before serving it since it was a new instruction.

This information had my mind racing as we drove towards the PGI and I started putting the pieces together. Obviously, events had moved very fast in Delhi and the decision on parole and back up release order was taken by the Delhi administration at the behest of the Prime Minister without the involvement of the members of the Sanjay coterie. Since things moved so fast, they had no control over the events and came into the picture late, by which time the Kohli-Sushil Kumar duo was already airborne. In a desperate move, they wanted to regain control and stall the whole move. Their assessment was that given his rebellious nature, JP would refuse to accept the parole order and perforce release order had to be served as per the PM's direction. This would have been devastating for the Sanjay coterie and they wanted to stop it. Hence Om Mehta's instruction, repeated twice, that either he or Dhawan, both members of the Sanjay coterie, should be consulted before serving the release order if need be. If this was the move, which I thought was most probable, I should defeat it, I decided.

The foursome–Kohli, Sushil Kumar, Bhanot and I–reached the

PGI around 9 pm Dr Mehra and RD Sharma were outside JP's room. I asked the others to wait outside and went into the room. JP was sleeping, cuddled up in bed, blanket pulled over the head. I called out twice or thrice and he stirred. At this point, impatient of waiting outside, the others trooped in and the noise woke JP. He was baffled to see so many people in the room, but when he saw me, he felt reassured. Collecting himself JP asked what the matter was. I introduced Kohli and Sushil Kumar to him and said that they had come to release him from detention. This I did to create a psychological impact that it was going to be a release, though the word parole would be used. JP nodded and was still looking perplexed. He had turned over to our side but still lying down, with the blanket up to the neck.

Kohli stepped forward, cleared his throat and said: "Sir, all of us are very much concerned about your health. The Prime Minister is specially concerned and worried about your health. In order to enable you to recover your health and get well soon, the government has decided to release you for the present." Following my lead, Kohli also used the word release. JP was listening intently and his face brightened on hearing this. Sushil Kumar took out the orders and read out: "The Administrator..." When he read the portion regarding release on parole for one month JP's face dimmed a little and he said '*hah*'. He then looked at me and I nodded. When Sushil Kumar read, "on the expiry of one month he was to report to DM, Chandigarh," JP obviously did not like it. He said, "What is the purpose in asking me to come back to Chandigarh? This place is too far and does not suit me. If I am to be arrested again, why not I be kept at Delhi itself?" Sushil Kumar and Kohli said that they had noted the point and would convey the same to the government.

By now JP had, with difficulty and support from Mehra and Bhanot, sat up on the bed. A look of relief crossed his face. He thanked Sushil Kumar and Kohli as well as the PM for her concern. So nice of Indira, he said. Sushil Kumar asked for JP's signature on the receipt on the order. The word 'parole' obviously troubled him and he looked at me questioningly. Thinking this was the time, I went near and whispered in his ears that the parole order was unconditional and as good as release and he could safely sign it. This dispelled his doubt and JP was willing to sign. Bhanot helped him to get a pen and pad. With a trembling hand, JP wrote "received original", signed the copy and handed over the papers to Sushil Kumar who returned the original copy of order to JP. Bhanot helped him to put it in a cover and keep it in between the row of books.

JP's face brightened as if a heavy load had been taken off his mind. "You have brought me happy news", he said and repeated that it was harsh on him to be asked to come back to Chandigarh. Not that Chandigarh was a bad place, the officials and doctors here had been very good. But it was far away. And he said in Hindi, "*vaise tho ek mahine ka time diya hai. Is ka kya zaroorat hai? Mera kaam tho sarkar ke nigrani mein hoga. Mein tho aisa koi kaam karnewala nahi hoon. Main tho kahin door chale jaaunga. Shaayad Madras chala jaaunga*" (You have put a one month restriction. What is the need for this? My work will be under the glare of the government. I am not going to do any objectionable work. I will go to a far off place. Probably I will go to Madras).

Kohli and Sushil Kumar promised to convey his feelings and request to the government and took leave. I told them to go to the car and we (I and Bhanot) would take a couple of more minutes with JP. Bhanot, Mehra and I stood around JP and I told him now that he had been released, he was a free man and we had no control over him. But we were deeply concerned over his health. He should strictly adhere to the advice of the doctors as to interviews and moving out of Chandigarh. We wanted him to recover as fast as possible. I said, from now on we (I and Bhanot) would also be under the control of the doctors, as far as JP was concerned. JP promised to abide by the advice of the doctors. We had been so kind to him and he could not go against our advice. Bhanot said that the policemen on duty were not there to restrict his movement but to serve and safeguard him. His security and safety was still our concern. JP said he understood and appreciated our position. He wanted his relatives to be informed, since he wanted them to come. I promised to do the needful, took leave of him and went out.

Kohli and Sushil Kumar were waiting outside the ward. We walked down to the car park and found C L Lakhanpal with about a dozen persons gathered there. Lakhanpal rushed up to me and said he wanted to see JP. I said he was sleeping and this was no time to see him (9.30 p.m.) and the doctors would not allow. He asked me whether it was true that JP had been released. I said yes. Is JP critically ill? I said no, he is in good health. "Can't I see him for one minute", he pleaded. I said, no, it was too late. Would he (JP) be here till tomorrow? I said, yes. "How can I see JP?", Lakhanpal asked again. I said JP was now a patient in the care of the PGI doctors. He should approach them tomorrow and seek permission. With difficulty, I disposed them off, sat in the car and drove to Mathur's residence. In the car Kohli and Sushil Kumar expressed their relief on the easy accomplishment of their task and admired the simplicity of the old man.

On reaching Mathur's residence, Kohli reported the accomplishment of the task and Mathur telephoned Om Mehta to convey this to him and handed over telephone to Kohli. He told Om Mehta that the task had been successfully accomplished and JP accepted the parole order meekly. He also reported the reaction and the words spoken by JP. Both sounded happy. Kohli then telephoned Dhawan and reported to him. Then Sushil Kumar took the phone from Kohli and talked to Dhawan. One of them – either Om Mehta or Dhawan – had instructed Kohli and Sushil Kumar to report to Bansi Lal, CM, Haryana. Sushil Kumar telephoned the CM's number and was asked to report to R C Mehtani, Private Secretary to Bansi Lal. Sushil Kumar called Mehtani and requested him to fix up time to meet Bansi Lal.

After a while, we proceeded to the guesthouse for dinner. Sushil Kumar went for a wash and I went to the toilet. As I came out, Kohli, Sushil Kumar and Bhanot were sitting in my staff car saying that they were going to Bansi Lal. I also got in and we drove straight to Bansi Lal's residence and reached there at about 10 pm. We waited in the drawing room. Bansi Lal came down, greeted us and then asked *kya hua?* Kohli reported completion of the task. JP had accepted the first order of parole gladly. In fact, he had expressed his gratitude and thanked the PM for his release on parole. We sat down on the sofa - Kohli and Sushil to his right and I and Bhanot to his left.

Bansi Lal, as is his wont, was in an expansive mood and loquacious, which indicated the mindset of Sanjay's men on dealing with JP, who they felt was the spoilsport and major hurdle to their ascendancy to absolute power. They seemed to be gloating, now that they had effectively 'removed' that hurdle. With JP 'a completely broken down and demoralised man', they did not see him as a threat any more.

Reflecting this mindset, Bansi Lal said: "*saala to* demoralised *tha* (the damn fellow was demoralised). *Agar 10 din ka parole dethe tho bhi le leta*" (The damn fellow was demoralized. Even if we had given 10 days parole he would have taken it). Kohli and Sushil Kumar endorsed the view. Bansi Lal continued, "*chalo achcha hua, musibat chutgae - saala yahin mar jaata to sirdardhi hota - aur kahin jakar pada rahe ya mar jaye to theek hai*". (OK, it is good. We got rid of the bother. If the damn fellow had died here it would have been a headache. It is all right if he lies sick or dies somewhere else) .

Kohli and Sushil Kumar repeated JP's words, after receiving the release orders. Bansi Lal said, "*thik hai, ye to bahut* demoralised *hai - abhi kya karega- khali Bihar nahi jane dena chahiye-aur kahin jakar pada rahe to koi nahin, maine behenji ko bhi yehi bataya tha*". (Alright, he was very demoralised. What will he do now? We should not allow him to go to Bihar. He will be of no consequence if he lies somewhere else. This is what I have also advised sister Indiraji).

Bansi Lal asked me for the details regarding JP's illness. I gave a low down, starting from the stomach pain about a month ago. Meanwhile tea, which was ordered earlier, came. Bhanot told Bansi Lal that though the GOI orders were to delay JP for a week at Chandigarh, it would be difficult to keep him for more than 3-4 days. I supported his point strongly. Bansi Lal asked about the reaction and Bhanot said it had already started. Lakhanpal, with 10-15 people, was already in the PGI when we came out after serving the parole order on JP. Bansi Lal pounced on the name of Lakhanpal and asked, *achcha* Lakhanpal is leading the dissent, now what explanation has Mathur got? Then he narrated his version of the Lakhanpal episode involving Om Mehta and Mathur. '*Saala Lakhanpal Mathur ka sasur lagta hai*' (This damn fellow Lakhanpal seem to be the father-in-law of Mathur). "I am going to talk to Om Mehta immediately. I will also write a DO letter tomorrow morning to the PM".

He asked for the telephone and got a call through to Om Mehta. Told him about the accomplishment of the mission and JP accepting the orders meekly, he being demoralised. He would be retained in Chandigarh for a couple of days. '*4-5 din mein usko yahan se phadak dena*'. (let us throw him out of this place in 4-5 days). Then Bansi Lal told Om Mehta about Lakhanpal's activities. "Now ask Mathur what he has to say, ask him immediately."

We took leave of Bansi Lal, went to the guesthouse and had dinner. We called Gupta, but he did not come. Both Kohli and Sushil Kumar were quite relieved at the easy accomplishment of the task. We finished dinner and both of them left at 11.30 p.m. Mohinder Singh took them in my car. Before leaving, Sushil Kumar gave me a copy of the parole orders. I received a call from Gupta saying that Dasgupta was coming by the early morning flight the next day. The same arrangements and secrecy was in place. I reserved a room for him and instructed Kushal Singh to pick him up from the airport.

I returned home at t about midnight. There were several telephone calls and many of those who called had abused Kamal, the telephone attendant, when he told them that I was not available. I looked at the list and returned only Rashpal's call. He complimented me and said that I was being discussed at top circles in Delhi with regard to the JP's affair. Rajan, a Deputy Secretary in GoI, had told him this a short while ago. Rajan had also asked whether I had any commendation before.

I smiled to myself at the irony of it all. Let alone commendation, I would be grateful if I escaped condemnation from the powers-that-be for what I had done. That was the way of the world, I thought wryly. Nevertheless, for the first time in several days, I went to sleep with a mind that was much less burdened.

'Delhi Durbar' Defied

On November 13, Kushal Singh picked up Dasgupta and lodged him in the guesthouse. Through Kushal, Dasgupta had sent a note to me saying that he wanted to meet JP early, before anyone else met him. He wanted to talk to me urgently, before going to JP. My getting ready got delayed due to a spate of telephone calls.

First, it was Rajeshwar Prasad calling from Bombay, asking about JP's health. There had been a lot of disturbing rumors about JP and his health. I said JP was all right and there was nothing to be panicky about. Rajeshwar said he was flying this evening and would be at Chandigarh next morning.

IP Anand telephoned from Delhi and wanted to meet JP. They had been old friends. Only social relationship. I asked him to come next morning. M R Masani's sister telephoned from Delhi saying Masani wanted to come and see JP on Saturday or Sunday. I said certainly, if JP was still here.

The DM, Patna called saying that he had located Gulab Yadav. Should he be sent now, since JP had been released on parole? I said yes, JP would be here for 3-4 days and let him come immediately. Gulab could go with JP when he left.

There was a telephone call from R K Misra, General Manager of the Indian Express Group. He said he had come to take JP to Delhi and would like to bring a special aircraft. I said JP would leave, depending on doctor's advice. Misra wanted to fly in specialists from the Christian Medical Hospital, Vellore. I said, I could not say anything on that and I would advise him to contact Dr Chuttani, Director, PGI. Misra then asked whether he could meet JP. I said certainly, he could and asked him to go to the PGI at 11a.m. and contact Dr Wahi. Soon thereafter, Misra came home and repeated the requests and I gave him the same answers.

I went to guesthouse at 9.30 a.m. Dasgupta was strolling on the lawns, waiting for me. He asked me how JP was. I said, not bad. He said that he had important messages for JP, who would be more cheerful when he heard the message he had brought.

This time he had come at the instance of Om Mehta. He was at Kanpur the day before Om Mehta had telephoned at about 4 p.m. and asked him to return to Delhi by 7 p.m., and arranged for a plane ticket within 15 minutes. Dasgupta had reached Delhi at 8.30 p.m., went to Om Mehta straight and was told to go to Chandigarh immediately.

Dasgupta said that JP's release had been contemplated for a while and my three-pronged move accelerated the process. He said that it was a masterstroke and could become a turning point in India's history. He was glad that his prediction, when he took leave of me on the 10th, had come true I told him about Masani's visit and IP Anand's telephone. Dasgupta expressed keenness to meet Masani before he (Masani) met JP. He wanted people like Minoo Masani and B.G. Varghese to persuade JP to keep away from active politics after his release.

JP's mention about going to a distant place, perhaps to Madras, had been well received in Delhi. Most probably government would make all the arrangements for his treatment and stay at Vellore or Madras, or anywhere else.

Dasgupta said that he would be giving a personal message from the PM to JP, conveyed through Om Mehta. Indira Gandhi had conveyed the message that her personal regards and respect for JP was the same as ever, inspite of political developments, and she was genuinely concerned about his health. Endorsing what Kohli told me last night, she had conveyed that though for technical reasons the release has been ordered on parole for one month, in fact, it is virtual release and JP was not likely to be detained again. Indira requested that JP should recoup his health by staying at Chandigarh for a week. After that, the government would arrange for his transport, stay and treatment anywhere in the country. If this was not acceptable to JP, he could go wherever and whenever he wished. I wondered whether this was Indira's message or Om Mehta's ploy to delay JP's departure.

Gupta said one Dr A C Sen would be coming to see JP in the evening. He was close to JP. Not much time should be given to him, though JP would like to spend a lot of time with him. This was because Sen was likely to turn JP's mind against the government. I thought, this time I found a change in Dasgupta's stance and attitude. Being a simple man, he seemed to have been taken in by the wily Om Mehta and was mouthing his thoughts like a parrot. In the process, though he did not realize it, Dasgupta was turning into a government agent instead of being an impartial interlocutor. I took a mental note of this.

I asked Dasgupta whether JP's release meant any relaxation of the Emergency and what about the other leaders? He said nothing was known since Indira kept her counsel. Dasgupta did not meet Dhar before coming to Chandigarh as he was away in Trivandrum. His thought that as a follow up to JP's release Sarvodaya and other similar workers were likely to be released. We went into JP's room and he was sitting on the chair, relaxed and relieved. The puffiness of his face had slightly decreased. He was glad to see Dasgupta and embraced him, sitting.

Dasgupta told him about his coming from Kanpur etc and said that for two weeks, the government had been thinking of his release. JP gave me a meaningful look and asked whether it took two weeks for such a small matter. Dasgupta protested and said that it was not a small matter, because the entire situation had to be assessed before a decision was taken. Dasgupta then gave the PM's and Om Mehta's messages about their well wishes and virtual release etc.

He than asked JP whether he was serious about going to Madras for treatment. JP said, no, not particularly, it was only a thought and he would decide in consultation with relatives and friends. JP then asked what about the other detainees and what about elections? Dasgupta responded by saying that he could not meet Dhar and did not know the details. He also said that he would stay in Chandigarh as long as JP stayed and would go back with him. The idea was to keep him company.

I found Dasgupta trying to say something to JP but hesitating. Sensing that he wanted to talk in private to JP, I got up to leave. Dasgupta said he would go back to the guesthouse by auto rickshaw. I took leave and left, wishing JP quick recovery. Before leaving, I asked JP about his meeting with Mishra. He said it was good and he did not know why Indira was after Goenka's blood. When I came out, Bhanot, Mohinder Singh and Krishan Lal were sitting in the adjoining room. We discussed briefly the changed arrangements. All of them resented Mathur's strange attitude in cutting off the DC and the SSP from all arrangements concerning JP and giving it over totally to the doctors. We felt that there was bound to be confusion.

In order to discuss the matter further, I sent for Dr Mehra and Dr Wahi. In the meanwhile, there was a message that Gupta was waiting in the corridor and wanted me or Bhanot to come out. Bhanot said Gupta has been sent by Mathur to sort out JP- related arrangement with the doctors. Both went out. Tandon was there and Dr Mehra also arrived.

Dr Mehra started the discussion by saying that he was being pestered by many persons to see JP. Digvijay Narain, who had come from Patna, and many others. Foreign journalists from ABC, Japan Radio, UPI had also been pestering him. With such rush, it would be difficult to handle JP's treatment. The matter was discussed at some length and a strategy was worked out:

- Wahi and Mehra to make themselves scarce, as far as possible. It was easy in view of their heavy clinical and surgical work. They should dodge ordinary visitors, saying that they did not know anything about JP
- Relatives and other important people would normally meet the DC first and he would handle them

- Certain others, whom the doctors felt were important should be allowed to meet JP only during the interview hours.
- In case of any doubt, the matter should be referred to the DC.

I came back to office. Mrs G B Singh telephoned and wanted to come with Vice Admiral Mahendru to discuss the issue of war widows' remarriage. I asked them to come at 11.30 a.m.

There was a telephone call from S N Prasad, Calcutta. How was JP? Was he critically ill? I said, not at all. Lot of rumors at Calcutta. I said there was nothing to worry. He wanted to come the next day, and I said he was welcome. I was sitting in Gupta's room when Mathur sent for us about 11a.m. I went over the arrangements made at the PGI and our talk with the doctors.

There was a phone call from Patna that I took at Mathur's office. Baxi was on the line and sounded shaky. How was JP? I said, alright. Had he recovered his senses? I said, what do you mean by recovering his senses? He never lost it. Was he still in a coma? I said no coma or full stop. JP was quite well. He had nausea and was a little weak. Baxi apologized for his questions and said every one was anxious because of the strong rumors in Patna that JP was in a coma, very serious, that is why he was released. I said, not to worry and JP was alright, with only some minor problems. He said he would come the next day and would bring Gulab along. I said both were welcome.

I came back to my office around 11. 30 a.m. Mrs G B Singh and the Vice Admiral were waiting. They discussed the war widows' remarriage issue and left at about 12.00 noon.

Foreign correspondents from ABC, BBC, Radio Japan and UPI, who were waiting for about 30 minutes, trooped into my office after that. They said that Dr Mehra had refused to tell them anything and had asked them to come to me. They asked several questions about JP's health, his release, his leaving Chandigarh, his meeting politicians etc. I answered many and parried some. They wanted to meet JP briefly. I said JP was a patient now, and not a prisoner and as such, I had no control over him or his time. It was for the doctors to decide to allow or not to allow interviews, depending on their assessment of JP's health.

Could we, at least, send in a slip to JP, they asked. Again, for the doctors to decide, I said.

The correspondents left. I passed them, going into Mathur's room, and heard one of them remarking, 'this DC fellow is quite a smart guy'. I went to Mathur and reported the contents of press interview. He said that I should insist that JP was an absolutely free man now, and I said, that is what I had precisely done.

Dasgupta telephoned and said he had a very useful meeting with JP, who was cheerful. He would be meeting JP again in the evening, along with A C Sen. JP wanted some clarification about the release orders. Was there any condition? None as far as I understood, I said. JP wanted to know specifically about giving public statements. I said I would check up with the DC, Delhi and clarify.

Bansi Lal called and said that some Indian Express correspondent was spreading the news that JP had not accepted the parole order. I said it was trash, he did so in my presence and the DC, Delhi had carried signed receipt from JP. He asked me to talk to Mehtani and give him the details. Then he asked about Mathur. I said, I found Mathur a bit gloomy this morning. Bansi Lal said, he deserved it for treating Lakhanpal as his father-in law-in-yin I spoke to Mahtani, explaining that the DC, Delhi had the receipt of the parole order, signed by JP himself. I asked him to warn the correspondent not to spread baseless tales, otherwise he would be in trouble.

In the evening, Dasgupta telephoned from the PGI to say that he was not being allowed to go in. I instructed the sub inspector of police, who was with him, to take Dasgupta to JP. After a while, DSP Kishan Lal telephoned asking whether to permit Dasgupta to see JP. The young doctor on duty was not letting him in, saying that Dasgupta had no chit from Dr Wahi or Dr Mehra. I said I allowed Dasgupta to visit JP and the duty doctor may be advised accordingly. This was the first indication of confusion being created by the new arrangement. I had specifically told Dr Mehra about Dasgupta and Sen, and he had promised to leave necessary instructions. Now he was not available and the duty doctor had refused to allow them to meet JP. I wondered as to how long, the JP- related arrangements– about which Mathur was so fussy – would hold good.

Bansi Lal called again and wanted to re-confirm regarding the service of the parole order. I asked what the matter was. He said there had been lots of rumors and queries from Delhi. The DC, Delhi had the original receipt, signed by JP wasn't it, he asked. I reconfirmed the service of the order, stating categorically that the DC, Delhi had the copy of the receipt, signed by JP. He then asked about Mathur and I gave the same reply that I had given him in the morning.

Bansi Lal then insisted that JP should be kept in the PGI at least for a week. If there was any difficulty, I should meet him along with Dr Wahi the next day. Though I told him that we were already working on those lines, this directive from Bansi Lal, along with his derisive comments on JP last night, rekindled my suspicion that somehow or the other, the Sanjay coterie wanted to keep JP in fetters, though he was now a free man. This would defeat the very purpose of our efforts to get JP released so that his ailment could be diagnosed in a good hospital and treated expeditiously. It also occurred to me that Dr Chuttani had conveniently gone out of station at this crucial time, and during his absence the doctors here would not be able to take any decision to discharge JP. I made a mental note of this.

R D Sharma later reported that when he got the jail register signed by JP, in token of his release, JP had commented with a sigh, "Thank God, now I am a free citizen of this country."

Among JP's relatives and friends, the first to arrive next day was Rajeshwar Prasad who came to my residence at 8.00 a.m. He was dressed in an overcoat and gloves, and looked shaken. I gave him a hot cup of tea and asked him to relax. He asked about JP's health and said that they were all very upset because of the rumors floating in Bombay. He had been getting a number of telephone calls. After his talk with me, he had tried to scotch the rumors and had some success.

Rajeshwar wanted to stay with JP. That would help the old man recover fast and keep a control on visitors. I thought it was a good idea. I telephoned R D Sharma to come immediately. Rajeshwar wanted a place to do his morning ablutions and change, before going to JP. I went up and telephoned Mathur and told him about Rajeshwar and his request to stay near JP. As if by instinct, Mathur said that leave everything to the doctors. You have nothing to do. Just send Rajeshwar to the doctors, they would decide. Given yesterday's mess up with Dasgupta and Sen, I couldn't stand this nonsense anymore. I lost my cool and asked him clearly to tell me whether I should completely cut off from the JP arrangement from now on. This would also mean that the police as well as the executive magistrate would also get out of the JP arrangement, leaving everything entirely to the doctors. I told him that I telephoned him to seek guidance regarding the administrative desirability of Rajeshwar staying with JP, and not medical advisability. My resentment must have registered. There was a clear mellowing down in his tone and he said that Rajeshwar should not stay with JP but could stay as near as possible. He advised me to talk to Chuttani, who had just returned from his Nepal trip.

When I telephoned Chuttani, he said Rajeshwar was welcome to stay in the PGI guesthouse. He asked me to send him along, and he would give necessary instructions. R D Sharma had arrived by now and I sent Rajeshwar to the PGI along with him.

I was doing the yogic kriyas when I P Anand came at 8.30 a.m. He waited for some time and then came to the drawing room. He said he was going to meet JP. He had traveled from Kathmandu on the same plane with Chuttani, and had already fixed 9 a.m. for meeting JP. He dropped in just to confirm the service of the parole order. There was so much of talk in Delhi that JP had refused to receive the parole orders, which had conditions. Even senior officers tended to believe it. I told him the real story and he was convinced. Anand spoke about his long-lasting family relationship with JP and left, after taking a cup of tea.

Dasgupta called up and requested me to go over to the guesthouse for him and Sen to have a talk with me.

There was a telephone call from the Welfare Officer of the J&K Government that he had a message from Sheikh Abdullah to JP. I asked him to meet me in the office later.

I then went to the guesthouse. Dasgupta took me aside and told me how receptive JP was, though not much ice was broken. It would take more time and efforts. He told me that JP wanted clarification as to whether there were any conditions in the parole. He also suggested that the rumors spreading about JP's health should be countered in two ways – one, a medical bulletin by doctors and second a statement to the press by JP's brother Rajeshwar Prasad. I said, I would have to think it over.

I went over to meet Sen and Dasgupta introduced me to him as the person 'who kept JP alive physically and psychologically'. Sen was grateful and he thanked me on behalf of JP's friends. "We do realize the value of the role played by you." Sen then asked, was JP a difficult prisoner? I said no. To start with, he was a bit difficult. Over a period of time, I had established a personal rapport with him and he was very understanding and cooperative. Had there been memorable events, he asked. I said quite a few, the most important was when he withdrew his fast threat on my request. Dasgupta said I could now write a book 'JP was my prisoner'. I told them I would get passes for them to go to JP's room, so that they won't have difficulties as they had on the previous day.

I went to see JP at 11 a.m. and was stopped by the hospital staff. The constable on duty snubbed him. JP was having a late breakfast and fiddling with a full-boiled egg, which was not properly boiled. He took a while and a young doctor sat like a stone, with a nurse hanging around. I observed that the young doctors were aimlessly hanging around, doing nothing to help JP. I asked the doctor to leave the room. He said he was Dr Raju. I said that did not make make any difference and asked him to clear the room, since I had something to talk to JP.

I asked JP how he was feeling. He said he was fine as the very news of his release had brought recovery fast. However, b being in the same atmosphere, was not conducive to quick recovery, he said.. He would like to shift from Chandigarh to Delhi or some other place, and would like to move the very next day, or if not, the day after. He strongly felt that his continuance at Chandigarh would adversely affect his recovery.

I told him that his brother had already arrived and Masani would be coming the next day. JP could talk it over with them and take a decision and he agreed. I also told him that I.P. Anand had come and he was happy. I asked him about Digvijay Narain Singh. JP said he was a big landlord in Bihar and a Congress (O) MP. He is a good person and he (JP) would like to meet him if he was here.

I left JP and went into Chuttani's room. Rajeshwar Prasad, Anand and Bhanot were there. Bhanot and I took Chuttani to the other room and told him of the Government of India requirement and JP's frame of mind. In an arrogant tone typical of Chuttani, he said, "cut off the entire official dance and leave it to the doctors. We will manage for as many days as necessary". He even suggested that Bhanot and I don't see JP at all. I told him not to be so sure. "You may land up in a mess", I told him. JP was not a normal type of patient. He was different and had to be dealt with differently. We had some argument and I left it at that.

On my saying that JP had finished breakfast, all of us trooped into JP's room. Digvijay Narain Singh was hanging around in the corridor and I took him along. JP embraced his brother and became emotional. Anand touched his feet. JP said "*aap paer kyun chu rahe ho?*(why are you touching my feet?)")" D N Singh also came and touched JP's feet and embraced. He whispered something in JP's ear for a few seconds and then left the room, saying he would meet in the evening again. Chuttani, I and Bhanot also left, with Anand sitting on the bed with JP asking him how everyone in the family was. As I left, I collected a few passes from Brig. Kataria, the security officer. Bhanot and I came back to my office together. In the car, we reviewed the situation and the main issue was how to handle Chuttani, who had vanished to Nepal to have a good time when we were splitting our heads and now he had returned to Chandigarh to order us around.. This man was clever and we knew we had to 'handle him with care'. We decided to think it over and went to Mathur's room to report on all that had happened in the morning.

Mathur received a telephone call from D N Singh. The two talked like old and very close friends. Mathur asked him what he had whispered in JP's ears. Singh was taken aback and said he told JP, "*aap ka kaam sab dhire dhire thik chal raha hai*" (your work is being accomplished slowly and steadily). He was going off to Delhi and would not do any 'golmal' (make trouble) in Chandigarh, Singh told Mathur.

I told Mathur about Dagupta's suggestions on how to control the rumors on JP's health. I said, a medical bulletin will be too technical, it would be better if JP's brother issued a statement. Mathur talked to Khurana, who did not approve of the idea. "What if the rumors are there?', Khurana had asked, it did not make any difference. "In any case, according to the rumours, JP has already died a couple of times." He advised that it would be better for us not to come into the picture at all and the rumors would die down on their own. I brought up our arguments with Chuttani and what was on JP's mind about leaving. As expected, Mathur asked us to keep off and let Chuttani handle everything. He told Khurana that though the DC and the SSP has different assessments, he was confident that Chuttani would handle JP successfully and make him stay in Chandigarh for a week. This was precisely what I did not want to happen, and I decided to do some maneuvering this time and draw on Bhanot's help, if necessary.

As I came back to my room, there was telephone from Dasgupta. He had been called by Dhar to Delhi immediately. He had not got the pass. Kushal Singh, who took the pass to the guesthouse, had missed them. I asked him to come over to my office at 1.15 p.m. M.R. Masani's sister called to say that Masani was flying in from Bombay on the same evening and would drive up to Chandigarh on the next day and would come straight to my office. Dasgupta came at 1.15 p.m.. He wanted to go to Delhi by the night train. I telephoned Tandon and fixed up a ticket and bed for him. Dasgupta said that he would meet JP in the evening, before going and he asked for my assessment. Would JP stick to his promise of not reviving the movement? I said it depended on the political developments and requirements. My reading was that if elections were held, as scheduled and as requested by JP, he wouldl stick to his promise. If elections were delayed on any pretext, he might not. I also told Dasgupta that the assessment in Delhi seemed to be that JP was demoralised and a spent force. Please tell Dhar that JP was not demoralised and could not be taken for granted. Indira might be gloating in the new-found glory and popularity and her sycophants would gladly tell her that she was the goddess of the country and that there was no dissent anywhere, but let her not fool herself. This situation would not continue for long. I told Dasgupta Masani was coming on the morrow. He was keen to meet Masani before he met JP, and said that after meeting Dhar he would come back the next day or the day after.

In the evening I learnt that a large number of people had met JP– to the extent that JP had got very tired. Utter confusion prevailed as neither Wahi nor Mehra was available and the security personnel allowed visitors at their whim and fancy. When I reported this to Mathur and Gupta, the latter said that JP needed Janta therapy (many people meeting him and sitting around him) than any other treatment, for quick recovery. JP was quite sentimental and emotional and was easily moved and he loved to be with people. That was okay, I said, but what about his security? That was our prime concern and we could not abdicate on it. Both Mathur and Gupta concurred with my point of view.

As the day progressed, I was felt uncomfortable about the prospect of JP being held back at the PGI by the 'Delhi Durbar', thereby defeating my real plan. Taking advantage of Bhanot's dislike of this move and his conversation with me earlier in the day about the possibility of trouble brewing in the university campus I, decided to defy the 'Durbar' and adopt a bold ploy to get JP discharged immediately so that Masani and the others arriving on the next day could decide the next step. So gathering all the authority I could muster, I called Dr Chuttani. After informing him about the chaos that prevailed at the hospital, with people thronging JP's room, possibly threatening his security, I said: "Though JP is no longer in my custody, I am the District Magistrate and am concerned with JP's security. I am also concerned with law and order, and I have information that students in the Punjab University campus, just across the PGI, have come to know of JP's release and are getting restive. They are also planning to visit JP in large groups. This may create dangerous law and order situation, which may get out of control. Please don't be offended, but I want an answer to this question - are you curing him or discharging him? Please take a decision and convey this to me by tomorrow. This is important because we have to make arrangements accordingly"

JP Departs with a Pledge: 'I Will Defeat That Woman'

The ultimatum worked and early next morning (November 15), Dr Chuttani decided to discharge JP and was the first to inform the old man. So, when I went to see JP at about 10 a.m., he was beaming and said that Dr Chuttani had met him in the morning and had cleared his departure. So, he would like to leave Chandigarh the next day and would like to pack his things. He found it difficult to pack his books. I promised to give him a wooden box for the books.

Bhanot had also come and remarked that JP was indeed looking relaxed and the puffiness of the face had practically gone. JP said that the emotional and psychological satisfaction of meeting people was restoring his health fast. He continued: *"I am emotional and give vent to my emotions while meeting people. Though I had best of medical care, and you have all been very kind to me, I was not well mainly because of the lack of company and opportunity to meet people."*

A doctor was hovering around and we asked him to go out. I told JP that we would talk with Dr Chuttani, plan his travel arrangements and get back to him in the evening or the next morning. I also said that Masani was coming to see me in the morning, I would have a word with him also. Then I gave JP the message of 'best wishes' from Sheikh Abdullah, conveyed though the Welfare Officer. He was glad and said he was grateful to the Sheikh. "Indeed, it was very thoughtful and considerate of him", remarked JP.

JP thanked Bhanot and me for being so kind to him though he was a prisoner. I told him that as far as I was concerned, I never thought of him as a prisoner.

Bhanot and I left JP and went up to Chuttani's room. On the piazza, we saw Rajeshwar Prasad, A C Sen and S N Prasad and called them over. D Baxi, Thomas Abraham and Gulab Yadav, who had just arrived from Patna, also joined us.

Sen said that JP had sent a message that Chuttani had cleared his departure and he wanted to leave the next day. They were going to the Indian Airlines office to book 6 tickets for tomorrow's IA flight to Delhi. They were just going to Chuttani to find out the name of the doctor he would be sending along.

I told him that JP had told us sos just now. "Please give us some time to think and talk things over. Don't make plans in a hurry. If plans keep changing it would upset JP. Since Masani was also arriving soon, it would only be proper to involve him also in the planning", I told them. They could come to see me at 3.30 p.m., by which time we also would have made up our minds. In the meantime, Baxi and Abraham could stay in the PGI guesthouse and Gulab could stay with JP. Gulab also gave me a letter from the DM, Patna.

We left them and came back to my office. Mathur had not arrived so far. I went to Gupta's room and told him about the developments. I enacted a drama of being furious that Dr Chuttani had discharged JP, without even informing us. Gupta telephoned Mathur, and he said he too had no knowledge whatsoever. He asked Gupta to go to Chuttani and sort out the matter. I said, now that JP has been discharged and had been informed about it, there was nothing to sort out and we should concentrate on the departure arrangements for JP and his entourage. Nevertheless, we resented Mathur as well as Chuttani belittling the SSP and me. In the end, Mathur also got the same treatment from Chuttani!

Mittal called up to say that Masani had come and I rushed down to my office. Masani walked in, a tall, slim personality. We had a facile and fluent conversation about JP and his health. He asked whether he could see JP. He would like to take him to Bombay straightaway. He had to halt at Delhi if he took a normal flight. He asked what our plans for JP's departure were. I said, we had not made up our minds. We had requested the GoI for a special aircraft and were awaiting a response.

Dasgupta telephoned from Delhi and asked about jP's departure programme. Obviously, he was talking from the office of P N Dhar. I mentioned about the possibility of the GoI providing an aircraft for his direct flight to Bombay. Mathur had already made the request to the Union Home Secretary. Dr Chuttani had cleared the departure and I could not hold JP in Chandigarh any longer, I said. Dasgupta asked whether there wasn't any way at all to hold JP in Chandigarh for a couple of days more. I said no, I had seen JP in the morning and he was all set to leave and was already feeling well. Retaining him here under any pretext could adversely affect his health. And since Dr Chuttani had cleared the departure, we could not think of any valid ground for prolonging his stay. Dasgupta complimented me on my role JP's release and hung up.

After spending a few more minutes with Masani, I gave him a pass to visit JP and asked him to come back at 4 p.m., by which time we would have made up our minds regarding JP's departure arrangements.

I met Mathur at 3 p.m. and briefed him on the developments. He telephoned Khurana and received a very unfavourable reply regarding a special aircraft. The message was 'let JP fend for himself'. Mathur felt that there was some annoyance at the GoI that we could not hold on to JP any further. I told him, now that JP was all set to leave, we should not even try to hold him back. Mathur agreed and approved the departure plan by normal flight the next day.

Masani and Sen came back sharp at 4 p.m. I told them that special aircraft was out and they could take JP by the normal Srinagar-Jammu-Chandigarh-Delhi flight next afternoon. They said they had planned to do so and JP would halt for one or two days in Delhi, and then would be taken directly to the Jaslok Hospital, Bombay for expert treatment for the kidney failure.

When I asked whether I could be of any help, Sen reluctantly said that they had only two tickets, one confirmed and one on wait list. They needed at least three confirmed tickets – for JP, brother Rajeshwar Prasad and attendant Gulab Yadav. I telephoned Ajit Singh, the airport manager and asked him to provide three confirmed seats to JP's party in the Delhi flight the next day. He mumbled something to the effect that the aircraft was overbooked from Chandigarh that day and it might not be possible. I said that it was urgent and top priority, and he had to get it done and I would call again in the morning.

I went to see JP in the evening. The box he had asked for had already reachedhim. I told him about the plan for his departure and he was quite happy. He felt relaxed, sitting with family members and other friends. For the first time in several days, JP had asked for a non-vegetarian meal. I told JP that I would return in the morning and left.

The DC, Delhi rang up at home in the evening and asked for JP's departure plan. I told him he was returning the next day by a routine IA flight. On this, he said why could we not keep him in Chandigarh for some more time. I told him bluntly that JP was now a free man and we could not hold him after doctors had discharged him.

November 16 was the day JP left Chandigarh, on his way to make history in fifteen months time. The day started with Rajeshwar Prasad coming home in the morning. He had brought two packets of sweets and gave them to me. I told him he should not have taken the trouble when he himself was under so much of worry. He said, whether I liked it or not, he had considered himself as one of my family and would continue to do so. The sweet packets were for my two little children, who used to call him uncle whenever he came to my place in connection with his visit to JP. I offered him tea. We had some conversation. He said that he, his family and all the friends and relatives were beholden to me for looking after JP so well. They would never forget this. He even went to the extent of saying that it was I who had kept the old man alive. I was overwhelmed and I told him that I was doing only my duty.

We talked about JP, his qualities and his illness. Rajeshwar nearly broke down when he talked about his brother. He said JP was like a child - simple, pure and sentimental. It was because of these characteristics that he came out of his political wilderness to fight the Congress and Indira Gandhi at the ripe age of 72. And JP had to pay the price of being imprisoned and becoming seriously ill. We did not know how long he would survive, he lamented. He then showed me the letter he had written to Indira as we had planned and gave me a copy. It was well drafted and worded and Nayantara Sahgal, in her book, claims that she had drafted the letter. I felt that this letter was one of the major factors, which clinched the issue in favor of releasing JP.

Our conversation slowly drifted to Indira Gandhi. Rajeshwar said that Indira was a competent lady but very mean and revengeful. He narrated his own case. He had been a senior personnel officer in the Dalmia/Birla group. After he retired a couple of years ago, the Kamani group employed him as a part-time adviser at Rs. 2000 per month. He was happy doing his work and looking after his family. But a few weeks after the JP movement stared, the Kamani group boss called him and in an embarrassing tone told him that it would be better if Rajeshwar resigned. He got the cue and resigned immediately. But he investigated into the matter and found out that Indira had told Kamani to sack him immediately. To what level could a prime minister stoop? What sort of country and democracy were we living in? I felt deeply perturbed. There were tears in Rajeshwar's eyes. We talked for a while more and then he took leave and we parted, promising to meet each other again.

I went to see JP at about 10 a.m. and was joined by Bhanot at the entrance. Both of us went to JP's room. Thomas Abraham and Gulab Yadav were in the room, with the former busy packing the books in the box given by Sharma. JP was giving him certain instructions as to which book was to be kept where. Rajeshwar Prasad and S.N. Prasad joined. It was decided that JP, Rajeshwar Prasad and Gulab Yadav would travel by air and others would go by road to Delhi.

JP felt satisfied about the arrangements. Some local people, including Lakhanpal, had come and were waiting outside. I told JP that the flight was at 1.10 p.m. and we should leave at 12.30 sharp to be on time. I said I would come back at 12.15 p.m.and went to my office.

At the office, Masani and Sen were waiting to check up about the Indian Airlines confirmed ticket. Since I had not received any call from Ajit Singh, I called him. He was evasive and said he had tried to off load two passengers at Jammu to accommodate my request but could not succeed. He was sorry he said. I did not like the story. I had made a specific request yesterday, saying that it was urgent and top priority. Yet he could not arrange for two seats, which was essential for JP to leave today. Obviously he had not taken it seriously and tried hard enough.

Given the extreme urgency, I had no option but to give a shock treatment to the airport manager. So I said: "Listen Mr. Ajit Singh. I think you have not taken my request seriously. Now this is my decision. As soon as the flight lands at Chandigarh airport, I will impound the aircraft on the tarmac and the flight will not leave except with the three passengers for whom I asked for confirmed ticket. If it is okay with you, well and good. If not, make the necessary arrangements as per my request and call me back immediately." Within minutes Ajit Singh called back saying that he had made the necessary arrangements for three confirmed tickets and these could be picked up. I asked him to waive the security regulations for JP and he instantly agreed.

I returned to JP's room at 12.15 p.m. Bhanot was already there. JP was in the toilet. He came out and started dressing. He wanted to be meticulously dressed since he would be seen in public for the first time after his arrest on 25/26 June night. He did not want people to feel that JP was a sick, old, demoralised man and a spent force. Gulab Yadav helpedin getting dressed, which was very slow since JP could not bend.

By 12.30, he was dressed and ready to leave and a wheel chair was brought in. Dr Chuttani and Dr Mehra also joined us. JP sat in the wheelchair and looked around at everyone standing there with misty eyes. I could see that he was getting emotional. There was absolute silence. No one even whispered. The wheel chair was taken to the lift to be brought down. At the lift, JP broke down, with tears in his eyes and in a faltering voice addressed me and Bhanot, "I came here as your prisoner and you treated me as a human being. I will never forget this." When I told him that it was our duty, he responded saying "you had gone much beyond your sphere of duty in giving a very humane treatment to me." We didn't speak.

These were not empty words, JP obviously meant them. Though the Alva Commission had castigated the PGI doctors for the shabby treatment meted out to JP, about my role this is what the Commission had to say: "Of the officials and doctors who met him in Chandigarh, Mr. Narayan had nice words to say about Mr Devasahayam, who was much concerned about his comfort. JP always looked forward to meeting this official because, during his visits, he would talk about many things besides his illness. This official left a very good impression on JP's mind. He did everything possible to make his eminent prisoner comfortable and happy, according to the Sarvodaya leader."

When the wheel chair was brought to where the cars were parked, JP bade affectionate farewell to Dr Chuttani and thanked him for everything. JP sat in the rear seat of my car, with me on the left and Bhanot on the right. We started at 12.40 p.m. Since JP wanted to have a look of the city he had been in confinement for nearly five months, we took the route via the engineering college and the lake. It was also to avoid possible crowds on the university side, and also to show the city around briefly to JP. Since the route was unexpected, there was no crowd anywhere.

In the car JP again broke down and repeated what he said earlier about coming as a prisoner and being treated as a human being. I told him now that he was free, everything would be all right, his health and the health of the nation, provided he did not give up.

JP said he planned to go to Bombay after a few days halt at Delhi, and would get treatment at the Jaslok Hospital. In fact, he was one of the trustees of that hospital. The board of the hospital wanted him to be the president last year but he had declined. Jaslok was one of the finest hospitals in this part of the world, he said. After getting cured, he would go to Patna and be with his people, he said. Since he could not run around much, he would do whatever his health permited him to do.

JP also complimented us that Chandigarh city was very well kept and clean.

We reached the airport at 1.10 p.m. and drove straight on the tarmac to the aircraft. The rotors were already running and the plane was about to take off. A small crowd was waiting near the gate of the tarmac, and we passed through them. JP located an old man - Mr Trikha - who was the chairman of the local Gandhi Samarak Nidhi. As soon as the car stopped near the aircraft, JP got out and asked for Mr. Trikha. One police inspector was asked to fetch him. Mr. Trikha came and touched JP's feet as he took leave of him. Rajeshwar Prasad had already got the security clearance for the baggage and was waiting.

JP took leave of Bhanot and me. He nearly broke down and had tears in his eyes. He said he would never forget our kindness. Dr Chuttani and an airport official helped him up the ladder. Bhanot accompanied him into the aircraft, saluted and came back. The door was closed and the ladder was about to be removed when all of a sudden, the door swung open and the airhostess asked for the Chandigarh DC. I answered and she said that JP wanted to see me. I hurried up the steps and went to JP, sitting in the second row from the rear. He took hold of my hands, and with tears rolling down his eyes, said that I was like a son he never had and he would never forget me in his life.

With most of the passengers looking at us, I felt embarrassed and at the same time elated. I slowly eased my hand from his and told him that I never took him to be my prisoner and had always held him as a father figure. Then I told him within the hearing of the passengers sitting near by that, he must take care of his health and I wanted to see his health restored as quickly as possible. Overcome by emotion, he slightly raised his voice and said: "My health is not important. It is the health of the nation that is important. I will defeat that woman and restore freedom. This will be my life's mission." I bid farewell and came down the stairs. The doors closed and the aircraft took off.

Bhanot told me that as JP entered the aircraft, G S Dhillon, Speaker of the Lok Sabha, who was seated inside the aircraft, came to JP and touched his feet. Pressmen and photographers were waiting at the entrance gate and we did not want to be cornered by them. So we got out through a side gate and hit the road back. I came back home and felt completely relieved and relaxed. The last words of JP showed that the fire was back in him and the transition of the 'Lok Nayak' from a defeated individual to a defiant icon was complete. I was confident that with this new spiri,t he would redeem his pledge of returning India to freedom and democracy.

What the 'Delhi Durbar' could not achieve in Chandigarh – delaying JP access to proper medical care at least by a week – they managed in Delhi, taking advantage of the gullibility of Rajeshwar Prasad. JP was virtually forced to spend a few days in the AIIMS and it was not till the morning of November 22 that he actually arrived in Bombay and was admitted to the Jaslok Hospital. This had meant about a week of needless delay in getting started with the treatment that he so badly required.

On this episode Mr Masani records: "As a result of my few minutes with JP that evening (the 22nd) and a long visit on the morning of the 23rd I noted in my diary:

"I may be wrong but I definitely have the feeling that he was a much weaker and frailer man than he was a few days earlier in Chandigarh. That, I suppose, is the contribution of the Prime Minister's Secretariat in delaying JP in Delhi"

'Better late than never'. Though late in arriving at Jaslok, JP went into the hands of the best specialists, led by Dr M K Mani, chief nephrologist at the Jaslok Hospital.

With failed Kidneys, JP Escapes Death by a Whisker

It was a very close shave, and but for providential intervention JP would not have lived to defeat 'that woman' and bring back democracy. Dr M K Mani, the man who saved JP, later moved from Bombay to Chennai and has been consulting nephrologist for the Appolo Group of Hospitals. I had a long chat with him at his residence some time in August 2003. He was categorical in his assertion that "if there had been a delay of two weeks in taking JP to Jaslok Hospital, he would have been dead." He was also equally emphatic that 'there was grievous failure on the part of PGI doctors in diagnosing JP's kidney damage.' I poignantly thought of the pincer assault of early November 1975 that had narrowly saved JP from death!

No wonder then that in February 1977, in the midst of elections, JP addressed an open letter to 'my dear brothers, sisters and young friends'. The letter dropped a bombshell when it said inter alia:

> "Suddenly on November 5, 1975 I was informed that both my kidneys had stopped functioning. I could not understand how and when I became a victim of the kidney disease. I was taking all the medicines prescribed to me at Chandigarh. I was also sticking to the diet given to me in detention. So the total collapse of my kidneys was beyond my comprehension. A number of my friends have expressed a doubt,

which I share, that my kidneys may have been deliberately damaged. Also no doctor (who has taken the Hippocratic oath) will be a party to such a heinous crime.

But the physicians who examined and treated me at Bombay were of the opinion that if I had gone in for their treatment fifteen days earlier, the functioning of the kidneys could have been partially restored. God alone knows how my kidneys were so totally affected. But this much is certain that I had been released only when the Indira Government was convinced that I would not survive for more than a few days."

Responding to this serious suspicion, the Janata Party-led Government of India appointed a Commission of Inquiry in May 1977 to enquire into the matter and bring out the truth. First it was headed by Dr Phillipose Koshy of the Christian Medical College, Vellore, who resigned within days amidst controversy that he used this position to get a job for his son at the PGI. Dr K Nagappa Alva, a physician-cum politician replaced him and went about the job with a missionary zeal, recording extensive and elaborate depositions from JP as well as all those connected with his detention and treatment at the PGI and the Jaslok Hospital. I have myself deposed before this Commission twice, lasting two days.

Dr Alva submitted his interim report in February 1978, which contained very damaging findings on the medical treatment providedt to JP while in detention: "The dysfunction of the kidneys, though detected on September 15, 1975, was left uninvestigated. This led to deterioration, without proper diabetic control and total mismanagement in the treatment of the case as a whole. Indiscriminate use of the drugs like dilantin, oral anti-diabetic drugs, which are contra-indicated in diabetic nephropathy, produced drug –induced nephropathy. The Commission finds that steps were not taken soon enough to investigate and correctly diagnose the main disease of diabetic nephropathy.... The diagnosis of kidney disease in Mr. Narayan was kept a secret for a considerable time."

The Commission went on: "The 43 days of detention at the guest-house from September 18 to October 30, 1975, were the darkest chapter in JP's life. This period caused permanent damage to JP's kidneys and his physical frame. During this period there was no nursing cover or any assistance to help him in his daily routine and to administer him drugs. His diabetic nephropathy was not investigated, the consultant services concerned were not made available and his condition was allowed to deteriorate further, consequent on cumulative toxic effects of 26 days when Dilantin was administered. Antidiabetic oral drugs are contraindicated in diabetic nephropathy. JP should have been treated with insulin therapy."

This interim report raised a ruckus in Parliament and outside. There was vociferous demand to place the report in Parliament and take strident follow up action. But Prime Minister Morarji Desai blocked this move at the instance of a powerful lobby. Soon thereafter, the Alva Commission was dragged to the Punjab & Haryana High Court, forcing Dr Nagappa Alva to resign from the Commission, which then collapsed. These factors, coupled with the cavalier manner in which such a sensitive issue was handled by the then Union Health Minister, Raj Narain ensured that the whole matter was pushed under the carpet and the truth about the damage of JP's kidney while in detention never saw the light of the day. Only rumors and insinuations persist even today.

Under the circumstances, Dr Chuttani, as Director of the PGI and the chief physician, should have met these 'damaging findings' head on with actual facts. He did not do this. Neither did he call upon the specialist nephrologist of the PGI, Dr K.S.Chugh to do so. Instead, he resorted to filibustering and firing from the shoulders of doctors who had nothing to do with JP's treatment. In this effort, he fielded Dr Christopher R. Blagg, Director, Northwest Kidney Center and Professor of Medicine, University of Washington, Seattle, USA and Dr B K Aikat, Professor of Pathology, PGI. This is what Dr Chuttani wrote in the booklet, "Politicisation of Health – JP's Documented Medical Profile" edited and published by him in 1995:

"Dr Christopher R Blagg, to whose center in the USA, JP had been flown when Jaslok Hospital could not effect the required shunt, was visiting India in February, 1979. Dr Nayar (Shushila Nayar, President of the PGI Governing Body) took advantage of the opportunity to refer JP's medical record to him for assessment. He concluded that the medical treatment of JP in Chandigarh was most appropriate in the light of the history and laboratory tests. Based on biochemical findings, there was no indication for dialysis prior to the time of JP's discharge from the PGI, he said.

Mention needs to be made of a detailed article by Professor B K Aikat, a former Dean of PGI. Professor Aikat was an outstanding pathologist of the country, who had been requested by no less a person than JBS Haldane to conduct an autopsy on him when he died in Orissa. His article 'JP at PGI-An inside view' published in *The Tribune* of March 31, 1978, showed his courage of conviction and exposed the vilification campaign unleashed by petty minds and time servers against the medical fraternity, which sedulously worked day and night to preserve the Lok Nayak for national service"

The Tribune article by Dr Aikat, so proudly referred to by Dr Chuttani, was nothing but a canard against the Jaslok Hospital: "I have very little doubt that the seeds of suspicion were sown at Jaslok Hospital, and Mr. Jayaprakash Narayan was given the impression that his life was saved by the efforts of the specialists in that hospital, who also told him that if he had come 15 days earlier the irreparable damage to his kidney could be prevented. Such an unprofessional and unethical statement appears to have been made by the specialists in that hospital. I am also of the opinion that the idea of poisoning his kidney during his long stay at the PGI emanates from that hospital. I am of the opinion that the malicious and distorted version of the specialists at Jaslok Hospital is a result of professional jealousy."

The person at the receiving end of Dr Aikat's wrath was Dr M K Mani, who as chief nephrologist of Bombay's Jaslok Hospital saved JP's life after he was taken there from the PGI and admitted on 22 November. But malice or vilification against the PGI seems to be the last thing on the mind of Dr Mani. In his autobiography, '*Yamaraja's Brother*' (Bharatiya Vidya Bhavan-1989), this is what Dr Mani writes: "I must state categorically that JP had kidney failure due to diabetic nephropathy, and not due to negligence or foul play. There was no medical means by which his kidneys could have been saved between June and November, 1975, (the period JP was in detention at PGI) for the disease process must have started long before 1975". But as we have seen earlier, he was categorical that 'there was grievous failure on the part of PGI doctors in diagnosing JP's kidney damage.'

I am a layman who does not understand a word of medical parlance, and one doctor's word is as good as the other, provided both are equally competent. Here are two doctors. One (M K Mani) an eminent nephrologist in the Jaslok Hospital who had taken JP in as a patient at the worst of his physical condition, diagnosed his real ailment and gave him the best of treatment possible under the circumstances. He also sustained JP's health for full four years, despite the patient's old age and being on dialysis twice a week. The other (B K Aikat) was a pathologist in the PGI and had nothing to do with the diagnosis and treatment of JP. He was only keen on doing 'autopsy on JP' in the event of his death in custody.

Administratively also this doctor, who boasts of officiating as Director, PGI during the absence of Dr Chuttani, was never in the picture as far as JP was concerned. The first time I saw him was during the middle of September when we were planning to shift JP to the PGI cottage. In the absence of Chuttani, he had come during the first inspection of the cottage and rambled on without understanding the requirements. Next, and the last time, I saw him was on November 12, when he had come to Mathur's office along with Dr Wahi to discuss the crisis caused by the deteriorating health of JP. He contributed little to the discussions and the medical opinion as well as advise emanated mostly from Dr Wahi. In fact, Dr Aikat was totally kept out on the crucial days between 7 November and 16 November and it was Dr Wahi, along with Dr Mehra, who handled JP-related matters till Chuttani returned from Nepal on the 14 November. With this reality and my observations and sixth-sense, I have no hesitation in endorsing the stand taken by Dr Mani and reject the insinuations of Dr Aikat.

Having closely watched the medical treatment given to JP as well as other developments inside and outside the PGI, I myself had serious doubts that the irreversible damage to JP's kidneys was caused due to failure in diagnosing the ailment in time despite the PGI having a full-fledged and well-equipped nephrology department, headed by Professor K S Chugh, a well-known and competent nephrologist. Whether it was intentional or not, only a thorough professional probe would have unveiled.

The intriguing part was that JP was never referred to Dr Chugh during his entire period of detention in the PGI. Dr Chug perhaps came into the picture only after JP's release on 12 November 1975, primarily for the purpose of appending to the discharge report. We had been receiving daily medical report on JP from the PGI from day one, and there was never a mention of kidney problem. Even the medical report on November 12 had no mention of any major kidney ailment, though there was reference to 'renal status':

> "Though he (JP) is as yet weak but this feeling according to him is less than before. We also feel that his condition in general is a little better. Aversion to food continues though he has taken small breakfast and a small lunch. He did not vomit today. His renal status is as yet below par but cardiac and diabetic state is well controlled. In general he was more alert and responsive today."
>
> — **Dr P L Wahi**
> **Professor of Cardiology**

Replying to a question by Rabi Ray that came up in Rajya Sabha on 8 January 1976 as to when JP's kidney trouble was detected, Dr Chuttani had replied: "When he was in detention at Chandigarh, the urinary infection reappeared on 8 November 1975 accompanied by kidney trouble precipitated by this infection." Yet there was no mention of this in the daily medical reports received by us on November 8, 9 and 10. The report on 11 November, signed by Dr H N Khatri just mentions, 'His (JP's) renal status is being re-evaluated'.

Only in the 'final diagnosis', contained in the discharge report prepared on 16 November, there was this entry: "Diabetes mellitus with peripheral neuropathy. Nephropathy with chronic renal failure."

What is more intriguing is that as early as September 27, the PGI doctors had identified the cause of JP's acute abdominal pain as 'intestinal colic'. This pain had continued on and off for over one-and-a-half months. Yet there was no proper examination of JP from the kidney damage point of view and the concerned specialist was not even called in!

There have been widespread suspicion and allegations about the failure of JP's kidneys in the PGI ranging from poisoning, deliberate damage, drug induced damage, and intentional non-diagnosis. Even JP had doubted on this score as we have seen from the letter above. Dr Alva was categorical in his indictment of the diagnosis and treatment of JP at the PGI. Dr Mani's observations only add to these doubts and suspicions. In the face of it, Dr Chuttani's and Dr Aikat's attempts at 'defending the undefendable' does not appear to be convincing.

I am not a medical practitioner and I cannot make value judgment on the adequacy or inadequacy, efficacy or inefficacy of the medical diagnosis and treatment given to JP while in detention. But as 'JP's custodian in jail' I was responsible for his safety and well-being that affected the whole nation. This was all the more so, since I have been seeing him very frequently. Therefore, I am morally bound to state my position in this vexing controversy that has a strong bearing on India's political culture and medical ethics.

My position is this: There was non-diagnosis of JP's serious ailments and lack of follow up when there was strong suspicion of kidney failure around mid- September. The objective seemed to be to 'put JP out of harm's way, if not eliminate him. This contention of mine is borne out from the 'circumstantial evidence' listed below:

- Non-reference of JP to nephrology specialists till the time he was released.
- Chuttani's resentment at the visit by Dr Bhatia, cardiologist from AIIMS to examine JP
- As per medical documents scanned by Dr Alva's Commission, doubts of renal failure had come up on – September 15 itself. Yet this was not followed up.

- Instead, JP was shifted to the guesthouse, precisely when he needed close attention and specialist treatment. During the days preceding this shifting, on September 18, Chuttani and Mathur behaved in a strange manner, sharing 'secrets' to be sorted out at Delhi about which I had no clue!
- Chuttani's repeated efforts to manage our minds with statements that JP's ailment was psychological and not physical.
- Admitted over-medication of JP
- Coincidences and happenings clearly indicate sabotage of reconciliation efforts including the serious one attempted by the Prime Minister through Lord Brockway.
- Sanjay's ambition to become Prime Minister while in his thirties and his coterie's assessment that JP was the only major hurdle to this ambition.
- Damaging and devious comments and remarks made by Bansi Lal at various times revealing the 'Delhi Durbar's' intentions.
- The despicable drama that preceded the release of JP and the desperate attempts to delay his departure from Chandigarh and Delhi.
- Chuttani's feeble and unconvincing attempts to deflect the main issue and to put the blame on the Jaslok Hospital doctors who, in fact, saved JP from the jaws of death and gave him a new lease of life.

Fact of the matter is that JP's kidney failed and there appears to be a purpose behind it - 'putting JP out of harms way' to facilitate the ascendancy of a dynastic greenhorn as Prime Minister. In the event, it is difficult to repudiate JP's charge that he was 'released only when the Indira government was convinced that I would not survive for more than a few days.' But due to certain swift moves, JP defied death and lived not for a 'few days' but for four more years and succeeded in liberating the country from the autocrats and restoring it to democracy. And Sanjay Gandhi never became Prime Minister.

JP Defeats That Woman

JP got his chance in early 1977. Emboldened by the reports of 'success' of the Emergency regime and the perception that opposition to her rule was crumbling and JP, the only mass leader, was sick and demoralised, Indira Gandhi called for the sixth General Election to Parliament in January 1977. The eye-ball to eye-ball confrontation between the autocrat and the democrat began with JP swinging into action to redeem his pledge: "I will defeat that woman and restore freedom."

And in his inimitable style, without wasting any time, he put into effect the political blueprint he had worked out while in detention and refined later. Due largely to his untiring efforts, immediately after coming out of jails, the Opposition leaders announced the merger of Congress (O), Jan Sangh, Bharatiya Lok Dal (BLD) and the Socialist Party into the new Janata Party. The Congress was dealt a blow by the sudden defection of Jagjivan Ram, H N Bahuguna and Nandini Sathpathy who formed the Congress for Democracy (CFD). Along with the DMK, the Akali Dal and the CPM, it forged a common front with the Janata Party in order to give a straight fight to the Congress and its allies, the CPI and the AIADMK in the elections to the Lok Sabha in March 1977.

The Opposition made the Emergency and its excesses and the restriction on civil liberties as its major issues for its election campaign.

The people also treated the elections as a referendum on the Emergency. JP created a public upsurge by touring the country intensively and addressing mammoth gatherings. This he did despite being tied down to dialysis twice a week. Dr Mani and his team of dedicated colleagues arranged for dialysis in certain centres like Delhi, Calcutta and Bombay to facilitate JP's uninterrupted election campaign. Because of this constraint, JP could not travel extensively and many areas in the country, especially South India was left out. At many places, large crowds intently listened to JP's appeal through pre-recorded tapes. He appealed to the Nation on the eve of the 6th Lok Sabha Elections:

Free India – Defeat the Dictators*

"In the name of all those who struggled for our country's freedom, I appeal to each one of you. Free India, defeat the dictators. This is the last chance. If you falter, 19 months of tyranny shall become 19 years of terror. Our goal is progress with justice.

Freedom is the first requisite to achieve this goal. We have seen in the past 19 months now, when freedom is crushed, the poor, the workers are intimidated to slave for enriching a small coterie at the top. When freedom is lost everything is lost. We want our officials and our elected representatives to be accountable to our people. Freedom alone can ensure that they are so. How will the rulers be accountable if the judiciary is robbed of all effectiveness? How can you end corruption if you cannot even talk or write about it? How can we have accountability if power is exercised by backroom operators who do not even hold office?

The terror of the black 19 months – herding hundreds of thousands into jails, the tortures inflicted on them, the untold sufferings of their families, mutilating laws so that a citizen does not even have the right to life, illicit as well as illegal extortions, destroying homes of the poor – these are not chance happenings, they are what dictatorship is about.

None of these atrocities could have happened in a free society. If you could have talked about them, if you could have met and organised

* Indian Express, 14 March 1977

to resist them, if the press could have written about them, an aroused and informed public opinion would have set its face against the oppressors. Contrast the black 19 months with the relative freedom of the last two months. The very rulers who were asserting that people do not want elections, who talked of gains of Emergency, these very rulers are today seeking alibis for that action and are compelled to make apologies. Just two months of freedom– and limited freedom at that–has forced them to once again take account of the people.

Do you want the irresponsibility, the brutality of the 19 months to return? Do you want your 30,000 brothers and sisters who have still not been released to continue in prison indefinitely? Do you want the set-up to continue in which each of you can be arrested without explanation? In which you can be held indefinitely without trial, in which the rulers are free to do what they will with you - and no one, not even your families – will know what is happening?

And my brothers and sisters in the minority communities must remember that fundamental rights and a free open society are even more important for them than for the majority. In addition to restoring fundamental rights and the rule of law, the Janata Party will establish civil rights commission to specifically protect the interests of minorities. Similarly, nothing will benefit the poor in general and minorities in particular as much as the Janata Party's pledge to make the right to work a fundamental right.

Many efforts have been made to hoodwink you and to distract you. Destabilisers who are responsible for splitting up all institutions in this country have talked about stability. They have tried to inflame communal passions, to frighten minorities, even to capitalize on Bapu's murder. They have tried to scare you with stories of violence, of external and internal threats. They have issued apologies. They have tried to pass on the blame for their dastardly deeds to officials, even to us who were in jails. They have tried to bribe you with last minute concessions. They have tried to mislead you with lies about the Janata Party's programme.

Do not let these mislead you. Be like Arjuna and like him do not let your eye wander from the central issue: Freedom or slavery, democracy or dynastic dictatorship. Remember that the ruling party still swears by the black laws and amendments that it used as the basis of its dictatorship. It will use them ruthlessly should it get another chance. Its leaders have clearly said that there is no room for differences of opinion in India, that they are the country. That far from being unhappy, the hundreds and thousands who were jailed should be grateful that they were shot to death.

The Janata Party, by contrast, is pledged to restore a free and open society. It is pledged to repealing black laws and amendments. The very process by which it will be acquiring power – that is, through the current struggle for freedom, through your support for the cause of freedom – will guarantee that it will fulfill its pledge.

Remember that each seat counts and that each vote counts. Translate the enthusiasm we have witnessed during the last few weeks into votes and vigilance for the Janata Party. Defeat the dictators. We can then build a free and Gandhian India. Vote for Janata Party; Vote for power to people; Vote for the 'man carrying the plough'.

This is what historian Bipan Chandra writes about India losing its freedom and getting it back in the seventies: "Whatever the character of the JP movement or of the Emergency regime, there is no doubt that the decision of Indira to hold genuine free elections, and her defeat and the Opposition's victory that followed were a remarkable achievement of Indian democracy." Indeed true and it was made possible by a man called Jayaprakash Narayan.

I was still the District Commissioner of Chandigarh and therefore the Returning Officer of the Chandigarh Parliamentary constituency. In that capacity, I had occasion to see this popular upsurge in person. What happened in Chandigarh was typical of the entire Indo-Gangetic belt where Indira's Congress was totally routed.

A day after the announcement of elections, Kedar Nath Sharma, the local Congress bigwig came to see me. Our conversation turned to the election prospects and Sharma was categorical in his assertion: "D C sahib, the elections are going to be a mere formality. Our candidates are strong and sure everywhere. Opposition people are either languishing in jail or lying in bed with leg or hand broken. They will not even find candidates to contest the polls. Even if they find candidates, they will have no means to contest. " I was distressed by this assessment and silently hoped it would misfire.

In the next couple of weeks, the election process of filing of nomination at Chandigarh commenced. It was then that I saw the 'truth' in the assertion of Sharma. One of the first to file nomination was Sat Pal Kapoor of the Congress (I), a millionaire liquor magnate, smelling of the best French scent all over. He came with all fanfare, in the manner of a conqueror, and went through the formalities with the kind of arrogance reserved for sure-shot winners. I felt uneasy about this semi-literate "Congress heavyweight" who might represent the most literate constituency in the Country.

A day or two later a mild, intellectual looking man in a crumpled '*kurta*' came to file his nomination with just a couple of men in tow. That was Krishan Kant, the Janata nee BLD candidate representing the Opposition. I had heard of Kant as a 'Young Turk', and this was the first time I met him. I was duly taken in by his simplicity but could not help making a mental comparison between the silk wearing, scent smelling Sat Pal with the *Khadi* clad and sweat smelling Krishan Kant. For once, I was genuinely concerned as to what a disaster it would be if Sharma's prediction came true.

Within days of filing nomination, the election battle began heating up. Sat Pal hit the ground with all cylinders firing and had the distinct advantage of money, muscle and material over the austere Krishan Kant and his supporters who were still reeling under the trauma of the Emergency and the fear psychosis that went with it. Every evening Sat Pal's minions spread out to the outlying 'labour colonies' with cases of liquor and wads of currency. Each voter was given 'one bottle and one note' (hundred rupees). Sat Pal's confidence rose with the ever-increasing number of bottles and currency notes disbursed and he made bold announcements of sure-shot victory.

But unknown to Sat Pal, a different scene was being enacted in the same 'labour colonies' when Krishan Kant went to seek vote in the early hours of the morning. The colony dwellers came out in large numbers and handed over the hundred rupee notes to him, saying: "This is part of Sat Pal's loot. We have finished the bottle. This note is for you, since you do not have money. Be assured of our votes too". This transformation happened after the massive rally at the Sector 17 parade ground, addressed by Chandra Shekhar, Jagjivan Ram and others. JP was scheduled to come but could not do so due to health reasons. However, a pre-recorded cassette of his speech was played to the vast crowd, moving them to tears.

The elections were conducted in a free and fair manner, leading to the resounding victory of Krishan Kant. Chandigarh's was the first election result to be announced and came as a precursor to the clean Janata sweep in the Indo-Gangetic belt of North and Central India.

When the eyeball-to-eyeball confrontation ended JP's Janata Party and its allies were victorious with 330 out of 542 seats. The Congress trailed far behind, with only 154 seats, with the CPI, its ally getting 7 and AIADMK 21 seats. The Congress Party was virtually wiped out in North India, with the party winning only 2 out of the 234 seats in seven northern States. Both Indira and Sanjay were defeated. Only because of South India, did the Congress survive. This was because the rigours of Emergency were felt much less in that region, and the voice of JP could not reach many parts.

As pledged, JP succeeded in 'defeating that woman' and removing the Congress Party from power at the Centre for the first time, replacing it with a 'Janata' Government. The democrat had defeated the autocrat.

'Janata' Fails: Kleptocracy on the Rise

But this success did not last long. Consequent upon the Janata victory, there was a near-crisis over the issue of prime ministership between the three aspirants, Morarji Desai, Charan Singh and Jagjivan Ram. The matter was referred to senior leaders, Jayaprakash Narayan and J B Kripalani, who ruled in favour of 81-year old Morarji Desai, who was sworn in as Prime Minister on 23 March 1977.

In the assembly elections held in June 1977, Janata and its allies came out victorious in most of the States except in Tamil Nadu, where the AIADMK won. Control over both the Parliament and the State assemblies enabled the Janata Party to elect unopposed its own candidate, N Sanjeeva Reddy, as the President of India in July, 1977.

The Janata government took immediate steps to dismantle the authoritarian features of the Emergency regime and to restore liberal democracy. It restored fundamental rights and full civil liberties to the press, political parties and individuals. Through the 44th Constitutional Amendment, it also modified the 42nd amendment, passed during the Emergency, repealing those of its provisions which had distorted the Constitution. The powers of the Supreme Court and the High Courts to decide on the validity of Central and State legislation were also restored.

Minoo Masani recalls his meeting with JP at the PGI on the day of his departure: "Before taking the car back to Delhi, I had another talk with JP. I found that he had not changed his angle of vision. He was determined to get the Opposition parties together and win the Parliamentary elections as and when they came. 'Give me two months', he said and he would defeat the Prime Minister. That's just about what he was to get later!" And he did defeat the Prime Minister.

Paying tribute to JP after his passing away on October 8, 1979, Nayantara Sahgal wrote in the *Indian Express*: "In detention JP was damaged for life, and it may have been assumed that he was out of action for the rest of his days. It must have been something of a shock when this old warrior summoned his remaining reserves to fight this last great crusade and consign the dictatorship to the rubbish heap."

JP was a man of his words and he did redeem his pledge of 'defeating that woman and restoring freedom' in full measure. But unfortunately, riddled with factionalism, internecine quarrels and petty politicking, the forces that JP brought together and catapulted to power disintegrated and dismantled, thereby betraying the cause of democracy for which JP gave his life.

"Public memory is short", goes the saying. So are personal memories. Recollecting the 'Emergency Era' of the mid-seventies and evaluating the same to draw 'lessons from the past and lessons for the future' is indeed daunting. This is particularly so when the minds of those in the target group – young men and women of the new generation born after this fateful era – for whom one is making the evaluation are filled with imaginations of 'super power' and screams of 'war on terror'. Little do they realise that real 'terror' struck the country in the mid-seventies in the form of the 'Emergency', putting thousands in jail, depriving millions of their fundamental rights, freedom and liberty, ravaging India's Constitution and severely debilitating institutions and instruments of governance. After-effects of this 'terror' still persist and the people in general and youth in particular are paying for it dearly.

It is therefore necessary to evaluate the 'Emergency' and learn lessons for the future. Because 'for those who do not remember the past, there is no future'. This is particularly so for a country with a hoary past that has been invaded, ravaged and subjugated by kings, emperors and trader-turned rulers. The factors that facilitated these merchants and marauders to achieve their conquest so easily is prevalent in this soil even today – a slavish and mendicanised mindset – among the majority.

Is there no one to speak up for freedom and democracy in India, particularly among the youth? Yes there are and all hope is not lost. A move reminiscent of the JP movement has made a humble beginning. It is named 'Youth 4 Democracy' and is led by a committed group of patriotic Indians with clarity of thought and foresight. This is their treatise with the nation:

The Treatise

Democracy in India has been hijacked by elites in business, bureaucracy and politics. The country is thus under the siege of kleptocrats. Since vested interests will not allow things to change for the better, there is a need to mobilise public opinion for the desired effect. And who represents the future of our people better than the youth?

When the Westminster Model of Parliament and governance was adopted, it was supposed to deliver greater goods to larger numbers. The experience of the last 60 years has, however, belied this simple expectation. Poverty is shown to be declining by arbitrary lowering of the BPL bar, even as we figure among the most corrupt countries in the world, with all the ill-gotten wealth going to a privileged few.

As of June 2009, 94 amendments had been made in the Indian Constitution, considered the most elaborate of all constitutions. Yet the system is failing to deliver. Education is now an expensive commodity; the public health system has been compromised as never before, and justice is not just and often affected by corruption. As for security, an ordinary citizen is safe only till nothing untoward has happened to her/him. We can be rescued from the system only through comprehensive reforms. However, this cannot be brought about by political parties. The agenda of governance is the last thing in the priority list of those who hanker after power. Merely replacing one government by another will thus not help.

The youth of this country must come together for the cause of institution building in a way that policy makers can no longer afford to stay status quoist. It is to realise this mission that Youth 4 Democracy has been established: to work towards attaining a better system. Let's turn Abraham Lincoln's philosophy of democracy as a government of the people, by the people and for the people into a reality.

We stand for

- A better India free of corruption;
- Promotion of demonstrable honesty and integrity in all functionaries of public offices;
- Transparent and more accountable democratic institutions;
- Comprehensive reforms in politics, police, bureaucracy, judiciary, electoral system, NGOs and the media;
- Promotion of equality so that all citizens are treated with dignity irrespective of class, caste, creed, religion, gender and other social divisions;
- Promotion of a liberal society with high degree of tolerance for dissenting opinions.

Oath for members: Inspired by the ideals mentioned above and with the intent to bring about systemic change, I pledge to abide by the values held by **Youth 4 Democracy**. If this pledge is to shape reality we need to revive the 'Agenda for Democracy' set forth before this generation of youth was even born.

JP's Democracy Agenda

JP, the man who defeated autocracy in 1977, had an 'agenda for Democracy' as early as 1959 which has been clearly laid down in his seminal essay, 'A Plea for the Reconstruction of the Indian Polity'. Even after five decades, every word of it rings true and relevant. Here it is in JP's own words:

I propose in this paper to describe the main outline of the polity which to my mind is not only most suited for us but also most rational and scientific, with a brief statement of the reasons for my views.

I have pleaded for our present political institutions to be based on the principles that had been enunciated and practiced in the ancient Indian polity because (a) I believe that would be in line with the natural course of social evolution and (b) those principles are more valid from the point of view of social science than any others.

Present Western polity is based upon an atomized society, the state being made up of an inorganic sum of individuals. This is both against the social nature of man and the scientific organization of society. Ancient Indian polity was much more consistent with both these. Let me make clear that this paper is not a treatise on democracy or government. I am dealing here with a practical and immediate question: what should be the principles and form of Indian polity at the present time.

I have not looked at this question from the point of view of any ready-made preconceptions and have avoided giving any label to the views expressed here. Even the phrase, communitarian, is reluctantly used, because a descriptive term sometimes becomes unavoidable. My search here has been for the forms of social life, particularly of political life, that would assure the preservation of human values about which there is hardly any dispute in the world today, and my approach has been non-partisan and non-sectarian.

On the very portals of democracy – irrespective of its form and structure – are words written that can never be wiped off without wiping off democracy itself. No kind of democracy can exist without the democratic freedoms – freedom of conscience, of association, of expression – and the rule of law. Where these freedoms do not exist, nor the rule of law, there can be no democracy. For my enquiry here I take these words as axiomatic and inscribe them in bold letters on the doorway before entering the house of Indian democracy.

If our present political institutions are to be soundly based, if they are to draw sustenance from Indian soil and, in turn, are to sustain, revive and strengthen the whole fabric of Indian society, they must be related to the social genius of India described above, and their texture must be woven again with an organically self- determining, self developing communal life in which occupations, professions and functions are integrated with the community.

This is not only a question of constitutional forms or political systems. It is a creative question in the widest sense of the term. It is a question of an ancient country finding its lost soul again.

The old village communities have survived in nothing else than their physical existence. They are no longer living communities acting jointly for the solution of individual or communal problems and for the development of their moral and material life. It is not necessary here to go into the story of the destruction of the village communities. It would be enough to note that it was a result of the deliberate policy of an alien government that neither understood the character of a communitarian polity nor felt secure in the presence of such strong traditions of self government and self help. Nevertheless, the very fact that the villages do exist physically provides us with a ready-made foundation to build upon.

A word that figures boldly on the ancient signpost is *dharma*. Indian polity held that the state was subject to the rule of *dharma*, which it was its duty to uphold and protect. The concept of *dharma* was of great importance in ancient India; it prescribed and regulated individual and group behaviour in all walks of life.

This concept of *dharma* and its role in Indian polity and the wider life of society is another example of that synthetic, organic, communal organization of India society which has been discussed above. Communities, territorial or functional, had developed laws and codes of behaviour to regulate the internal life of their communities and groups and their relations with the rest of society. There were in addition codes and laws that were common to and accepted by all of them and that made up the universal social ethics. The ensemble of these social ethics exercised a powerful influence over the state.

Communal life having been completely destroyed, the roots of *dharma* have no soil from which to draw sustenance. *Dharma* has therefore declined and ceased to exercise any influence not only upon the present polity, which is a wholly foreign implantation and has no roots in the India soil, but upon all social activities such as commerce, education, labour, administration, priesthood. Unless life in India is again organized on the basis of self-determining and mutually coordinating and integrating communities, that organic self-regulation of society, which the concept of *dharma* represented, will not be possible. To that extent democracy will remain distantly removed from the life of the people.

The ancient concept of *dharma* has to be revived and the appropriate *dharma* for a democracy has to be evolved. This, as of old, will not be brought about by a legislative process. It can be done only in an organic manner: *dharma* must arise from life itself – life that is vital enough, real enough, organic enough to be able to throw up codes and laws for its internal regulation. The experience of recent social engineering may and should be drawn upon, but the main mould of life must be indigenous and consistent with the genius of Indian social organization.

I believe it would be fair to say that even the most ardent defenders of parliamentary democracy agree that it has serious defects. But they console themselves with the thought (a) that there is no better alternative; and (b) that, within limits, it is possible to amend and improve it. No one will deny that the system is capable of much improvement and it is undergoing change all the time, though not always for the better. But no matter how much improved, its fundamental defects will yet remain because they are the very premises on which its entire structure has been raised.

The fundamental defect, from which other serious defects arise, is that this form of democracy is based on the vote of the individual. We have already examined this situation and found that it is the atomization of society that is responsible for this kind of political system. But that does not alter the fact that the system is based on a false premise; the state cannot be an arithmetical sum of individuals. The people, the nation, the community can never be equated with the sum of individual voters.

The partisans of parliamentary democracy claim that under it the government is at least representative of the majority of the voters, if not of the people. First of all, this is not true. More often than not it is commonly believed that governments elected under universal adult suffrage are minority governments, in the sense that they represent a minority of the voters. Wherever there are more than two parties, this happens quite often, but even under two party systems it is not a rare phenomenon. At the last general election in this country, for instance, minority governments were established in a majority of the states, i.e., in seven out of the thirteen states, excluding Union Territories.

It will not do to brush aside, as it has been done in this country, such serious anomalies and glaring defects in the parliamentary democratic system by the smug remark that such things are inevitable under a multi-party system. If such things are inevitable and if we are serious about democracy we must seriously set about to find a better type of democracy. The alternatives of plural constituencies, proportional representation, alternative vote cannot, even if there was general agreement about them, which there is not, take us far.

The claim that parliamentary democratic governments at least represent a majority of the voters breaks down in a still more serious manner. Experience has shown that present-day mass elections, manipulated by powerful, centrally controlled parties, with the aid of high finance and diabolically clever methods and super media of communication, represent far less the electorate than the forces and interests behind the parties and the propaganda machines. It is not only in the totalitarian countries that the 'rape of the masses' happens. The basic difference is that in a democracy there is a competition between the violators while there is no competition in totalitarianism.

Here we are face to face with another serious defect of parliamentary democracy – demagoguery. The need to 'catch' votes creates an unlimited opportunity for indulging in half-truths, even outright lies sometimes; for exciting the passions, more often than not, the base passions; for arousing false hopes by making dishonest, but pleasing promises. Hardly any issue of public policy is presented to the people in its true light; everything gets distorted by partisan demagoguery. The consequence of all this is that the real interests of the nation are sacrificed, more often than not, at the altar of demagoguery.

Perhaps the most serious fault of parliamentary democracy, from the point of view of democracy itself, is its inherent tendency toward centralism. At one extreme of its political spectrum is the nation state and at the other the individual voter, with a blank in between.

The local bodies that may exist have (a) little self-government powers, and (b) no direct or indirect influence on the nation state. Add to this the complexities of a highly industrialized civilization that are beyond even the understanding of the ordinary citizen, and you have a central state of overwhelming power and resources and the individual voter reduced to abject helplessness. The 'sovereign people' being dispersed over the length and breadth of the country like particles of sand over the desert and having no other organized political force than the nation state itself to interpose between themselves and that state, the latter naturally becomes all powerful. The issue of power in such states is decided not by the fictitious 'people', but by a balance between political parties and such organized interests as industrialists and bankers and powerful labour unions. The people represent wholeness, while the organized interests are sectional. Even a sum of the sections cannot make up the whole. Only their organic integration can do so. Such integration takes place only in the community – at its various levels. In the communal or communitarian democracy that we are advocating there is natural decentralization and a multi-central pluralistic state.

A natural outcome of centralization of power and administration is bureaucracy. The central executive or cabinet is so overburdened with work that it is compelled to leave more and more to, and depend more and more upon, the permanent officials, who in course of time gather more and more power for themselves. This soon leads to a dangerous autocracy, the autocracy of the bureaucrat, which is difficult to fight because it 'works in the shadows' and is hard to get at.

The only answer to the problem of bureaucracy is more and more decentralization so that the people directly participate in the administration of their affairs and control the civil servants who owe their jobs and are directly responsible to them. This is exactly what will happen in the communitarian democracy outlined here. The communal administrations might make mistakes and there might be inefficiency. But as they themselves will be the sufferers, they will learn and improve things. Moreover, during the British rule did we not say to ourselves repeatedly that good government was no substitute for self-government? Is that less true now?

An inevitable concomitant of parliamentary democracy is the party system. So much has been written in criticism of this system that it seems unnecessary to dwell upon it here at any length. Some criticism of it has been implicit in what has been said above. It is clear that parliamentary democracy cannot work without parties. Parties of a sort will perhaps exist everywhere and at all times. Even in the family there may be 'parties'. In the ancient Indian republics, which were aristocratic democracies, parties and factions were a common feature.

But the highly organized, centralized mass parties of modern times are a far cry from the factions of old, whether of the ancient Indian republics or the Greek city states.

The old democracies were small and the factions and the people were not so far removed from one another. The people therefore could judge them and the issues that were raised with intimate understanding. The issues in those days were also simple enough. All this has changed now and parties have become a sort of state within the state. They are now the real arbiters of the people's fate, whose control over them is fictional. The citizens who cast their votes for the parties have nothing to do with the running of the parties: they are complete outsiders. Even the enrolled members of the parties have no say either in the policy-making or the inner administration of the parties. The parties are run by caucuses that are beyond democratic control.

Party rivalries, we have seen above, give birth to demagoguery, depress political ethics, put a premium on unscrupulousness and aptitude for manipulation and intrigue. Parties create dissensions where unity is called for, exaggerate differences where they should be minimized. Parties often put party interests over the national interests because centralization of power prevents the citizen from participating in government; the parties, that is to say, small caucuses of politicians, rule in the name of the people and create the illusion of democracy and self-government.

No doubt the party system has its good points and because parliamentary democracy cannot work without it, those who swear by that type of democracy and see no alternative to it, are prepared to accept the evils of the party system as inevitable and satisfy themselves by pointing out their virtues. For my part, it is not the party system that is the main culprit, but parliamentary democracy itself, which gives rise to it. In the communitarian democracy that I have proposed here, there may conceivably be parties, but they are likely to be local factions, and, in any case, their role in the state will not be as commanding as that of the parties in the parliamentary system.

Another serious fault of parliamentary democracy is the system of elections that it fosters and requires for its proper functioning.

First of all, the system is very expensive and appallingly wasteful. The fabulous expenses involved have the effect of mortgaging democracy to moneyed interests or large sectional organizations like trade unions. As compared with this, elections in the communitarian system would cost practically nothing.

It would have been a matter of some consolation if the huge expenditure had resulted in any public good. In fact, the result is just the contrary. A general election, as noted above, creates unnecessary passion and excitement; instead of educating and enlightening the people it befogs their mind; instead of resulting in the election of able and good men, it tends to favour demagoguery. Serious political and economic issues and other questions of policy, it is obvious, should be considered calmly and dispassionately and not in the heat of partisan warfare. That is why I hold that the practice of general elections should be abolished. The elected houses should be continuous in nature, with a part of them being renewed periodically.

It is time now to gather all the threads of the argument and tie them together. Ancient Indian thought and tradition; social nature of man; social science; ethical and spiritual goals of civilization; the demand of democracy that the citizen should participate in the ordering and running of his life; the need of saving man from himself and from the fate of robotism; the requirement that the state and other institutions of society be reduced to a human scale; the ideal, above all, that man should become the centre of civilization – all these point in the same direction: to a communal or communitarian way of life; communitarian ethics and education; communitarian social, economic and political organization. In this paper I have been mainly interested in the political aspect of the matter: the shape of the political organization, or polity, most desirable for our country.

The foundation of this polity, as I have pointed out, must necessarily be self-governing, self-sufficient, agro-industrial, urbo-rural local communities. The existing villages and townships provide the physical base for such reconstruction. The highest political institution of the local community should be the General Assembly – the gram sabha – of which all the adults should be considered members. The selection of the Executive – the panchayat – should be by general consensus of opinion in the sabha. There should be no 'candidates', i.e. no one should 'stand' for any post. There should be clear-cut qualifications, as in ancient times, laid down for all selective posts. No individual should hold the same post for more than a defined period of time. The panchayat should function through subcommittees charged with different responsibilities. There should be no official or member appointed or nominated by the state government in the panchayat or its sub-committees.

It may be questioned if there can ever be a general consensus of opinion amongst villagers who are divided into castes and factions and have conflicting interests. We have seen already how for thousands of years the villages of India elected their executive councils by general agreement. Those villages were by no means homogeneous and ideal communities. Therefore, there is no reason to believe that the experience of centuries cannot be repeated again.

We may also recall that the only alternative method of election of village councils or panchayats was that of drawing lots. There is nothing undemocratic in selection by general agreement or by drawing lots; alternatively, it might be provided that the villages first try the former method, and failing therein take recourse to the latter. Something similar happens in the Bhoodan movement. When the landless families are unable to agree about the distribution of *bhoodan* lands between themselves, the issue is decided by drawing lots. It is not our experience that there has been in any case dissatisfaction with decisions reached in this manner.

The question may also be asked if the village panchayats, as they are today, would be able to function in the manner visualized above. There is no better way to teach the young except by giving them responsibility. In the same manner the only way to make the villages self-governing, self-reliant and self-sufficient is to throw upon them real responsibilities. There was a time when the Indian village republics were self-created, like the Swiss communes, and their powers and functions were not given to them from above. But in the present conditions they have to be recreated by a deliberate and bold process of devolution and decentralization if Indian democracy is to have a firm base and living reality.

I believe that the responsibility given to the gram sabha and the panchayat should be in things that really do matter. For instance, it should be the responsibility of the gram sabha and its panchayat to ensure that no one in the village goes without food, clothing and shelter; no child without primary education; every one receives primary medical care. The sabha and panchayat should see that the village becomes self-sufficient in the matter of food and clothing as soon as possible. Further, they should so plan that within five years, let us say, there is no unemployment in the village and every family reaches a minimum standard of living. Self-government, to be real, should be about essential problems of life.

It would be necessary for some time to help the village from above, but the responsibility must be clearly defined and the demand for help must come from the village in specific terms, meant to supplement what has been or is proposed to be done by the collective effort of the village. No help should be given until the village has proved that it has done that and is prepared to do its best to help itself. Eventually such help will have to come from the next larger communal organization, the regional community, but at the beginning it will have to come from the state government. Social and political workers must go in large numbers to the villages, not to make promises but to preach self-reliance and to help them to practice it.

The development of the rest of the polity need not wait till the villages and townships become real communities as visualized here. Our work must begin at all levels simultaneously, otherwise it will not succeed at any level.

The next level of the political structure would obviously be that of the regional community. Here, as already indicated, the gram panchayats will have to be integrated into the panchayat samiti, as recommended by the Balvantrai Mehta team, with this difference that the nature and functions of the samiti should be those of an autonomous self-governing community as discussed in the previous section: the samiti should have powers and obligations to do all that may be within its competence. As suggested already, the panchayat samiti, comprising the optimum community as defined above, would play a key role in the political and economic life of the country, particularly in the processes of planning and development.

There is one important point which I wish to emphasize in connection with the formation of the panchayat samiti. The samiti should be elected by the gram panchayats and not by their members. This at first might appear to be a distinction between six and half-a-dozen. But that is not so. We have here a major principle of communal life involved. It is the gram panchayat as a body that represents the village community and not its members. The panchayat samiti, in its turn, is a representative of the gram panchayats, and it is the latter that should be represented as such and not their members.

Following the pattern of social organization described in the previous section, the political structure would rise storey by storey from the foundation. The next storey above the panchayat samiti would be that of the district council (or whatever name given to it), which will be formed by the integration of the panchayat samitis of the district – again the samitis as such electing their representatives and not their members. The district councils, in their turn, should have all the powers and obligations necessary to do everything that may be within their competence.

In a similar manner all the district councils of a state would come together to create the state assembly. The state assemblies, in like manner, would bring into being the Lok Sabha. Thus the political institution at each level is an integration of all the institutions at the lower level.

The picture drawn here of the polity of India, and of social organization in general, might perhaps appear to be idealistic. If so, I would not consider that to be a disqualification. An ideal cannot but be idealistic. The question is if the ideal is impractical, unscientific or otherwise ill-conceived. I have tried in the preceding pages to show that all relevant considerations lead irresistibly towards it.

The achievement of this ideal would, however, be a colossal task.

Thousands, perhaps hundreds of thousands, of voluntary workers would be needed over a number of years to accomplish it.

The governments should lend their full support; but it is necessary to remember that the main burden of the task would have to be borne by voluntary political and social workers and institutions. The heart of the problem is to create the 'spirit of community', without which the whole body politic would be without life and soul. This is a task of moral regeneration to be brought about by example, service, sacrifice and love. Those who occupy high places in society – in politics, business, the professions – bear the heavy responsibility of leading the people by personal example.

The task also is one of social engineering, needing the help of the state; of scientists, experts, educationists, businessmen, experimenters; of men and women; of young and old. It is a task of dedication; of creation; of self-discovery. It is a task that defines India's destiny. It spells a challenge to India's sons and daughters. Will they accept the challenge?

This is the challenge for the youth of today. The advent of 'Brashtachar Raj' (corrupt kleptocracy), ushered in by the Liberalisation era and Panchayat Raj (grass roots democracy) expounded by JP coincided in the early nineties. While high-end kleptocracy that came through executive action is flourishing today and has taken over the country, grass roots democracy established through Constitutional amendments in 1992 is in shatters. Redeeming this basic democracy and putting it on strong footing should be the task of the 'Youth 4 Democracy'. For this, the spirit of the JP movement should be reignited to extinguish corruption and ruthlessly defeat the kleptocrats who are getting deeply entrenched!

Epilogue – "Lest We Forget"

Couple of years ego, after three decades of gathering dust, two notebooks containing Nelson Mandela's 'writings in jail' that an apartheid agent had kept in safe custody was handed over to him. Accepting the notebooks in an 'emotional ceremony of restitution' Mr. Mandela said: "The history of our country is characterised by too much forgetting.

The [notebooks] represent the hope that we can recover memories and stories suppressed by the apartheid regime."

How true of India. It is well over three decades since the 'extinction of freedom through emergency' happened. Despite this and the rise of fascism and kleptocracy, the 'lotus eating' and laid-back populace of this country is taking freedom and democracy for granted and have given up the vigil required to upkeep these precious gifts. Historians and 'Intellectuals' have written off JP as a 'champion of lost causes' and an 'unlikely hero'. For a huge populace 'Emergency' meant nothing and JP not even a speck in their memory. India is also characterised by far too much forgetting.

Reasons are not far to seek. Janata government collapsed in mid-1979 due to intrigues and betrayals. JP passed away in October 1979 and Congress returned to power in January 1980. Despite being a crucial chapter of India's post-Independence history, JP Movement and Emergency have been blacked-out from school-texts, books, forums, media and other avenues. BJP, with its own self-promotion agenda, was disinterested in perpetuating the memory of JP and in fact betrayed him!

Ironically, the most poignant of tribute to JP had come from that Poet-Prime Minister Atal Behari Vajpayee way back in 1978: "JP was not merely the name of one person; it symbolised humanity. When one remembered Mr Narayan two pictures came to one's mind. One was reminded of Bishmapitamah lying on a bed of arrows. There was only one difference between Bishmapitamah and Mr Narayan; while the former fought for the Kauravas, the latter fought for Justice. The second picture was one of Christ on the Cross and Mr Narayan's life reminded one of Christ's sacrifices". As it was, this turned out to be sheer hypocrisy!

Shortly after the collapse of Janata Government in mid-1979, I visited JP in his Kadam Kuan residence at Patna. He was on dialysis, but made me sit beside him. That he had taken Janata's collapse to heart was evident when he said with tears welling in his eyes, 'Devasahayam, I have failed yet again'. The hard-boiled revolutionary, who was a foot-soldier for the Mahatma in his fight for Independence and who almost single-handedly won India's second freedom was a sad man when he died weeks later in October! Today he stands near-totally forgotten with 'media-manufactured messiahs' leading 'Second Freedom' struggle. Can there be a worse form of ingratitude?

'Freedom-killing' autocrat Indira, who institutionalized corruption, extinguished democracy and imploded all institutions of governance in this country, was voted the 'woman of the Millennium' by a BBC poll and is still being celebrated as India's 'Iron Lady'! Almost every populist scheme of Government of India, many state government schemes, projects, townships, government buildings, hospitals, roads, airports, railway stations, institutions, colleges and universities are named after her, her father, mother and sons as if this family owns them!

But 'Freedom-loving' democrat JP, who defied 'death and disease' to fight corruption and restore freedom and democracy did not even find mention among the list of persons polled. Except naming a few odd buildings after him, nothing has been done to remember him. What is worse, decades ego, JP had led the largest and the most powerful of youth movements India had ever witnessed. Yet the youth of today does not even know him!

The savant of all savants, Leo Tolstoy has rightly said: "It is by those who have suffered that the world has been advanced." JP is one such man and betraying him is the worst form of ingratitude. Tamil Saint-Savant Thiruvalluvar poignantly said: "*Ennantri kontarkum vuivundam, vuivillai seinantri kontra maharku*" (There is forgiveness to every sin except ingratitude!).

The least the youth of the country could do to wipe out this sin is to remember JP and revive his Movement through the **Youth 4 Democracy** that will cleanse up and bring about rejuvenation in the Indian polity.

Index

T

U

V

W

Y

Z